In Praise of *Perseverance* . . .

———

People can't relate to six million deaths. The number is incomprehensible. What they can relate to is one. This is the best way to tell the story of the Holocaust. I am grateful for Melvin's life and testimony.

—Susan T. Hessel, *Journalist and Author*

A tremendously stirring story . . . [told] through thick description of one Jewish man's life in Poland, and later, in America following the Second World War. By situating this book in the details of the "local," the co-authors offer a personalized story of how the Holocaust unfolded in one man's life and how that same man emerged with an outlook that was nothing less than amazing.

—*Rabbi Aaron Benjamin Bisno*
Rodef Shalom Congregation, Pittsburgh

Perseverance is the testimony of a Holocaust survivor and his daughter to one man's journey and spirit. Melvin Goldman's experience was in some ways typical of the torture and starvation by the Nazis, but it is also deeply particular and gripping. It is an inspiring book, a record of a life well lived after unbearable suffering and loss.

—Meredith Sue Willis, *author,* Out of the Mountains, Their Houses, *and* Oradell at Sea, *among other books*

The premise of local history is that every story is worth telling, provided you have enough documentation to support it. Melvin Goldman did the hard work of creating and preserving that documentation, and his daughter, Lee, did the hard work of bringing it together into a narrative. The result is a local, individualized look at a communal experience. The section about Squirrel Hill is particularly valuable, as that story is only just beginning to be told in detail.

—*Eric S. Lidji*
Director, Rauh Jewish History Program & Archives
Senator John Heinz History Center, Pittsburgh,
in association with the Smithsonian Institution

I have been on the Greater Altoona Jewish Federation's annual International Film Festival committee for ten years and was in the audience for years before that. So, I have seen more than my share of Shoah films. Reading this brought the experience into "view" better than any film. But, you know what they say—the book is always better. Reading *Perseverance* I felt almost as if I knew nothing about the depth of depravity and suffering of the Holocaust, even though I may be better informed than the average American Christian.

—Valerie Metzler, Archivist/Historian

With this book, Mrs. Kikel has managed to bring to life her father's words. You can really imagine Melvin's voice as if he were there telling you his personal history. This, together with Lee's subsequent perspective, makes for a wonderful father/daughter memoir.

—Martine Groman-Marks, London
Supporter of Holocaust Education

Survivors have been through such atrocities and lived, while others died by something that seems as simple as "wrong place, wrong time." We are fortunate that some of those who lived have carried the story and given it to us. I love that this book is not just about the Holocaust: it begins with a boy's loving family, tells of his hardships in the Nazi death camps, and finally blossoms into the portrait of a man in full.

—McCall Goughneour
Cultural Literacy High School Teacher

PERSEVERANCE
ONE HOLOCAUST SURVIVOR'S JOURNEY
from Poland to America

Melvin Goldman
Lee Goldman Kikel

Goldman–Ceder Forge
Pittsburgh, Pennsylvania

Perseverance: One Holocaust Survivor's Journey from Poland to America
© 2019 Lee Goldman Kikel

All rights reserved. This book or parts thereof may not be reproduced or transmitted in any form by any means without prior written permission of the co-author, with the exception of use for educational or promotional purposes, and as provided by United States of America copyright law. For permission requests, contact the co-author at the email address below.

ISBN: 978-0-578-45752-9
Library of Congress Control Number: 2019905929

Lee Goldman Kikel
lee@leekikel.com
www.leekikel.com
Goldman–Ceder Forge
Pittsburgh, Pennsylvania

Production by:
Populore®
Populore Publishing Company, Morgantown, West Virginia

My father said one of us had to eat from the earth and survive in order that our name stays alive. Remembering this kept me going.

—M. G.

Dedication

At Melvin Goldman's request, this book is dedicated to all the young children of the world, in hope for peace and harmony.

Contents

Dear Reader ix
Introduction xiii

Part I: In Melvin's Words

1. My Beautiful Childhood Years, 1923–1939 3
2. The Germans March into Łódź, 1939–1944 23
3. Prisoner 64277, 1944–1945 47
4. "If I Survive and Live . . .", 1945 69
5. My Will Was Strong, 1946–1949 79
6. I Was Going to Make It, 1949–1970s 97
7. Looking Back . . . Looking Forward 117

Part II: In Lee's Words

1. A Thriving Jewish Community 131
2. Melvin and Mildred Meet 134
3. A Personal Journey to Find His Way 136
4. These Were Happy Times 139
5. A Pearl, A Golden Totem Pole, and a Garbage Truck with Diamonds and Rubies 140
6. He Put His Heart into Every Piece 149
7. He Always Made Himself Available 154
8. They Were Looking for Answers and a Place to Start Over 160
9. Aron: My Father's Brother 161
10. Becoming Me 165
11. He Was Driven by Principle—To Have Things Made Right 169
12. A Sad Time, but Looking Forward 172
13. A Nice Backyard, a Garden, and Peacefulness 173
14. Dad Remains with Us 176

15. An Accomplished Woman 177
16. In My Father's Footsteps 180

Epilogue 189
Editor's Note 193

Appendices
1. The War in Europe, Poland, and Łódź 199
2. Family Trees
    Notes 204
    Melvin's Immediate Family 206
    Melvin's Paternal Ancestors 207
    Melvin's Maternal Ancestors 208
3. Maps
    Łódź Ghetto 209
    Melvin's Journey in Postwar Germany 210
    Squirrel Hill, Pittsburgh 211
4. Documents and Photos
    Melvin's Timeline, 1923–1996 212
    Melvin's Family, 1898–1939 213
    War Years, 1939–1945 227
    Liberation, 1945 231
    Rehabilitation, 1945–1950 232
    Emigration, 1950 237
    Early Pittsburgh Years, 1950s 243
    Relatives Abroad 251
    Restitution and Reparation Efforts 253
    US Holocaust Memorial Museum Testimony 284

Acknowledgments 287
Sources and Credits 289
Index 291
About Lee Goldman Kikel 303

Dear Reader

This book is a tribute to my father, Melvin Goldman, and his family. On the audiocassettes he recorded in the late 1970s, while in his mid-fifties, he clearly said he wanted the story he was telling to be preserved in a book, and finally the time seemed right for me to see that through. With this book, I honor his request.

It wasn't until fairly recently that I realized how significant it is that my father recorded his story on his own initiative, and in the late 1970s. My father simply "talked to his tape recorder" in snippets, when he had free moments at his jewelry store, with no one asking questions for clarification or to shape his narrative. He worked alone. That makes his story rare among Holocaust survivor accounts in the United States. The great majority of them were collected years later than this, and in collaboration with organized institutional efforts. Yale University's Fortunoff Video Archive for Holocaust Testimonies was established in 1981, and it was only in 1993 that the US Holocaust Memorial Museum opened.

In 1994, filmmaker Steven Spielberg founded the Shoah Foundation, with the explicit purpose of recording oral histories of survivors of, and witnesses to, the Holocaust. In its first five years, the foundation conducted 52,000 interviews around the world; this initiative raised awareness of the importance of gathering and listening to these stories, and offered a path by which survivors could finally open up and share their experiences. Without any prompting, and at a time when the relatively fresh collective trauma of the Holocaust inspired silence rather than reflection, my father knew that he had an obligation—to his family, to himself, and to the world—to give voice to his own experiences. Reliving his most painful years through telling his story took tremendous courage, and wanting a book published took great foresight and wisdom.

It is not an easy story to hear. My father's family was murdered. He was imprisoned and was a slave laborer, and he was forced to witness incomprehensible atrocities, but he hoped that sharing the story might serve a purpose. Unfortunately, hatred, upheaval, and genocide continue today. Jewish people use the phrase "never again," and vow to not let the world forget the depths to which people can sink. Stories and testimonies like my father's are vital to keeping this vow. Their memory is, for us, a blessing.

The Goldmans and Ceders were large, tight-knit Jewish families in Poland, happy and thriving. Then one maniac and his followers murdered nearly all of them—along with millions of others—and scattered the few survivors. I never had the chance to grow up with the normal joys of family traditions, or of times spent with grandparents, aunts, uncles, cousins, and family friends. My son, Jason, has also missed out on these joys, and this book will hopefully help fill some voids for him. Because my father's family was violently wrenched apart when my father was young, most of their stories are gone forever. I'm keenly aware that not knowing these stories weighed heavily on him. My father would be pleased knowing Jason now has more family stories.

Writing this book was extremely difficult at times—heart-rending and exhausting. Sometimes, I had to displace myself in order to get through the material, while listening to my own father's voice on his tapes. Yet his words drove me to complete the task. He said that the book would have "the sole purpose to dramatize to all the people so that they can understand the inhumanity from man to man, what can happen when a people, no matter what race, is pointed out for religious, racial, or ethnic discrimination, humiliation, or persecution—and even annihilation." I am still overcome, trying to fathom how anyone could endure such depravity and not let himself be defined by it.

But somehow he did not let hatred and loss define him. He was marked by it and transcended it too. He was a man of hope. Once he said that his book should be dedicated "to all the young children of the world. I hope for them to have a better world, a future, a peaceful and harmonious life for all these kids, and not the way my youth was cut down." When he sent his written testimony to the US Holocaust Memorial Museum, he wrote, "Writing and dictating my story wrenched and tore my heart. I have finally spoken up as requested. Please don't let this go to waste. Use it, and use me, if necessary."

Yes, it is necessary. This is a story of survival, of beating the odds. But also of hope, tenacity, and perseverance. My father struggled, and won. Once he began to recuperate, he promised himself he would learn as much as he could and work hard, and become the best person he could be. He found his place in life, and left a lasting influence on those who knew him. May this book carry his influence to others.

L'Shalom
Lee Goldman Kikel
Summer 2019

Introduction

When my son was born in 1992, I began to realize how very important our family history was. A few short years later, in 1996, my father passed away. It wasn't until 2015 that I was finally inspired to listen to my father's taped memories and ready to begin this project. Also, at that time, Jason had an opportunity to study in Berlin for a month. My husband and I joined him, then we three traveled to Poland together to retrace some of my father's footsteps. When we returned, I got to work in earnest.

This book is arranged in three parts: Part I is my father's account of his life from his earliest memories through when he was first getting settled in Pittsburgh. In Part II, I continue his story for four and a half decades, through his death—then, a bit beyond. The Appendices offer extensive and significant supplemental information and documentation that give the reader a better picture of Melvin's life and the times.

Part I is my father telling his story *through his own words*, apart from some light editing to preserve continuity or clarity. The bulk of this part comes directly from those priceless audiotapes. At the beginning of each of the seven chapters, I've added a brief introduction to provide context for the narrative that follows. These fill in some of the facts my father could not have known at the time from his individual perspective. A few footnotes have been added within some chapters to give the reader more detailed information.

Especially considering the circumstances, my father's memory was exceptional. The prewar times, especially, were many years past when he recorded his tapes. Then came the horror of war, and the confusion of a Europe flooded with millions of displaced persons. He passed through various refugee centers, hospitals, rehabilitation facilities, and administrative offices amid the chaos that was postwar Europe. His memories were limited, and no doubt some of them were blurred. I checked many details to clarify some confusions on the transcripts (e.g., unintelligible words), but this remains a personal history and not a scholarly work.

Reading this story now, I am struck by some wonderful surprises. My father's father, Chaim Goldman, owned an important metalworking factory in Łódź, and my father worked and learned his trade there. They made official liter measures, certified by the government Bureau of Measurements, and my grandfather had some patents, including a machine to clean the air in textile factories and lessen the threat to the health of the workers. And, this image I'll never forget: One time, after the war, my father and two other death camp survivors made their way to a Polish DP (displaced persons) camp. The Poles in the camp were astonished to see them. They thought Jews had been completely exterminated. In joy, they knelt down and made the sign of the cross. Another story I find so poignant: The day he arrived in America, when my father was trying to sleep on the train from New York City to Pittsburgh, a kind lady paid the porter for the use of a pillow and gave it to him. They had a pleasant exchange, despite not knowing a word of each other's languages, and later they became friends.

My father arrived in Pittsburgh in 1950 as Melvin Goldman. No longer would he officially answer to "Mieczyslaw" or "Mordka." He had very little besides what he carried inside—hope and determination, a strong will, and the memory of his terrible loss.

I wrote Part II, the story of his new life in America, largely from my own memories and research, to create a more complete depiction of his entire life journey. It seemed necessary to expand the book beyond his own words—that is, his tape recorded recollections—so I picked up the narrative of his years in Pittsburgh and described the dear father I knew as a child and young adult. I'm especially gratified to be able to highlight his devotion to his family and to emphasize his long, successful career, including comments from some of his customers-turned-friends.

When I was a child, my dad didn't discuss his life much, including talking about the Holocaust. It was when I was in college that Dad recorded the tapes. I took a few Holocaust studies classes, and we began discussing what had happened. I took notes as he told stories about the Goldmans and the Ceders, and provided lovely memories of Łódź, family vacations, the factory, and prewar life. He remembered all of the camps, hospitals, doctors, zones, and events with so many specifics. This helped me "audit" the tape transcripts for this project. I was very touched by his sharing, but interestingly, it was years before I was ready to begin my more serious inquiries, exploration, and study.

A wealth of materials can be found in the appendices. These items were placed in the back of the book as to not distract from my father's story, and to give him a place for his words to stand on their own—in Part I. The first three appendices—The War . . . , Family Trees, and Maps—plus the timeline page of my father's life, were added to help illustrate his remarkable journey. There are precious few remaining family artifacts from the prewar period; those are included in an appendix, along with a number of photographs from the Polish State Archives depicting the Łódź my father would have known before the invasion. Additionally, when I began organizing this material, I found that my father had saved an enormous amount of paperwork. He came to America with some documents, and in the sixties began submitting what became volumes of forms, letters, and supporting writeups to various restitution programs, applying for compensation for the severe injuries and permanent damage from his imprisonment and forced labor. Only a small, representative sample is included here.

—

With this project, I have come to a greater understanding of who my father was and what he had endured. I had no way of knowing where this process would take me when I first set my sights on a book, or what the final product would look like. However, I am grateful for both the process and result. No book would be able to fully encapsulate my father; nevertheless, this book is a moving and faithful depiction of his strength and abiding humanity. While this world can be dark at times, and we are not free from the hatred that changed the course of my father's life, his story is a beacon that continues to shine in these pages, and in our memories.

PART I

IN MELVIN'S WORDS

1. My Beautiful Childhood Years
1923–1939

1923–1939 *The Goldmans are a hard-working, respectable, middle-class family in Łódź, Poland. Chaim Goldman, the family patriarch, is an accomplished and inventive fabricator of metal fixtures and a veteran of the Polish–Soviet War, as well as a leader in his local trade group. Son Mieczyslaw is the oldest of seven children. As a teenager, he has aspirations to become an engineer but also spends hours at his father's factory learning the metalworking trade. The Goldmans have the means to vacation in the countryside in summers . . . and they are Jewish. The dark clouds of the Great Depression are gathering over Łódź, and an undercurrent of anti-Semitism is growing throughout Europe. The family is not oblivious to their nation's political and economic troubles, nor to the bellicose rhetoric coming from its aggressive neighbor to the west—the Third Reich. Several extended family members have left the country, but like so many of their Jewish neighbors, the Goldmans do not feel the need to flee. They have a good life. Their businesses are prospering. Family is nearby and ties are strong.*

For related documentation, see appendix pages 204–208 (family trees), 213–226.

Photo: The Goldman children on vacation, 1934. Left to right, Chaja Sura, Aron, Natan, Rojza, Josef, and Mieczyslaw, sitting behind Lajb.

I was born in Łódź, Poland, the second largest city after Warsaw. It was an industrial city with over a half million, comparable to the Pittsburgh population when I arrived here in 1950. Most are employed in the textile industry, like the Eitingon Company, the Oscar Kon Company, and other Polish companies. I was the oldest of my parents' seven children. My family was, I would say, middle class; that is, I never had a want for anything. We got almost anything we wanted. My father, Chaim Goldman, was very industrious, very intelligent. My mother, Bajla Maria, was a sweet, gentle woman who would do anything for her family, but she was also independent.

I went to kindergarten and then to public schools, but there was an interruption when I was enrolled in Edelstein school, the most expensive private Hebrew school. I attended for about three years before transferring back to public schools in order to get certification. While in public school, I used to come home like an average kid and do the lessons, and then usually I was very much interested in what went on in our sheet metal shop or factory. It was a relatively small place. There are other manufacturing plants in Łódź; some are diversified and large, others are smaller like ours.

In general, Łódź is not a very clean city. But there are some beautiful places also, like Piotrkowska Street—a long street, attractive—and the Freedom Square, Plac Wolności. There lived before the war about 100,000 Jews and about as many Germans in the town. There were also clothing bazaars, and hucksters would bring various produce to town on Friday. The farmers used to come to town, especially in the summertime, with horse and buggy selling fresh butter, potatoes, and lots of fresh produce, and the people used to go out from their houses and buy whatever they needed. The outlying district is very lovely, like Atamorek [?] and the Cherry Mountains, Wiśniówa Góra.

My mother and father loved to go to the theater, and since I was the oldest grandchild and son, they took me along, and I still remember most of the performances and songs. From five years old, my mom used to take me from time to time on Friday afternoons in a horse and buggy. She used to love the theater or the Philharmonic. The last time I went with my dad, I remember, we went to see the *Yellow Star*. It was 1937 and a well-known artist who had immigrated to the United States, Alexander Granach, came to perform it. I also saw Lola Folman who was a singer and soloist with the Moshe Schneur Choir.

— — — — —

Some things I remember about my father, Chaim Goldman. He was self-employed, in ownership with two other people in a sheet metal factory. Also he owned a separate workshop. My father was fifteen years honorary secretary of so-called *cech* [guild] for metal workers. His secretary was Miss Friedman.

As an officer in the army, my father had fought under Marshal Józef Piłsudski for Poland's liberation from Russia for eighteen months [1919–1921] in the ditches of Brest-Litovsk until Poland was free. He received three distinguished medals for fighting, especially for valor. Since my dad was the only military man, at the table we always talked about the topics of the military.

My dad is a very modern man, but he is also very religious. He went to synagogue every Saturday morning where he had a special place as a Kohain, a Jewish religious order of highest degree, of which there are three degrees. He is looking forward to taking us to buy clothes and other special things for the holidays. This, for holidays, is the first time he took me to Kolski's, his barber, to have a shave.

My dad belongs to the oldest synagogue [Altshtot synagogue] in Łódź, like my grandfather who is also in the metal business.

My father was on the board of the Chamber of Commerce of Łódź. As can be understood in Europe, you have to begin as an apprentice, then a fellowcraft [craftsman], and then a master. In each category you have to pass a written exam and also create a masterpiece in order to get certification for this trade. In the fall and winter my dad sat on the examinations to prepare applicants to become masters of the trade. So Saturday, after the synagogue and after he ate, he always dressed in a three-piece suit to go sit on the commission for the tests. He worked with a Pole, the head of the commission, whose name was Mr. Dobjinski, and also served on the sheet metal preparation committee for examinations.

I went with my dad to cech meetings whenever he had to make a speech to the members. These were one- to two-and-a-half–hour speeches. He took me to the meetings in the chamber and afterward asked my opinion of how he did, what I thought of his remarks. We had a closeness. Also he took me to lectures. One I will never forget—the name of the lecturer was Noah Prilutzki. He talked about the Jewish dialectics. I could not understand it, but I enjoyed being there with all the grown-ups.

In the middle of the week, after the meetings at the club, we used to go down and eat the most delicious food—me, my dad, and his buddies.

He was also thoughtful of the kids, the family at home, so we always stopped and bought a cake or some other delicacy on the way home. He worked at a strenuous business, but my dad always took time to think of the family and his friends. He never forgot courteousness and congeniality and compassion for other people. He gave devotedly. In addition to making money, half of his time or more was helping in the preparation and examination of people working toward their certifications.

My dad was a workhorse. He loved his profession and inspired everybody, including me, to love work. He used to tell me, "Work is the medicine of the soul and also part of the enjoyment in life." My mom, on the other hand, taught me how to respect people by using old-fashioned ways, maybe, but they sound not so old-fashioned today but rather rightful,

> *"My dad always took time to think of the family and his friends. He never forgot courteousness and congeniality and compassion for other people. He gave devotedly."*

as I can see now. For example, when I talked about a neighbor, she told me, "First you have to clean your own porch steps before telling your neighbor to clean his house."

Dad had to go to Warsaw once every two months in order to get the parts needed for the shop. The last time he was there was before my bar mitzvah. He brought me back as a gift a *tallis* [prayer shawl], a set of *tefillin* [small leather boxes containing Torah scrolls], and a little *siddur* [Jewish prayer book] with a gold bookmark. My name was printed on the siddur. Up until I became bar mitzvah, Dad made me go to synagogue each week. Afterwards—no pressure.

Saturday morning was my dad's day to walk. He got up about 9:00 a.m., later than during the week. Once he told me in a conversation, "Common sense is not so common. Period." The rest of the week he got up about 7:00 a.m., put on the tallis, sat down for breakfast, read the paper, and went to work while my mom attended to the kids. I remember how he hated cleaning, especially floors or laundry, but he wanted the house to be impeccably clean. He was an impeccable person, but he did not like to see the cleaning being done. Every time my mother started it, he used to walk out. I guess we all have funny ways about us. He used to say also, "When it's your day, it's your day. Keep on going! It is meant for work, for play, try not to get entwined in one thing. Be worldly! Respect another person's opinion and you'll be happy."

I remember some of my mother's cousins—Ceders. One lived about three and a half kilometers away. Another cousin was in his late fifties, near sixty, and he had three daughters. I used to go down Saturday night from time to time. The daughters used to go out for a walk, stroll with me in the park and neighborhood, take me along, and I was terribly proud of it. Also, now and then, on Saturday afternoons I used to go to visit Aunt Rachel Berger, my mother's sister, whose husband had a shoelace factory. I used to go down and eat an evening meal with them. Also, they had about six orchards where we would spend a few days in the summer. My mother's younger sister, Chaja Sura, who married early to my recollection, left for Buenos Aires, Argentina. I keep in touch with her now [late 1970s]. Her son and daughter are my cousins. The son is a dentist, married with children.

At the time, my father's sister, my aunt Sala, had about fifteen girls and they did embroidery work. She had a shop. Also, [most likely Goldman aunts]

I had one aunt working at a chocolate factory, and another, Aunt Wrobleska [?] who had a shoe factory and store.

From time to time, and especially one time I remember right before the outbreak of the war, my dad took me on a Saturday afternoon to a matinee, which was unusual because I usually went by myself. But this time he asked me if we could take along a friend. I did not know what he had in mind but said it was fine to invite a friend. He had a friend by the name of Green with a daughter, blonde, a nice girl, and all of a sudden he picks her up and we go down to cross the Piotrkowska Street to the biggest delicatessen in town. He goes and leaves me and says, "You talk to the girl and then I'll come out. I'll buy some things and we'll go to the movies."

He always used psychology on me in the old-fashioned way. It was beautiful. It took ten to twenty years for me to realize what the man had done for me, for my mom. Of course we went to the movies. Afterward, he asked if I would mind if we got a cottage in Atamorek next year with the Green family. And I could not understand. The next year I go out just reminiscing, and there is the girl and her family on the weekends. He tried to get me together with that girl!

I used to go out and play soccer ball. I was the oldest grandchild, the oldest son out of seven kids. I had very good rapport with my parents most of the time. In the meantime I am finishing school. We have friends. My father runs the factory. My mother tends to the home and the children who are all in school except little Josef who has blond hair and blue-green eyes, who is now three and a half and Lajb, five and a half, with the same blondish hair but with brownish eyes. The others, the older children, at least learned the alphabet, and we teach them at home certain things.

When summer comes, it is the custom in our house that my mother is preparing to go on vacation with the kids, which is what she does every year that I can remember. They go to the Cherry Mountains, to Wiśniówa. She leaves about end of May or middle of June and stays every year until mid-September up to the High Holidays.

While I am the oldest child and grandchild, I stay at home with my dad to help attend to business. We actually enjoy ourselves. He gives me instructions before he leaves for the day. He is gone the whole day attending to other businesses, like the construction of new buildings, where he has people on the outside doing all kinds of work. Meanwhile, I'm taking care of the business at the factory—taking in the money and whatever else has to be done. When he comes home in the evening, we go out to eat or I go for the food.

The factory is closed every Friday at noon. Apprentices clean the tools, and after that my father and I go out to shop for special things, such as medications and delicacies, that we will take along when we join our family for the weekend. First we take the train, where sometimes I would get a delicacy, like Eskimo ice creams. My dad puts his hat on my head sometimes and loans me his pocket watch. We hire a horse and buggy for the remaining five and a half kilometers to the cottage. There is always a celebration when we arrive. The kids come running. My dad always buys anything the kids want when he gets there.

My friend there is Moniek. On Saturday nights he plays the mandolin, and we go into the forest and play and sing and have a nice time. Sometimes my brother and sister come along. It is very sad when we have to leave Sunday afternoon to go back to the city.

The scenery here is beautiful, seventeen kilometers of forest. In order to get into these forests in the summer you have to have a special pass with your picture on it from the government of Poland, and you pay a small fee. Every member of our family has a pass. It has to be shown at all times on your hip, or on the outside of your clothes, for the Polish rangers to see. Having that pass and going to the Polish forest we also did some mischievous things, like all the youth, except not as strong as it is done now in America, but we used to go and take blackberries and blueberries, or do some damage in the forest. The Polish rangers caught me once and sent the dogs after me, which tore up my pants.

There were other little things, minor skirmishes that I remember, playing soccer ball where you weren't suppose to and breaking a window and then being admonished by your father. Coming before him, very disciplined like, and he asked you, "Did you do it intentionally?" If it was intentionally, I was punished like four or five weeks, and not given any pocket money to go to the movies in the wintertime. If it was not intentionally, he paid for the window or whatever I broke.

The summer is over and my mother is coming home to make preparations for the High Holidays. There was a standing joke that I understood later. When my mom came back from vacation, my dad asked her how come she gained some weight. She used to answer, "It's the air, dear, the air."

Life in the wintertime is also beautiful. As in summer, Friday at noon the shop is closed, but my dad and the whole family dressed up for Friday night. There was a helper in the house who made potato soup or other soup. The main meal on Friday is going to be served in the evening after my dad comes home from the synagogue. My mother does her praying over the candles and we sat down for the Sabbath sacrament, which my dad would say, and drink the wine. Our Sabbath was performed in the normal Jewish traditional way. Then we enjoyed the delicious, well-prepared meal. During the holidays, we are very enthusiastic. We dress up especially in new clothes and shoes. We would also get extra things, like a soccer ball. Everyone is eager and animated.

> "My mother does her praying over the candles and we sat down for the Sabbath sacrament... Then we enjoyed the delicious, well-prepared meal."

In the fall my dad's friends, like Silverberg, Klaussner, Himelfarb and many more I don't remember, used to rotate for parties at each other's house with kegs of beer, pretzels, goose meat, and salami.

Dad would sometimes take me, every two or three weeks, on Saturdays to the most honorable and nicest family, that of Moshe Chaim Senderovicz. They lived on Zawadzka [?] Street in the PKO Bank building near the Polish Treasury. Nobody lived in that building except these people. We were only allowed to go in by invitation. A policeman had to let you in. The Senderoviczs did not have children and considered me their own. When I entered, I had to bow down and kiss the lady's hand. My dad trained me that when you walk in, you kiss the lady's hand. It was a nice old-fashioned way in which I was raised. The people present were Mr. Senderovicz, who was president of the cech, Mr. Biegelman, a mechanical engineer, a lawyer by the name of Machtinger, and a Mr. Friedman. They discussed politics and other topics.

I would sit with Dad when he had his breakfast. He gets up about 7:00 in the morning, has breakfast that my mother serves, and reads the paper, the *Folksblat*. From the time I was young, we discussed many things, for instance, the Spanish Revolution and Civil War in the papers and all kinds of intrigue, but this time, since I am after bar mitzvah and becoming a man, he says, "*Tachlis* [getting to the heart of the matter], we have to start tachlis." By this he means, "What am I going to do?" He always wanted me to go to school.

The school he had in mind was Jarocinski Engineering School. We talked about it day in and day out. My father wanted me to become a mechanical engineer and run the factory later on when he retires. My father's friend, Biegelman, was the best mechanical engineer in town and owned a factory. In Europe, you have to ask a person—a father or master—if they want you in the factory. Since I didn't have enough sense to ask, I talked to my mom. She advised me to ask Biegelman if he would want me. I asked and I told him I would like to learn the trade and go to Jarocinski. He says, "Not exactly. I would like you to go and work for somebody else first."

— — — — —

Meanwhile, my dad gives me a piece of paper. He already had corresponded with somebody, another friend of his, a designer of children's clothes, and he sent me up to this gentleman. In those days if you are an apprentice, you sign a contract and stay for four weeks. I remember it is a hot day in July, probably 1938, and I go up and introduce myself to the gentleman. We never talk about money. He says, "Oh, I know, yes. I talked to your father. Now do you know how to clean up the house or the factory? You have to clean up all of this. You have to do this and that. You have to make yourself busy all day and then after about a month, I will let you know if I can use you."

I stayed there for two weeks, but what did I know about children's clothes or designing children's clothes? The only thing I knew was that my dad and mom went out to buy them or bought me a pair of boots. I didn't have the slightest idea about clothes. One day I quit, came home, and told my mom I'm not interested in being a children's clothing designer or any kind of designer for that matter. I would like to be in a factory, sign a contract, and at the same time go to school—Jarocinski school it is.

So my mom talked it over with my dad. I didn't know it. My dad one morning said he would take a half an hour extra to sit down and talk to me. He asked me questions: Do you know what you have to do? Do you realize that you have to sign a contract for three years? You get a black book, your name is in it and whatever you have to do, and you cannot talk back to the master. Money is of no consequence because you won't get any. You only get so much, a *złoty* a week or something, whatever is necessary. After you finish the apprenticeship, then you have to do three more years as a craftsman. That means you are already above the apprentice level where you're only given orders. Instead, you are working on metal, whatever there is to be done. You are independent and, after three years of being a craftsman then it is the responsibility of the master to prepare you for the master level, which takes another four years.

Now I wasn't worried at all about that, and the reason for this is: The way I was told, we go back in Poland around four hundred years, on both sides, in the business. My mother's father was in the metal business, but I also heard that his family was the first to build tile stoves in Końskie. My father's father was in the metal business. My father's father's father's father was in the metal business. My aunt, who went away as a young woman and is now in Argentina, her husband was in the metal business. I was surrounded by metal, and that is where I wanted to stay. I crawled around and walked around in the midst of metal. And I thought I knew a lot about metal. On the other hand, I figured the engineering scientifically would come in handy, among other things, in reorganizing the factory, and my dad agreed.

I learned the metal trade from my father and his father. When I came home from school, I used to watch the apprentices and the skilled workers and learned some things. When I was fourteen, I had already made a few art pieces, like a little milk can and stuff like that. My dad showed off that milk can that took me about four weeks, evenings, to do, showing it off to other masters, friends of his, who used to come in to our company. They praised it as a beautiful piece of art. I walked over one evening and asked Dad why he never tells me it is good. He sat down, smiled with his bright smile and said to me, "If I tell you this was done good, would you ever do better?"

So I signed a contract with my dad to be an apprentice for three years. In the evenings, three times a week, I went to Jarocinski Engineering School. In order to qualify, I had to pass a test for aptitude. Also, my father made sure that I kept on going to school, private school, for about six months. I studied the Talmud for about six months—Rashi's Gemara [part of the Talmud]. It was like taking civil law.

— — — — —

I used to go through a particular drawer that I loved. It had my dad's and mom's and other family pictures, and also souvenirs, like the ones from my dad, especially from the war, small souvenirs. An other drawer was where he kept a bit of money, coming in from the customers, also some silver coins, so-called "Piłsudskis," named for the late marshal of Poland. One day I was looking through it when my dad came in. He said, "It's time we talked about finances." He had seen me puttering around with the money. We talked about finances a little bit, and he explained some things and then sang me a song in Jewish and here's how it goes . . . here's how it goes.[1] When my father sang that song, with its message, I saw what a nice and beautiful person he was. This song and his behavior towards us and other people showed what a person should be:

> Little person,
> when it is going good for you,
> and you are rich,
> without limits,
> think of what a responsibility lays on you,
> when a poor person comes into your house,
> empty handed,
> don't let them,
> out of your apartment,
> because today,
> I have it.
> Tomorrow,
> somebody else,
> and later it might be winding up in others' hands.
> Since with money,
> you shouldn't be proud,
> you can easily lose it,
> so throw away your foolish pride,
> your foolish pride,
> and a person you should be.

I am also reminiscent about the two older gentlemen, Froyam and Bayer, in their sixties or seventies. Froyam was eighteen years in the Russian Army, and he comes back and finds another way to Poland. He lived right across the street from us. The other gentleman was a coppersmith, one of the finest. These two were retired and they did not have anywhere to go, so sometimes they would come to our factory.

---

1 On one of his cassette tapes, Melvin sings his father's song in Yiddish. At another time, he recorded the translation given here. The song's origin is unknown.

They were also very attached to our house. In winter they would sometimes come for whole days, day in and day out. We had a coal stove in the front where the old men baked potatoes and *milch* [roe] of herring and kept the conversation going, kibitzing all day. My mom used to lay out herring and cut it up for them. They would also have hot tea in a glass and bite a piece of sugar. That was the custom, throughout Eastern Europe. They used to enjoy themselves, and it was a pleasure having them around. They were like guests all the time, all year round.

I talked to them a lot, and they told me old stories. From them I got a real education, besides what I learned from my father and going to school. These two old gentlemen always used to talk to me and question me, either about the Hebrew Bible or they talked to me about politics.

The wife of one of those gentlemen had a vegetable stand at a place that was like a modern mall with meat and the newest figs and stuff like that. On Saturday night my mom would shop there. From time to time we would invite them on Saturday for supper. Our home was real open and welcoming. Evenings, we often had guests at the house.

We also took in at least two boys who needed a home. In 1937, a man brought in a boy whose mother had died and whose father didn't want him. His name was Reuben. He stayed with us till the start of the war, worked in the shop. Dad made him an apprentice in his factory and we adopted him.

Another boy that was an apprentice was named Kudlik. His father was sick and had to go for treatments in Vienna and he lost everything. That was the first time I had heard about cancer of the neck. We took him in and signed a contract with him. And, my uncle Jake also goes to our factory.

— — — — —

The work in the factory was of various kinds. We did specialized work in sheet metal and other metals. Our products were sold in hardware stores as well as directly to factories and other businesses. We had three patents. One was the liter patent that my dad and grandfather had, the only ones in the whole city that were allowed to do it. You made these liters [measuring containers] that were extremely difficult, precision made. The two guys that worked on that specialty made about sixty of them a week. They had to be tested with water, brimming the water with a glass moving over it to check for leaks. We had a woman and her daughter who used to clean them with a special cleaner. They had to shine to perfection. After that you had to take them down to the Bureau of Measurements where they stamped each one of them. Very seldom do I remember that any were thrown out or not approved at a later date. These liters we sold to stores.

Also before the war we made *tassen* [cups] cleaners for restaurants. It was a special patent that my dad discovered and we used to do it for the Berman brothers and others. It was square or oblong, made of brass. On top it had sticking out a six-point piece with two hoses and when you pushed a glass on top of the spoke, it cleaned outside and inside of the glass, and the dirty water ran out on the other side. I used to carry in the summertime two of them to be nickeled at Voss's—a friend of my father at Piotrkowska Street who had a big factory for nickeling jobs and silvering jobs, and then I'd go pick them up. They were beautiful. I sometimes got ten or twenty *groszy* to go on the streetcar, but most of the time I kept the money.

We also made our own power stanchions [?]. Mr. Voss also nickeled these. I used to go once a week or once every two weeks to deliver them.

The third patented item, *rozpylacie powietrza* [air sprayer], was something used in all the textile factories. It was approximately two and a half feet in diameter inverted, and it was screwed up into the ceiling. It caught the dust so that the factory workers did not get tuberculosis. I was sent on horse and buggy to the Oscar Kon Company every Friday to deliver those machines; usually two pieces were made in the week that we finished. I remember well that sprawling factory, the gates with the security guards. I was so impressed with it. It felt like I was like a big man with much responsibility. I even talked to my friends about it and they envied me.

Also we made big containers, with metal called "new silver," and enameled pots, cutting off the ears [side handles], for restaurants to put in containers. It had to be run right, otherwise it would rust. We had two-and-a-half-foot cutters set in a wooden log, and I learned how to do that. We also made for some retired military men incubators from metal to raise chicks. When I delivered one, I got a big bonus.

- - - - -

The work in the factory was fascinating. Everything was done by hand as if the workers were making art pieces, especially the custom pieces. They used various metals including nickel and brass. I used to stay up evenings and watch. We used to work on Primus machines and on electricity. And it was funny, up to the date when I hear a buzz of a Primus machine, or naphtha burning,

I could fall asleep because that was how I used to sit as a little boy in front and watch how they soldered and did those jobs. Sometimes I went out on jobs, especially to help out my uncle or the apprentices or even the craftsmen when I was out of school in the summer.

> "The work in the factory was fascinating. Everything was done by hand as if the workers were making art pieces, especially the custom pieces. . . . I used to stay up evenings and watch."

We had a sheet metal guillotine to cut metal. We had many machines, like Sieg [?] machines, and all the other machinery and it was rarely quiet. He was very particular, my dad, a very particular person. The minute the apprentices cut something they had to lift off the leftovers from the metal and put it into containers.

There was an exchange program every fifth week if we completed a big job. We had a big party and exchanged gifts with my father's friends. We had beer that was tapped, salted matzos, and other delicacies that you very seldom see around here. It was usually on a Saturday. If we finished a very, very big job, my dad used to take me and the workers to Schmuel's or Krell's, big restaurants where we had *kishke* [stuffed beef casings] or something like that. From time to time he was generous and let us take the copper or brass that we salvaged from buildings. We would sell it as scrap and have a little bit of extra pocket money.

Aside from the other things we did in the factory and shop, we also undertook construction—building of buildings, doing roofing and gutters. We had special people for winter and summertime—my dad used to go out and buy furs for them and boots. The last building we did was Cichtikers [?] building, Zavawadz [?] #53, a four-story building. We even worked on that in the winter, and my dad bought the guys sheepskin coats. We did all the work on buildings for some German gymnasiums [high schools]. It was about fifteen kilometers away and you took a train to go out there, of course, in the summertime.

— — — — —

In Poland it is the custom to take the military test. The first thing you do is you are sent up to a local test site. I took an aptitude test given by a lieutenant and a sergeant. If you wanted to go into college life, you had to take that aptitude test to see if you are mechanically inclined for the profession you want. I received an A. After that, my dad filed the papers, and about three weeks later

I got the book for me to become a full apprentice at the company. At the same time, if you want to go to college [secondary education], you have to enroll, and I did.

Also, the custom was that young men in Poland prepared for military service—when you are fourteen years old. You bought your own uniform and your own personal items. In the wintertime while you go through the lessons in school in the college, a few times a week you have to spend an evening training with a Polish lieutenant by the name of Shermans. You trained inside—gymnastics and everything, including to prepare to use a rifle but only artificially without real bullets. Every Sunday, you have to get up at 4:30 in the morning and walk eight kilometers for drill. You began at 6:00 at a place called Haller's Square, named after General Haller. We wore uniforms and used live ammunition, a Mauser [rifle], and hand grenades. It was actual practice, the same like you go here to boot camp. After doing that for two years you get a certificate, and of course, if your time comes up to serve in the armed forces, you go in and serve.

For many years the marshal of Poland was Edward Rydz-Śmigły, a youngish man who became marshal of Poland because Marshal Piłsudski who died favored him. The Polish have a joke about Rydz-Śmigły that he can be a president of Poland or run the country as if every Pole can be a ballet dancer. That is how talented he is. It was true. The reason I heard this was, in time of war, 1939, it was a rumor, that the minute the war started, that this general flew with his family and entourage to Romania and took as much money as he could.

Now the year is 1939. I am sixteen years old. The Polish government is calling for all the citizens, including children, school children, anybody who can help, to go out and dig ditches around certain perimeters of the city. Also my father becomes the chief of the district in civil defense. The Polish government says there is nothing to worry about; Germans cannot attack Poland and win. The Polish president had speeches on the radio, advising the Polish citizens the Germans would fight until the last drop of blood, but the Germans could never invade Poland. They will never take Poland.

In the meantime, we prepared for civil defense, the ditches, the training; and the Polish government

"We prepared for civil defense, the ditches, the training; and the Polish government issued orders on how to behave during a civil emergency. Everybody was trained."

issued orders on how to behave during a civil emergency. Everybody was trained. Everyone had to have a flashlight and it was covered with blue, and be prepared to cover the windows [in case of nighttime bombing]. After 7:00 the doors of the big buildings, the front doors, had to be closed and it was somewhat confusing. You had to go four or five kilometers down the road to do exercises and people spoke to you, instructors, telling you what to prepare for and what to do, but all in all, it was a fiasco. It was not organized.

— — — — —

We were still most of the time carefree. We cannot foresee what is going to happen. We have food, life goes as pleasant as possible, what we try to make out of it. I always had a dream to become an engineer and enjoyed school very much. I was on my way.

My childhood years were very beautiful. Of course I omitted certain things here, not consciously but because it is very hard to remember. While you go to school, you have a run-in with Polish boys. They call you Jew or you have a fight in Łódź; there is a big place where you play soccer ball. There are other incidents. You have good times and bad, but the Poles never showed any love for the Jews. They used to write on the walls: "Down with the Jews" and "The Jews are with us." We saw it all the time. They sometimes broke windows. It wasn't a country where you could live in peace. There were 30 million Poles and among them 3.5 million Jews.

Before the war we used to go around playing soccer ball. We'd go up to school and also played in the *aleike* [?]. The Poles used to come and harass us and always wanted to fight. The Club Maccabee played there and whenever they played the Polish ŁKS and we won, we had trouble.

I cannot say there weren't good times then. I was born there, but there was always something going wrong, such as a drunk coming in from the post office, into the Jewish section, and starting trouble. The Jews in Poland had begun to defend themselves for the last fifty or sixty years. My dad told me, my uncle, and my aunts, and I understood that when they come in, we start to fight back. We started realizing that we cannot be passive. I don't believe now in passivity. But with all of the things going on, my dad told me, "You have to hold your head up high. You have to be a proud person. You didn't take anybody's wealth away. You didn't steal. You don't do nothing wrong. You should be proud. And on top of it you should be a proud Jew. The reason for this is . . . you never took away from their literature . . . it's these people that took ours . . . they learn from us, they interpreted our Bible. . . you don't have nothing to worry about."

I still cannot understand how that country survived. I have a feeling, a deep feeling, that if it wasn't for the Jewish people, the Ukrainians, and other minorities, I don't know how the Poles would run a country. That is my opinion. I don't think too greatly about the Polish people, and the reason for this is they were instigating, even the preachers.

My dad used to tell me negatives even at that time. Even though, I would consider him a patriot. He fought for Poland. He got wounded in Poland, for them. He was awarded the Polish Iron Cross, but still in all, they did not love Jews. Not only didn't they love them, I think that the majority hated them. They were jealous. They were not educated enough, I don't think. They always tried to keep the Jews down. Every once in a while you heard things, like in little towns, where they had a riot against the Jews, like you would have a riot in the United States in the South against the blacks. It was always something. If the economy didn't work or if anything happens, it was the Jews' fault. If they didn't have enough bread or didn't work hard enough or it was bad times, it was always caused by the Jews. The Jews were at fault for everything. They were scapegoats that suffered.

─────

Now that I am middle-aged, I look back and I think maybe Poland is not a country like England and France. They at least were more technologically advanced and more civilized countries, more than Poland. Poland was not technologically advanced, like Germany. The hatred in Poland, though, the Germans had a perfect ally in the Poles when it came to annihilating the Jews. Very, very few . . . maybe counting on your fingers . . . did Polish people help hide a Jewish person at the time of the war or help them out otherwise. They were always jealous. They said the Jews had everything, while they had nothing. They didn't realize that the Jews worked like dogs in order to accumulate something to be able to send their kids to school or to be able to advance themselves. But for the Poles, it was always the Jews' fault.

> "If there was a Catholic church on one side, the Jew had to walk on the other side."

And the reason I don't have anything good to say about it maybe is because of the bad memories. I remember as a kid when I went out with my mom to the Cherry Mountains or to visit my aunt Rachel who had a big orchard. Walking off the train and here were four Polish boys who tried to take away my soccer ball. I got in a fight with them and got beaten up and beat up one or two of them, but it was always, always the Jews.

Another thing that aggravates the life out of me now especially is thinking back that a Polish Jew after being there for four to five hundred years and being rooted in the culture, speaking perfect Polish, writing their literature, doing their things, paying their taxes and everything, fighting their wars, even the thousands who died right before the Germans invaded Poland, Jewish boys dying, they still had to walk off the sidewalk. If there was a Catholic church on one side, the Jew had to walk on the other side most of the time. As far as religion itself, it was very hard for me to understand at that time that little towns had *pogroms*.[2] A few windows broken in a bakery. It was always a nagging problem.

In the meantime the Jewish population of Łódź is represented by an official organization, and they had a spokesman at that time. Anti-Semitism is becoming bad. The Polish fascist party is starting to show its cockiness by throwing stones—what is not new—in the windows of Jewish stores but with a little bit more cockiness. They also demolished Polish newspapers, the Polish socialist newspaper, by destroying their equipment. This is all what we hear. Even the police were never friendly and were showing their hostility even more.

Life in Europe is not as tranquil as it used to be a few years back. What I mean is it sounds like the whole world is talking war talk. People stay in groups discussing the newspaper stories about war and the increasing power of the Nazis in Germany, that they would make war, what is going to happen to Poland and all the European countries. Of course nobody, even diplomats and government officials, could predict at this time the calamity, the atrocities, the terror, the hardship that were to follow, or the lies of fascism. We did not know that the forces of evil were at work. In the meantime you hear about the German Jews and Nazism, but it is strictly from the paper's point of view. You cannot make up your mind what is going to happen actually. You hear things and it is all rumors.

> *"We did not know that the forces of evil were at work. You cannot make up your mind what is going to happen actually. You hear things and it's all rumors."*

— — — — —

---

2   Organized persecution of a religious or ethnic group, especially Jews.

As far as living at that time, my recollection comes from reading the papers about the fight that went on in the senate, the Polish senate, about Jewish slaughtering of animals for meat; that the Jews should not be able to slaughter their way. The Jewish senate at that time, leaders Mincberg and Sommerstein, kept telling the Polish people to worry about the German armaments industry and that they had a feeling, they said, that we had more important things to worry about than painting houses and Jewish slaughtering traditions. I think about a Polish debutante who was the most outspoken on the senate floor from what we read in the papers and heard on the radio. She kept up that stupid agenda for a whole year and a half while the Germans already planned how to occupy the country. We can see it now in retrospect. They invited back the Polish minister, that I have a feeling was a German, invited Göring and the others, to hunt bear in the Polish forest while they were stealing the documents about the country, the strengths, the military, and other secrets. Of course they helped themselves to all these Polish plans and whatever they needed for the invasion of the country.

2. The Germans March into Łódź
1939–1944

1939-1944 *The timing of the German invasion of Poland, one result of secret negotiations between the Soviets and Germany, is unexpected, both to Poland and the world. Polish forces are quickly subdued. More surprising, though, is the swift and powerful Nazi takeover of Polish cities, along with rapid appropriation of industrial and manufacturing sites, and the brutal subjugation of the Jewish population. The formation of the ghetto in Łódź begins. The Goldmans, like the rest of the Jews in Łódź, are caught off guard, and the family must now readjust their lives and make difficult decisions, often very quickly. Surrounded by turmoil and destruction, they don't know what is going on nor do they know whom to trust. They live with curfews and rationing, and in constant fear. But, they do have one thing in their favor: the Goldman family is strong and resourceful.*

For related documentation, see appendices pages 199–203, 209 (map of Łódź ghetto), 227.

Photo: Elderly women carrying young children and bundles of personal belongings trudge along a street in the Łódź ghetto toward the assembly point for deportations to Chełmno. The first of the Nazi extermination camps, it was about 50 kilometers (30 miles) north of Łódź. (From US Holocaust Memorial Museum, courtesy of Muzeum Sztuki w Łódźi.)

We heard that the Germans had invaded Poland [on September 1, 1939] when the Polish president made an announcement over the radio. We did not know which way they would come. We heard rumors that in Kunów, the Polish military were preparing some divisions to start fighting the Germans. All of that was over Danzig and Leipzig. First, the Germans do not want nothing else but Leipzig. Now they want Danzig, the corridor. It went on for a while and everybody talked about it constantly. Then suddenly, a cry went up: All Polish citizens—keep cool, calm. We will fight back the enemy. That kind of talk.

At this time many Poles start realizing the presence of a fifth column, an element later called Volksdeutsche.[1] They are Polish citizens who are ethnically, racially, German and non-Jewish. They are the ones to be feared most because they become the spies. Jewish people began to listen as these spies talked about who owned the buildings, advising the Germans coming with planes and pointing out focal points of population or the factories where

---

1 Volksdeutsche (German people), People of German ancestry or ethnicity living outside the Reich. Before the war, some Volksdeutsche in Poland and other targeted territories organized to help pave the way for Nazi occupation.

everything is. These Volksdeutsche not only spied out Jewish businesses but also Polish businesses, everything that was strategic, the plans and everything.

At that time there is turmoil, nothing organized at all, absolutely turmoil. No organization. No preparation. No nothing.

Within a week the Germans marched into Łódź in the most horrible, horrible way. People were running all over the place, moving around, afraid, not knowing where to go. Some people started to leave Łódź for the small towns like Zgierz, only about twelve to fifteen kilometers away, or to the countryside. Then there were rumors that the Germans came down with planes and strafed these travelers, killing them all on the highways by the thousands.

First, they come and demolish the synagogue, the oldest synagogue in Łódź, called the Altshtot.[2] They climbed to the top, to the roof, and doused the wooden structure with gasoline. It burned to the ground. For two weeks after the burning of the synagogue, my sister and I collected charcoal from the site for use at home.

A "house of prayers" was located behind the synagogue for the less affluent people. I remember my father telling me that he donated thousands of bricks and so much money, and that my grandfather donated the silver and beautiful covers for the Torahs for both the synagogue and the house of prayers.

The next thing, the Germans got together a few Jews, dressed them up like olden times with scrolls in their hands. A little bit farther down the street there was an area, like a garden, with a few trees where they took pictures of these people for propaganda purposes to send around the world showing how good the people are treated—that they are even allowed to pray. They wear the holy shawls and the whole thing. And after that the Germans put them on transports.

> "... every day there was tension and horrible feelings. You did not understand what was coming on."

Of course, every day there was tension and horrible feelings. You did not understand what was coming on. We found out that the smaller kids were useless to the Germans and were taken away. We worried about their being killed because there was no resistance among the residents, nothing, when the Germans walked in. Those first two days we saw thousands of trucks and

---

2 Altshtot (old town) synagogue at 20 Wolborska Street. Also known as the Stara (old) synagogue, it was Łódź's main Orthodox synagogue. Rebuilt between 1897 and 1900, initial construction was circa 1861. This building replaced Łódź's first synagogue, which was wooden and built in 1809 at 8 Wolborska.

motorcycles and machinery and armaments and planes flying over. Thousands. Now who can be strong enough to refuse an order when you see all those thousands of soldiers, hundreds of thousands of trucks and jeeps and armaments? How are you going to resist that kind of force? Yet I remain to this day still in awe that nobody . . . nobody . . .[3]

My dad and mom sat us down and we had a session. We decided not to go no place, to stay put, to keep our family together. There was a jalousie [blind] in front of the factory. Instead of staying in our house, we moved into the front of the shop, and covered the jalousie. At first we had food. My dad had nearly a thousand pounds of wood—planks that we used for other things—and three houses down was our warehouse at #31. We figured that from time to time we would go out and get some of that wood or chop it, so there would be enough heating material. Food, we had a little bit, only for about a month, so nothing to worry about for the time being, we thought. No need to panic. And we don't go no place. We still have family members living close by.

– – – – –

My mother got a letter from her father, Icek Ceder, saying he could no longer live in Końskie because of anti-Semitism. He was driven out of his house; his factory and all his property were confiscated. My father found a place for him about ten blocks from us, set up a shop for him, and gave him some tools so he could make a living. I was a boy—I didn't know that my mother's mother had died. Icek had a son and a daughter with him, and the reason I remember it is because the girl had a soprano voice and always sang to me. My grandfather Icek died in the ghetto.

Every Sunday, my father's father, Eli Melech [Majlech Goldman], used to go out with a samovar and sugar cubes for the poor. He had lived on Lutomierska Street. He moved to Görlitz with his wife, Rajzla Goldman, but the rest of the sixty-nine members of our family were still in the city of Łódź. When Grandfather left, he took a little coal stove, put a double bottom in it and hid silver coins in it. He also told my dad he had concealed

---

3 Though it no doubt seemed to those in the Łódź ghetto (Litzmannstadt) that their Polish neighbors had forgotten them, there were several attempts to help. A church in Łódź issued fake birth certificates with Christian names. Some residents helped Jews live in hiding, at great risk to themselves. Catholic convents harbored Jewish children. A number of Poles from Łódź were later awarded titles of "Righteous among the Nations" by Yad Vashem, the World Holocaust Remembrance Center in Israel. In the end, these efforts were tragically inadequate for the more than 200,000 Jews living in Łódź before the war.

10,000 silver złotys, coin money, in the chimney of his home in case he didn't come back.

Eli Melech and his wife lived about 750 kilometers away. In the year 1942 he came back to visit us and stayed with us for a couple of months but had to go back to my grandmother. I never knew how he, being seventy-two years of age, could make a 750-kilometer trek to town to see us in the winter and then go back to his home. He had actually come back to retrieve the złotys, which was about equal to 2,000 US dollars. He had hidden the silver coins in the chimney so he and my grandmother could live off of it. That is what I found out later. Then, of course, we never heard from him again.

– – – – –

When the war broke out and they started to close in the ghetto, my dad went to a German friend and started talking to him about what we can do, if he has any ideas. He says, "No, I cannot do anything." And, that my dad has to forget about it, never to call him, to stay away, he cannot do anything about it. I remember we had been the best friends. He used to come and have a drink and come for supper and he used to love my mom. He used to play around with us kids. He was a very wealthy guy with a couple of cars. We also worked for the Garmalinskis, who told us the same thing.

My dad used to tell me how Uncle Joel, Dad's brother, had a rough time in Constantinople after being smuggled out from Poland, on his way to Israel. I never found out why he left. I guess, restlessness. After a few years and struggling through, he opened a nice shop in the Tel Aviv area and got a motorboat on the Jordan. He was well off. He wrote for us to come. My dad made fun of him: "Who needs America or Israel when we have it here—we have a normal life." He finally admitted this to me in the ghetto, when our normal life was gone.

My mother's cousin, a Ceder staying on Lagiewnicka Street, also left about the same time, because he was wealthy. He left his wife and kids, and then took them over to Israel when I was a little kid. He even came to visit for three months before the war and left quite a tidbit to the poor side of the family. He was a well-to-do person who left some things to relatives. When he left Poland, he had only a tallis and a prayer book, but when he visited us in Poland, he was a nice wealthy man. He had three or four buildings, one of them in Jerusalem. His daughter, Sarah Appel, is now [late 1970s] in Jerusalem, and we stay in touch by writing.

– – – – –

In Łódź, after the occupation of Poland, the Germans began to take away Jewish businesses. They confiscated everything from the Jews and relocated them to one small area of the city, which became the ghetto. During this process many were killed. Our rooms were demolished and our houses and property were taken away. They allowed five days to move all Jews, who didn't already live within the confines of the ghetto, into the ghetto that will be closed in. My family was in with everyone else. Jews were formally sealed in on May 1, 1940. Electric wires were put up with German soldiers behind them, and nobody was allowed to go within fifty feet of the wires or they got shot.

> *"The Germans began to take away Jewish businesses. They confiscated everything from the Jews and relocated them to one small area of the city."*

The ghetto was about as large as a city area that could contain 50,000 people in the United States; there were 150,000 Jews in that ghetto in May 1940.

There were pronouncements telling what the inhabitants of the ghetto were supposed to do and not allowed to do. There were hundreds and hundreds of decrees later on to be put up on the walls that everybody reads, the Jewish population especially. The first pronouncement was plastered on the walls all over the ghetto, saying all Jews—including old people, the middle-aged, the young and the kids—had to wear a yellow David's star [Star of David], ten centimeters, on the breast. In the center of the star was written "Jude" [Jew].

The next order was no persons allowed outside after 6:00 p.m., except in certain cases where they either worked or were functionaries of the ghetto administration. Such people had to wear white armbands and carry identification passes. Curfew hours were harshly and one hundred percent enforced. If somebody was caught after curfew, he was taken and you never heard of him again.

Other orders followed that all able-bodied people had to work. So-called "resorts" were established, which were the various factories. I worked at the metal factory in the ghetto. Also, anytime the Germans needed workers, they grabbed people in the street, boys and men, and took them away, often never to be heard of again.

There are no words ever written that adequately describe or explain what went on in the ghetto. To me, it feels like we're in a zoo. Some of them stand outside the wires, the Poles, and look in at us.

— — — — —

The parish house of St. Mary's Assumption Church, in the center of the ghetto, was used as headquarters for the Criminal Police, the Kripo.[4] There, was the torture house, made of red brick and called the Red House.[5] The Kripo took people down there after the ghetto was electric wired. We could see it down the street, only about a quarter kilometer away.

They used to take everybody that anybody knew from before who had any wealth or any belongings and keep them incarcerated. In 1942, my dad got a so-called "invitation" by the Gestapo,[6] the Kripo. Everyone knew what that meant.

I knew an old man, a tailor with two sons, who was paralyzed on one side. I was always nice to him. One of his sons, Yuma, was a stool pigeon for the Germans. We knew by his clothes and the food he ate. I went to the old man and begged him to plead with his son on behalf of my father. He did and so my father came home. He never talked about what happened to him there. He thanked me and we were a family again, the only family of nine people in the whole ghetto.

I remember well the day my dad came back from the Red House after eight days. He was so beaten up that he was about five days in bed. He looked at me, looked at my mom, and then starts saying to us, "Now I understand, but I don't understand why. I don't understand the brutality of it." We put compresses on him for five days. My father said he was able to live through it only because he was thinking about us, about me especially, because I was the oldest and someday maybe times will get better.

Walking home with my dad from the factory, I talk to him and he talks to me. And I know he did not get over yet the beatings he got by the Kripo. You can tell in his eyes, in the way he looks, and the way he thinks, but he keeps on talking to me with optimism. He is trying to give me a hopeful view of the future. He always talks about nice things. He says, "We will survive, we will survive. The only thing you have to do is just hold on. It couldn't happen, bad things can't happen while the whole world is looking on. There is a France.

---

4 Kripo (Kriminalpolizei), The German Criminal Police Department, under control of the SS during the Nazi years.

5 Red House, A church building, converted into the headquarters of the Kripo, where they carried out interrogations, torture, and murder of Jews. The house still stands, owned again by the Catholic church.

6 Gestapo (Geheime Staatspolizei, Secret State Police), Formed out of the existing state police after the Nazis took power.

There is an England. There is a United States. All these nations, they are righteous nations. Somehow, somewhere I hope pretty soon they will come and help us or get us out." But we don't understand.

My dad also reminisced and told me what his father had told him about World War I, that when the Germans came into Poland, they were very good to the Jews. They were nice. At first we didn't understand that it is a different world. He started realizing some of it as he read before the war about the Nazis and everything, but nobody could understand the calamity, nobody could understand the beast, the barbarism that would go on.

In the meantime, day in and day out, even though we are working and we have the police and you are surrounded, they still come in from the Criminal Police or SS or SA,[7] like guards at a zoo. They keep on looking at you, walking down the street, rounding people up, taking them away, and you never hear of them again. That goes on day in and day out, day in and day out.

— — — — —

We thought the Kripo had taken all of our belongings of worth, but the Germans came in and plundered through the ghetto and took out everything, all the valuables, even furniture. Trucks are rolling day and night. First from the homes, cleaning out the ghetto, then the factories, searching every place thoroughly. Everything goes, textiles, leather, copper, everything. This is going on while the wretched life, unbearable from hunger, goes on.

The Hitler Youth[8] also came in. They would roam the streets and come into houses looking for copper and brass for their war machines, for bullets and stuff. These young punks were indoctrinated and hated Jews. They thought nothing of pulling a man's beard or putting a knife in you. They were the worst kind of kids. It was like watching a monster movie.

Luckily, I had a pass because I worked. I got beaten up a few times, including while being on *Montage* [assembly-line] work. Two Germans knocked out five of my upper teeth for no reason. I was not guilty of anything besides crossing the sidewalk inside the factory.

---

7 SS (Schutzstaffel, Protection Squadron), Nazi security forces, the major paramilitary security apparatus under Hitler. SA (Sturmabteilung, Storm Detachment), the infamous "brownshirts," the main perpetrators of escalating violence against the Jews in the late 1930s.

8 Hitler Youth, The young people's arm of the Nazi Party, and the only youth organization permitted in Germany after 1934. Membership became virtually compulsory for boys and girls over ten years old. Over time, the Hitler Youth became increasingly militarized.

Some people, like our friends three streets down—Silibeck, a good friend of my dad—moved in with us because the Nazis or the Hitler Youth still rioted, still came in and caught people, and made all kinds of problems. We did not know all the terrible things going on. It was a time of not knowing what is going to happen.

One day, after what you call a day's work, we heard some commotion in the factory. Something is in the air. We did not know what, but we knew that the Hitler Youth was coming in and they were going to show off to themselves what they are doing to the Jews.

It was about 5:00 in the afternoon on a Sunday. A couple of Hitler Youth came in with a man from the Criminal Police and went down the street. We were looking out the window and saw them coming, looking out the window. I told my little brother Josef to go hide. When my mom used to go on vacation, one of the last years, my dad built a galley [attic space] in the back of the factory. It was a nice little galley with beautiful little steps going up. I told Josef, the only one home, to go upstairs, to go up there and hide in the galley. There was a little couch. I said get under the couch so they cannot find him.

They came in and plundered the house. They found twenty or thirty pounds of copper, nails like, and took that with them. They roughed me up a little bit and asked me if anybody was there. They went up the steps and lifted up a cover on the couch and saw my little brother. I thought for sure they were going to kill him or take him with them, but they just looked at him. Later they came back, gave me a couple of beatings, and left.

They did not go into the house through the back door. If they had, they would have found a few hundred pounds of copper or brass or English tin that we used for soldering that was very, very expensive now in the ghetto. It was leftover from when we stopped production in the shop. We kept it under a bed. If they had found that, they would have waited for my mom and dad, and the whole family would have gone up in the smoke.

When my dad came home in the evening, he went out to see the neighbors. I told him about the incident with the Hitler Youth, and he said, "Well, tonight we will have to do something about it." He got us some bags, made from material, that we put around the middle of the belly. Then my sister Rojza, my brother Aron, and I walked down the street in the evening wearing our white armbands—my father loaned my sister his, and my brother and I had ours. We had them because we worked. Aron, two years younger than I, worked in a factory too. At that time Aron worked with an artist and only on certain projects, like cages for birds and brass, really beautiful things. He had a very good aptitude for that. Anyhow we took all that stuff, put it around our waists in the material bags like belts, and went down the street one by one and threw it in the toilets.

There was no running water and no sewer system. There were house toilets [outhouses], like in the backyard of a big building. There were sixty or seventy people living in the building. We went down to each building and threw all this material into the toilets, the copper and brass and all that English tin. We also had some small valuables and materials, like new silver and stuff. All of that went. We must have put about 150 to 200 pounds of metal in the toilets. My dad said it is not worth the aggravation of keeping it; it is not worth dying for. After the war, if anything happens, whatever happened, we know we had put it away. But he left himself enough English tin and a little bit of material so that we, my brother and I, could do something with it in the evenings.

Ration cards were issued, of course. They were distributed for each working person, and didn't distinguish between a child or an older person yet.

After about a month and a half or two, the rations came up, and each one got so much bread and so much kohlrabi [turnip cabbage] or potatoes. Each person got half a gram of sugar a day. You got about ten grams of bread, a couple of frozen potatoes in the winter, a piece of kohlrabi. That was it. You had to spare yourself, be careful of every scrap of food. Mothers and the fathers often did not eat, giving their portions instead to their kids. My mother did that—gave us most of hers—so we could keep some strength. It was not enough to live on, but not enough to die from either. Everybody still had a little bit, or someone sold something. People tried to survive, and a little underground market and exchange went up.

It was a miserable life, always being hungry. If you were a big eater, you were gone the first year. The first summer in the ghetto even though you were on a starvation diet, you could survive for a short while. But when the winter came along, there were no heating materials except what you broke up and wood that you used.

We kept our spirits up because we were a whole family. Also we got the *Beirat* [advisory council] designation, a privileged class in the ghetto. But even with an extra ration of food you still starved. My dad brought home a little bottle of liquid. Each of us got a couple of drops because we were so weak that we couldn't lift our feet to go on the sidewalk. After the drops we felt better. We also got a parcel of land about one hundred feet by five feet, where we could grow vegetables in the summer. For two years we grew carrots, beets, potatoes, and some greens. On Sunday we used to go to that little garden and tend it. As weak as we were, we liked to do it because it helped the family.

You get small food rations that barely can keep you on your feet, but you have to produce piecework. You have to work hard and produce like you would on a normal diet, under normal circumstances. It seems impossible, but we did it. As time went on, rations got smaller. By the end, a diet of about three hundred calories a day would be tops for each person.

> *"You get small food rations that barely can keep you on your feet, but you have to produce piecework. You have to work hard and produce like you would on a normal diet, under normal circumstances."*

Besides being fenced in by electric wires, we had to get up in the morning and walk to work, a long walk when you are hungry. Everybody had to work; otherwise, you did not get a ration card. You go to sleep hungry. You get up hungry, and you have to go to work to produce for these beasts. If you are lucky, by 12:00, the factory would hand out soups. You had your own metal container, called a *menażke* [mess kit]. You went over and get a soup, which was like dirty water, barely a quarter of one potato in the whole soup that had to last you until the evening. It was absolutely impossible to live on.

It is a constant nightmare and also cold. There was no coal in the winter. You are numb all the time. Trudging in the wintertime and in the summer with always that terrible feeling. Maybe you get one slice of bread a day when you were working, always on an empty stomach. Certain horrible things happen that simply cannot be forgotten.

— — — — —

People were dying like flies. My dad and I walking to work heard screams all the time. The stench was terrible, absolutely horrible, almost unbearable, but that is the way people had to survive. You walk through and smell death. In order to collect additional coupons, some people would probably go out and kill other people just to keep alive. In the morning you might hear cries of a daughter sobbing that the mother died, but people kept the mother for eight or ten days in order to get her coupons.

On average the population of the ghetto could hardly walk at all. The ones who could walk could not walk up a step. Their bones were dry, in the wintertime especially. There was no heating material, only what you smuggled away or hid, and you preserved it. You had to lift up your foot with the right hand or left hand in order to make a step.

There is also the agony of looking at your mother, once a beautiful blonde, blue-green-eyed woman, now with swollen legs, looking at the kids and not being able to help. My mother never complained about herself. She lost a lot of weight but still shared her small portions with the children. We dipped out only one spoonful of sugar every second day for each of the kids. Some of us could not walk up the sidewalk.

No one would believe the attention given the things that women did to help their families survive. For example, my mother made chicory spinach hamburgers [patties]. She took a little bit of spinach and chicory and mixed that up with a drop of sugar. You ate it with a lot of water just to keep something in your stomach. You lied to yourself just to keep the stomach full.

Thousands of families from little towns were brought into Łódź and also German Jews. These people were not used to the hardships we were accustomed to, and by the hundreds, they jumped off the man-made wooden bridges. One family that was brought was as large as ours—seven children, mother and father. The oldest was Schmuel, who became my friend. They lived on the third floor in the back of a building that had a hidden attic. My friend Schmuel died in the ghetto.

It was horrifying, but at the same time, on the other side, the Jews did really stick together. It was out of necessity. Not only this, but there were times in the ghetto when they sang more songs and dedicated more songs and wrote more songs. One guy in his forties, I don't remember his name, used to go all over the ghetto, composing songs and singing them in order to lighten up the hearts of everybody.

My family was still together, my parents and all seven of us kids. We tried to be as industrious as possible. We still had a little bit left of what we kept at a third place. We had hidden rations and warehoused metal. We were also working, my father, my brother, and me. We were considered lucky since we got the rations, and my father, a master worker, received an extra ration. That way we could almost make soup. As for my mother, she worked at a factory that had once been a textile factory. She made boots from straw. The soldiers who went to invade Russia put these over their shoes to keep their feet warm and stave off frostbite.

Always, all times, we don't feel good. We hurt and are uncomfortable. In the wintertime especially, it is very hard, with not very much clothes and no coal, so we cannot be warm. And hungry too. The gloom and dreariness, it's not to be forgotten. It's a hell, having to work feeling like this. And we have to walk, dragging oneself, going heavily. The stomach is usually empty. People started to feel despairing with no food. Aron and I went out from time to time and tried to organize, to figure out ways to get food. Instead of calling it stealing, we threw ropes over like snares to "catch" a frozen kohlrabi or a potato and bring it home.

There was no medical help anywhere, no prescriptions. You were lucky, no matter what the sickness, if you had an aspirin. Absolutely you could not complain. There was nothing anybody could do to help you.

— — — — —

It became a wretched life in the ghetto. I do not think anybody, nobody unless they went through this horrible mess, could understand what the ghetto really means. In the ghetto there were always Germans around with guns, armored trucks, and dogs. We heard all kinds of rumors but didn't know what was actually happening outside. From time to time, somebody smuggled in a German paper and we read it. But we couldn't make out how the war was really going. We had hopes that on the Stalingrad Front or anywhere the Germans were fighting that they would lose. We heard rumors about England coming to help. So many rumors, always talk, always with uncertainty, but always with some hope.

One evening we were sitting down and reflecting on the past, and we all, one by one, started to cry except my father. He believed we will survive and go back to normal. He saw the misery as a passing thing. He believed that somehow someone in the world will think about us as being worldly and intelligent, as worthy human beings. He thought we will be able to withstand this catastrophe. Who could believe, he used to say, these barbarous acts occurring against civilians from a highly intellectual nation. This was more than a war, more than military. It was against civilians, especially pointed out to liquidate the Jews. All people, children and women, my mother, the beautiful woman, no gossip please, be righteous, all for family, and now what?

My brother Aron and I stood up to everybody and told them we were disciplined, we were trained right. We went to *cheder* [a school teaching the basics of Judaism and Hebrew], but for once we told them, we sat up. We needed to learn how to organize for food so that the kids don't go hungry. We took food and anything else. We started picking up potatoes, charcoal from the burned synagogues, every day so the younger kids have something to eat. My mom kept begging us to stop. We knew the consequences. Even as small as we were, if we were caught, we could be hanged or maimed by the Germans, but after a year we just didn't care anymore.

Under these circumstances, my father still kept faith and kept telling us why as we walked to and from work. He would remind my brother and me constantly that he survived the war where he was eighteen months in the ditches. We should never forget, no matter what happens, and he did not know what would happen, and that if we have to eat sand or grass or anything, some of us—especially me, the oldest—must survive in order to show these people that not only are we better human beings working for a better future but also for the preservation of the name that he handed down.

He used to lecture me and tell me about the Spanish Inquisition, the pogroms in Russia, or about the Beilis Affair in Russia. He often talked to me about the persecutions that Jewish people went through—that for two to three thousand years the Jewish people went through horrible things for one reason or another, such as that we were responsible for Christ's crucifixion. During those walks, he told me how we would live after the war. I would be an engineer and run the factory. How beautiful life would be. He used to prop us up with the idea that everything would get back to normal. I think that he meant it earnestly. Even though he was an educated and very bright person, I don't think he realized the calamity that was coming on. Many did not.

Immediately after the Nazis came in and surrounded the ghetto, they started picking up people to do any kind of dirty work and beat them up many times.

Then they started asking people to come to work voluntarily. If there were no volunteers, they grabbed people off the street, chased them like animals, threw them into a car, pushed them with bayonets, and took them to work. The Germans roamed the streets shooting, which caused riots. In the beginning they took hundreds of people out of the ghetto supposedly for work. They would haul them in packs, saying they need people to work. But those people were never heard of again. The Germans also took away the most intelligent people—the doctors, lawyers, and accountants, and also the rabbis but the flock stayed behind.

Early on, it was a while before people started realizing what was happening, but over the months and years, intermittent roundups and deportations became common and everyone lived in fear. From time to time the Germans came in unannounced, usually in the morning, and rounded people up, especially the old and very young. They would tear children away from their mothers and fathers, or grandparents away from their families. These people never came back.

Sometime in 1942, the Germans started asking the ghetto to supply so many thousands of people for export. They said they were taking these people to nice camps with good working conditions to work near the Russian Front or other fronts because they had to support the military, which is fighting. Or they needed civilians for other uses to take the place of people serving in the military. We did not know where these people were going. Even at the last minute we did not know.

Every day, the Judenrat,[9] a committee of Jewish elders, had to pick people to go. Once you got that card, you knew in your heart, you knew you would never see your family again. They did not usually take whole families. They might have sent out a card for a man, and the man went and left the wife and so many kids. The family went, if they were grown up, altogether.

That is how it started out, five or six thousand Jews a day. Every day you dreaded that this little card is going to come to your house or be delivered from the police. You would then have to show up a few days later at a designated time at the station, to be deported. One consolation they gave you, trying to perpetuate a myth, is that you can take your personal belongings,

---

9 Judenrat (Jewish Council), Administrative bodies made up of Jews in the ghettos, organized by the Nazis in order to help control the communities. They are largely seen as having been complicit in the Holocaust.

pack up a suitcase. You will be treated right; you'll have good food. Of course you did not know what to do. It was very mixed up.

I remember when the Germans called a *szpera*,[10] and we were not allowed to go to the factory or do anything for six days. They went house to house looking, who to take. They rounded up children, old people, and those who were sick and sent them out—to where, we still did not know. We learned by then how to hide in Schmuel's attic.

Winter 1943 was the worst, with starvation and the insecurity of being picked up on the szperas for mass deportations. We avoided being caught a few times because my father had friends in the police and fire departments who told us to let the jalousie down from the inside and to be quiet. We avoided being deported a few times that way. Up until 1944 the Germans came, sometimes with the head of the Gestapo and Kripo. They went through the ghetto streets announcing through megaphones that we will have a better life than in the ghetto by going to work for Germany, to take what we can with us including utensils, baby carriages, and other personal belongings. Director Chaimovich at the factory told my father that if he agrees for him and my mother to go, my sister and I could stay another few months. But my father said no.

> *"Every day you dreaded that this little card is going to come to your house or be delivered from the police. You would then have to show up a few days later at a designated time, at the station to be deported."*

─ ─ ─ ─ ─

One day I remember my dad came to me in the factory. He said, "There is something going on." He had heard from the higher echelon that they are asking for people. Besides the people they had working in the factories, the Germans wanted a certain number of people, three or four hundred a day, with special cards for such jobs as gardening or repair work and hauling—things like that. The ghetto functionaries had to pick them and send them to the Germans living outside the ghetto.

Now people started to get scared, afraid they were going to be taken away. We did not know about concentration camps at that time, of course, but

---

10   Szpera (Polish for the German *Sperre*—barrier, lockout, suspension of movement), The term was applied to mass confiscations of property and deportations. One of the most tragic events in the history of the Łódź ghetto was the deportations from September 5 to 12, 1942, when more than 15,000 elderly over sixty-five and children under ten were selected for murder in Chełmno.

many people were disappearing. At first we didn't know that they would never come back. Sometimes the people that worked would get a few marks together and buy themselves out for the day, like an older man giving a few marks to a younger man. The younger man goes out and works. Of these people, actually seventy percent came back every day to the ghetto.

The Nazi ghetto administration was headed by Hans Biebow, a man specially chosen by Himmler. He had set up the Judenrat, a committee of the oldest Jews, and they took a Jew by the name of Chaim Rumkowski, who would become the president of the ghetto. They called him the "king of the ghetto." Biebow had established Jewish police, a special command, and he issued ghetto money. Also, they had set up workshops and factories. Only a privileged few Jews were chosen to be in charge. These were the ones who supervised workers; these were the few that were allowed to go out after the evening hours. These people also had all the aggravation.

The functionaries, of course, lived better with better rations. The director of the sheet metal factory was Chaimovich, and his brother Leon was under him. They always wore commanders' police uniforms. They were German Jews who came into the ghetto as big shots and then took over the factory. Chaimovich was an impeccable man whom my dad had known, along with his brother, before the war. Chaimovich had been a Polish officer. He wore a tunic and used to walk around like the king of the world, not like the refugee. He comes into the ghetto the first time to see our metal factory, to talk to my dad, and figure out what he is going to do. He was also a womanizer.

In 1942 the Germans incorporated all of the Jewish factories. These were factories of all sorts, located in various parts of the ghetto, to produce for the Germans: textile factories, metal factories, and others. That resulting conglomerate had over 70,000 people working for the Germans. I worked in the metal factory at Brzezinska Street #56, and later moved to Metal #L on Lagiewnicka Street #63, as a slave under conditions well known and described thousands of times by people who were in this ghetto.

The first winter, my dad worked for the electric company in Łódź. After two months, they opened the metal factory and he became top master, the *Obermeister* [upper master], of 650 people. As an Obermeister, you belonged to the buyer, and were a special group that got extra food. That helped the family a lot; otherwise, we would have starved to death.

My dad handed over the job at the electric company to Mr. Himelfarb and me. I was there for three months, then was moved back to the metal factory. I had a little bench in a corner where I worked. I did about 250 nozzles, soldering and all. I hadn't been working there for long when one day Chaimovich came in and started watching me. He stayed behind me when I was soldering, with an electric soldering iron, pieces used for gardening to spray water on gardening tools. He watched and it felt like the hangman was standing behind me. Everyone was scared of him. At the factory our lives were in his hands. He could make you or break you, and one day he could report you. He watched me for a while and came back a few days later, called my dad over, and said he was making me an instructor. This is how at sixteen and a half years old I became the youngest instructor in the history of the sheet metal business. He had watched my hands. He saw them moving. He saw what I was able to do, how I put out production.

As an instructor, I had a bunch of kids under me. We prepared buckles for the German Army, metal containers used as hand warmers at the front, and many other items. We walked to work all the time. In the morning, you got up around 7:00. You went to the factory. You walked.

After the ghetto was sealed, my dad had taught me and my brother how to make a stove, similar to coal stoves, from black metal. He made a model for us, and once a week, on a Wednesday or Thursday night, we worked on it. It took us one week to make the first one. After that we made one stove a week and used them to barter for food—potatoes, bread—or other things. We also made menaźkes. We used to smuggle out some of the pieces —it was duraluminum, made by a special process of softening and heating it over a fire that my dad knew how to do. We made about two of them a week.

The hand-warming containers [braziers] we made at the factory were called *Spitzcolencassen* [?]. We used leftover iron and constructed them with special machinery. The container was a squared-off box with a longer opening on the top and two handles to pick it up. The boxes could hold at least ten pounds of coal, enough to fuel the stoves at home for a day. Two people had to sit together on chairs, one held the box while one riveted the handle. Then I came up with an idea to make it a one-person job. I took a two-by-two fastened to the bench from the handle to the top, and I did not need a helper anymore. They put me on the night shift, gave me the whole group, and we produced sixty or seventy pieces a week. The finished products were put in the backyard for inspection and were always perfect. Our group was the most accomplished, the most productive.

We worked in slave conditions. We were given one soup a day in a metal container that was handed to us with ten grams of bread. The factory was tremendous. When the Germans came in to look it over, it was like an inspection. It was like an orchestra, orchestrated. Everybody kept their heads down and worked. Young kids under fifteen were not allowed to be seen by the Germans. Many young kids worked there. We knew the Nazis were going to take them out and send them away, so each instructor that had a group took two or three smaller kids and hid them behind the big ones. That way we got ration cards for them for food. The ghetto functionaries issued cards for these kids.

> "I worked in the metal factory . . . as a slave. . . . We worked in slave conditions. We were given one soup a day in a metal container that was handed to us with ten grams of bread."

I ended up stuck with about thirty of these kids working for me in 1942. They handed me first thirty people with about ten kids, and then I had around sixty-five people with about fifteen of them kids. The protection of children had to keep going because the inspectors kept coming unexpectedly to the factory for roundups. Every day there was some excitement, something frightening. It's funny that as bad and sickly as you are and as hungry as you are, as many people that you've seen taken away, you keep holding on to the last hope that you will be able to survive.

One day my dad came up with an idea to make square lanterns. In Europe when you make a square frame and put milk glass behind the frame, it looks like there is light, like light inserted into the wall. You put the frame in and cemented it to the wall and it displayed the number of the house. I watched him working at it. He always had to have one helper to hold the angles in order to soft-solder the edges to make them come around square. You have to soft-solder in order to hold all four edges and then you solder the angles. I took a piece of marble that we had and built a wooden frame outside the frame where the brass was and put the brass frame right in so that you did not need anybody to hold it. This time my dad said, "That's a beautiful idea, but you are not getting the credit for it unless you speak up. We are going to get an extra pound of meat for that from Chaimovich because we have a new idea." He went over to his office, and sure enough, two weeks later we start to get a pound of meat. That was like getting a fortune because there was no money in the world that could buy a pound of meat.

I was also sent on a job with another master of the sheet metal factory to take care of a big company to do some metal work for them. Leather belt machines, for shoes. We, though, didn't have shoes. It was wintertime, and we went in without shoes.

– – – – –

The second youngest in our family was Lajb, or Leon, who was my favorite brother—I called him "Laibusz." He always slept with me, always stuck around with me. I loved him so much, and that is why I named my daughter, Lee, after him. I remember right before the war, Laibusz, who was blond, was standing and curling my hair. A Polish photographer that happened to be there caught it, and we were in the Polish paper for two days. I still think about him a lot.

Leon was the most courageous little boy, and even under the circumstances in the ghetto he tried to show us that he can bring home some extra food and share it. He got a job at a factory that made uniforms for the Germans. He worked as a helping boy. He had to stand in front of the door to let people in who wanted to talk with the director. He also made appointments for that big shot. He was nine years old by then and was very, very smart. He would come home and tell us stories of who he let in and who he didn't let in to see the factory director.

All the kids worked and had cards except Josef, the youngest who stayed with my mom.

– – – – –

There was a library in the ghetto at Franciszkańska Street #36. It was clandestine, underground. I used to go there even though it was dangerous. My mother begged me not to, but I sneaked up there anyway. There was a handicapped girl, about twenty-two years old, who kept about five hundred books stocked in that library, all kinds of books, and people would walk up from all over the ghetto and get a book to read. I took books out to read at night.

My family was hysterical about it. If I am discovered, they say, I would be hung or deported. If I were caught with the kind of books I liked, the worst could happen. My mother was always pleading with me, sometimes crying. She sat up with me and begged me to stop it. From time to time, in order for me to look forward and not to do the things that I did, she would remind me about the beautiful time before the war when we went to the opera or the Philharmonic with my dad. Or she would talk about the time he took us to a movie at Piotrkowska Street and tried to match me up with a beautiful girl—Mr. Green's daughter.

Since I wore a white armband, in addition to the David's star on my chest, I was allowed to go out, but it was very, very dangerous. I didn't care. I felt I wanted to read something. There was nothing to do and I wanted to get educated. There was no school. So I went to Franciszkańska Street and picked up books. I liked to read about the Russian Revolution, and Russian writers like Maxim Gorky.

The library was very secret, on the third floor, hidden behind a back door. You had to open one door in order to go into another door and then through a third door into the bedroom where there was a hole in the wall that opened a piece. You went in and then chose a book. And, she had to know you. You had to be recommended. I knew the family. We had been raised three blocks apart and she knew me, so I got the books. But by the time you got to the library from my street it was eight or ten blocks. The only time I could go was after work. So I had to walk down one street and then through an alley, then another street; in other words it was like an underground. By the time you got there, you were full of sweat because you didn't know who might stop you, who might do something to you. But you made it and brought the book home.

At night I went into the last bedroom, only took a little light with me, and I sat up in the night until 2:00 or 3:00 and read these books. They were fascinating because they opened a new world. They only had books such as Polish literature, which was forbidden to read, the Russian books, and Jewish books that were for grown-up people. It was very, very hard for me to understand some of these, but I labored through them and tried to understand the Russian books, a few of them translated to Polish. Jewish books were very few because—at least as far as our reading and language were concerned—we were more Polish than Jewish. I was good at learning languages. Once the war came around, we started smuggling in a German newspaper, which helped me learn the language. Soon I was able to translate and lead for a group of people in learning

> "I sat up in the night until 2:00 or 3:00 and read these books. They were fascinating because they opened a new world."

a bit of German. Within a year in the ghetto, I was reading German almost fluently.

— — — — —

Life often seemed unbearable, but still in all we as a family stayed together only because my father and I kept good jobs. We also had some friends who protected us, like the chief of the fire department who was a good friend of my dad's and looked out for us. Then one day in 1944, the Germans, including Biebow, the Nazi head man of the Łódź ghetto, came and promised us that we would all go to work in Germany. We could take all the things we needed, get good jobs, and be treated well. They started coming five or six times a day. Both the Germans and the representatives of the ghetto would stand on a stool or a bench and give these speeches in the street and promised us all that—good jobs and good treatment.

About two weeks before the deportation, German officers came into the ghetto, drunk, of course, and knocking out doors and molesting women. They acted like the Hitler Youth had, only the Hitler Youth were worse.

3. Prisoner 64277
1944–1945

1944–1945 *The Goldmans have been imprisoned in the Łódź ghetto for almost five years. During that time, while fighting the Allies, the Nazis have also been rounding up Jews and other "undesirables" who are then either imprisoned in concentration camps to be starved, tortured, and used as slave labor, or sent to extermination camps, where they become victims of the industrial-scale mass murder. By summer 1944, the German Army is in retreat. American and British forces have begun an approach from the west, while the Soviets are coming from the east. The Nazis begin to consolidate or close down many of their operations. This means emptying the ghettos and deporting the inhabitants to camps. As part of the liquidation of Łódź, the Goldmans find themselves packed in a cattle car with countless others, headed to an unknown future. At their destination, prisoners who are initially spared are forced into labor; if they are not worked to death, they are killed when they become too sickly to be useful. Suddenly separated from his family, Mieczyslaw, forced into labor, must fend for himself in the most barbaric and terrifying of conditions.*

For related documentation, see appendix pages 210 (map with camp locations), 227–230.

Photo: Auschwitz concentration camp gate. (From US Holocaust Memorial Museum, courtesy of National Archives and Records Administration, College Park.)

I remember my mother one time in the ghetto when she leaned her head against an icy window muffling sobs, thinking, dreading what was going to happen to us, which is exactly how I felt at the time. It was like solitary confinement, an aloneness, being a person who has done nothing, and at only seventeen years of age or eighteen. Who says you cannot smell in your dreams, she used to tell me. She could not explain it in psychological terms.

My dad told me about a conversation he had with Chaimovich, the director of the factory. He called my dad into his office and said, "Mr. Goldman, something is coming up. I want to tell you something. There is a girl that works for your son . . ." At that time I was an instructor. The girl's name was Sasza Hartstein [?], and her grandfather was the chief rabbi in Łódź. Chaimovich says, "She is on the list to be deported." I loved that girl. She was a nice little girl. I said, "Please intervene on my behalf. I never asked a favor of you, Dad, in the last couple of years. Please make sure that this girl doesn't go."

My father went back to Chaimovich and talked to him, and they held up the deportation for three months. Meanwhile, I kept that girl working. Her brother was a policeman and he could not do anything about it either. They held it off, but eventually she was deported. She had, I think, some kidney trouble. She was a nice, beautiful little girl. I saw her after the war in Frankfurt am Main, which I will come back to later and talk about. Later on in Auschwitz I kept looking for her policeman brother. I heard he was in the transport, but I never found him.

Another time my dad said to me as we walked home from our factory jobs, "I have to tell you something that is serious. I don't want you to tell your mother until I say so, especially if the kids are around. Chaimovich called me in again and said there might be a way we can move quietly." The director had another gentleman by the name of Drachman, who is now [1970s] I think in Uruguay, and a few other people, other factory masters, and he told them that they can save themselves. If you take only one kid you could go with your wife and that kid. You would go to another place to work where you would have privilege, where they will keep you for as long as they could. No transports. But if you have more than one kid they cannot help you.

I asked, "What did you tell him?" Dad said, "I told him that without my wife and all my children, I am not going." If he had decided to be selfish and had taken only me and maybe my mother, just forget about the rest of the kids, he might have survived. Because Drachman, I saw him after the war, he came to visit me all the way to a hospital I was in, and told me that his wife and his little boy are alive. That boy was about ten years old when they left.

> "Dad said, 'I told him that without my wife and all my children, I am not going.'"

Drachman told me how they were hidden and what was done for him, as if he was special. They needed such people's talents for the work. Maybe they just had to keep some on until the last minute. They didn't know what was going to happen. But when my dad was given the opportunity for special treatment, he said, "Absolutely not. Without my whole family, I won't go." That is what happened. So his fate was sealed.

The only good memory of that time was the uprising of the Jews in the Warsaw ghetto. That was in 1943, in the spring, over a few weeks. Those Poles did not go freely to a camp. They fought the beast, and the glory of fighting is beautiful. I wish I had had a gun. If we all had known what was going to happen, the Germans would have paid a dear, dear price. But who could have imagined what would happen?

— — — — —

In July 1944, they started moving large numbers of people out of the Łódź ghetto. My family and I were taken in wagons to railroad cars. Each car was packed full with people, probably fifty or sixty. We were kept without water and without food except what we had hidden and brought with us. They put a soldier on each car, and the train started rolling. We did not know where we were going or what to expect. There were nine in my family, seven children and my mother and father. Other family members, uncles, aunts, and grandparents were already gone from the ghetto. To where, we did not know. Our family had consisted of sixty-eight or sixty-nine persons in Łódź alone.

We could not take a lot of stuff on the transport. Our clothes were wretched, nearly worn out after more than four years. We took a little bit of food and a few necessities, but after two or three days our food was gone. Sixty people were locked in a cattle car for days. I cannot describe in detail what happened when you had to go to the bathroom. We were very uncomfortable, very miserable. A few people even died in the car. And that was only the beginning.

> *"We were very uncomfortable, very miserable. A few people even died in the car. And that was only the beginning."*

After a while, my dad tried to have a conversation with my mother. Her name was Bajla Maria, but he called her all the time "Balcia." Now, he was using that endearing name. "Balcia," he said, "do you remember the time . . ." And he would talk about earlier days, trying to take her thoughts away because she was sitting very sadly as if doomsday is coming. She had a premonition and kept on touching the kids. He said, "Do you remember when we were in Atamorek?" It was a resort where we had once vacationed. He had hired a photographer to take pictures of the kids with a car behind. The photographer came on a weekend and we had a beautiful time. It was a picnic day, and my dad said it would be a good idea to take the pictures and send one to his brother Joel in Israel and one to Bajla's sister in Argentina. After the war I got that picture, that I have now, of the kids.

The train finally stopped [220 km (135 miles) south of Łódź]. We had arrived at Auschwitz, the well-known concentration camp.

— — — — —

Auschwitz [Auschwitz-Birkenau] was actually a network of several concentration camps built around the town of Oświęcim, the small town's Polish name before the area was annexed by Germany. The Auschwitz camp we were brought to was nothing like anybody could imagine. We thought we were rid of the ghetto, out of hell, but actually hell had just begun. It was the hell of the earth, and I hope to God that it never happens again to anybody.

We were herded off the trains and put into groups. There were hundreds of officers and military men, particularly SS men, and also dogs. There was a terrible smell in the air. We were sent to be cleaned. They undressed us and shaved us, our heads and every place else. They shaved the middle of the head especially. Women were present, and for the first time I saw a woman looking at me naked. We went through a bath [no doubt for disinfecting] before we were taken in. On the entrance to the camp was written: "ARBEIT MACHT FREI" [work makes you free].

For identification, we were given numbers—tattooed or, like me, otherwise given. I got a metal bracelet with the number stamped on. One of the first things we learned was there were quite a few denominations and religions. Regardless, everybody had a number. There were all kinds of Jews in Auschwitz. Some of them called themselves half Jews or quarter Jews. Some even went over to being Catholic, but whether they said they were Catholics, Lutherans, or agnostics, they were Jews. The great assimilated. At one with the Hasidim. The Germans did not make distinctions about where you came from. A Polish or Hungarian Jew or a German Jew, a quarter, a half Jew, or a Jewish doctor, lawyer, or a professional therapist, all of this did not count. You were a Jew and you were treated like one. And you didn't need anything to help you remember that.

When I got into Auschwitz, I had with me about 20,000 złotys in notes hidden that was outstanding debt we did not collect since the war broke out. That is not all. My dad, mom, and my sister Rojza also had notes, but of course all of this was taken away, even the shoes that we hid some gold pieces in.

> "They touched our muscles and that's how they decided. You went to the left or to the right, which meant for work."

They separated us, but I was still with my brother Aron. We even saw one of the Ceder boys on a train and he waved to us.

— — — — —

I remember a particular person who I later learned was Dr. Josef Mengele, the well-known Nazi doctor in Auschwitz, the murderer, who always pointed his finger. They touched our muscles and that's how they decided. You went to the left or to the right, which meant for work. Well, my family, my parents and five siblings, went to the left. It was the last time I saw them. We had no idea what it meant. Me and my brother, they looked you in the face, looked at your muscles, went to the right. Aron and I at that time were healthier than the rest of them. My family, I eventually learned, was sent to the gas chambers. Only Aron and I survived out of our family.[1]

On the right, things proceeded fast and in a brutal way. We were herded with sticks, and that was how it went. We were chased in groups into Camp Birkenau, what I learned later was known as the Gypsy Camp because the first people brought there were Gypsies. Ninety percent of them were eventually eliminated. Birkenau is well known for the treatments they gave the prisoners the first night. My brother and I were directed to Block #12, under block leader Willie, who was a *Kapo*. Kapos were also captives but ones the SS had enlisted to help keep order.

That night, believe me, we did not sleep. There were more than five hundred of us, and the beatings started off right away. They beat us indiscriminately for hours with unmistakable sadism. Kapos with whips stood on each end of a wall. One beats you and then makes you run to the other side where another one whipped you, then back to the other side. They wore only pants, no shirts, and were strong like the horses. These people thrived on brutality; they were criminals. They asked for your gold, your diamonds, any precious property if you still had anything. Sometimes if they saw you swallow, they X-rayed your stomach to see if you had swallowed your valuables. Finally, after hours of scaring us with beatings, when the sun came up, we were relieved to hear that we were going to get a hot soup. But we have to behave, follow orders, and work hard.

> "One beats you and then makes you run to the other side where another one whipped you, then back to the other side."

We were marched into big buildings once used by the Polish military. Block #13 was where Aron and I were assigned. We slept one body into the other on the cement floor. Two or three hundred prisoners were crammed into a room designed to hold fifty. In the morning, we were called onto a

---

1 Actually, the three oldest siblings—ages nineteen, twenty, and twenty-one—did not perish in the Auschwitz gas chambers. The two boys were put to work as slave laborers, and their sister Rojza was transferred to the Stutthof concentration camp.

field, and there was that Dr. Mengele with a stick in his hand pointing out who is going and who will stay.

I might have been frightened, but since I was with my brother, after the things we had gone through, I was okay. We were together, we shared. The procedure was that you got a small piece of mostly stale bread, and a little bit of soup, actually more water than soup. You had to catch it fast in a little hat, a cap that they handed you to wear. Either you burned your hands or your mouth, or you went hungry. That is how fast you had to get it. That is how you ate it. Besides the hat, the clothes you were given were like a blue-and-white striped pajama uniform and a pair of wooden shoes. That was the extent of the dress.

— — — — —

Going outside, you smelled something. You hadn't been told yet, but you knew deep down that it was human flesh. We had been in Auschwitz for three days or so when the block leaders started pointing out the crematoriums. We saw the smoke, a constant dark billow from the smokestacks, and understood that we smelled the flesh and bones from the ovens. Sometimes even the ashes drifted down and settled around us like gray snow.

> "Going outside, you smelled something. You hadn't been told yet, but you knew deep down that it was human flesh."

Our work was carrying bricks from one camp to another to make the highways of Auschwitz where thousands died. We also brought blocks and worked in the gardens. We were pushed around back and forth and beaten without warning or provocation. They moved us randomly to different jobs. We might be picked up from the toilet and taken out to the kitchen to work or bring in meals or take out the garbage or push garbage wagons. I was chosen to cut squares of grass for artificial lawns in another camp. We worked at Birkenau where we were staying or we went through the gates to work at Auschwitz. At that time we were forced in and out by the soldiers.

Auschwitz had electric wires around it, and the watchtowers were manned with armed guards day and night. I witnessed plenty of prisoners who went to the wires. If you touched them, you became blue and ash, burned. I remember some Russian prisoners who tried to get through.

When you got up in the morning, by whistle or beatings, the place was like a lime pit, mass graves. We smelled the poison gas, the ovens, and the dead bodies. Oh God, those smells! It's something you don't forget. Nor do you forget hearing about the injection experiments, survivors unable to eat, or seeing skeletons, corpses by the thousands, cadavers.

If we thought life in the ghetto was bad, life in Auschwitz was horrendously bad. You took one day at a time, never certain what would happen to you next. You always wondered if you were going to live through the night. There was always some block leader or an officer who might want to have a little fun in the middle of the night, and always there were times for the picking. They used to come in, point their finger at one or two or ten, take them away, and you never knew what happened. That is why even today I keep things and always say to myself, "If I forget these, I'm willing to go through the whole schmear because I believe in God. It is a way of remembering." Ritual is a form of remembering.

After some time had passed, they asked if anybody had relatives. We did not know any better so we said, "We are." They divided me and my brother. Aron ended up being sent to work in a coal mine in Görlitz. I was beaten up twice because I tried to get into the transport with him. From that time on, I was alone. I did not know what happened to my brother until later.

> "They divided me and my brother.... I was beaten up twice because I tried to get into the transport with him. From that time on I was alone."

— — — — —

You were taken out once in a while on what is called morning selection alertness. You were put out in a place where they would go through us for whoever feels weak. We later found out it was for removal to Block #11 and from there to the crematorium. Also, they had *Appell*, or roll call, outside almost every second or third day, even in bad weather, starting in early morning. If someone was missing or the numbers were miscounted, we had to stay out there until they got it right. Sometimes we would stand for two or three hours.

Auschwitz had once been a post of the Polish cavalry. The former horse stalls were rebuilt as toilets, each stall with about sixteen or eighteen or twenty toilets, where you sat down and you let your pants down. All told, it was actually holes where about a hundred people sat openly. You didn't want to be caught lingering in there for too long. If you were wanted for work, they came in, beat you up with your pants down, and that's how you had to run into the formation.

One time, five friends and I were standing in Appell. We were examined by Mengele. We were then pushed to the left, the way to the crematoriums. We thought we were finished, but they took us instead to the *Lazarett*. It was a little hospital, a field hospital, and we were sent, I guess, because we had dysentery. I was taken to a room where I was supposed to be helped. Funny, the German people made themselves, before, a reputation of being honest. That they are straightforward, like if they gave you their word, it is one hundred percent, you can bet on it. That's a joke. At the Lazarett, was a Mr. Hoffman and his son. Mr. Hoffman said that hospital was a hoax and that people were really being sent to the crematorium. He brought me a handful of flour and put it in my mouth.

Mr. Hoffman knew my father. He was a bit stronger and helped us, dragged us, to get out of there and back to the block. He was like a watchman or a guard. He and his son were supposed to herd you in and keep you there. It was very dangerous what he did. He pushed us behind a door. We hid there while two officers and one Kapo came through for the selection. They rounded up about forty people but didn't see us. It was me and another boy—Moniek Taub, who is now [1970s] in Sweden. I knew him from the metal factory back home in the ghetto. We were safe behind the door.

I was lucky like that a few times. I think sometimes it was meant to be. When my dad and I used to walk on Sundays in the ghetto to do our gardening, he stopped once and said one of us has to eat from the earth and survive in order that our name stays alive. Remembering this kept me going, even though sometimes I felt like committing suicide.

— — — —

Three days after the hiding incident, after being two months in Auschwitz, at an Appell, Mengele himself pointed out about fifty-five people in my block's group. He and various camp officers picked what were called *Muselmänner*,[2] people who were dying and were no longer capable of working. They touched prisoners' buttocks and the muscles in arms. I was moved to Block #11, notorious for taking our people and sending them to the gas chamber.

In the daylight in that block, under a lucky star, I met somebody who owed my father a favor. My father had helped the man before the war. His name was Irvin, a pickpocket and a thief. A Polish policeman was chasing him one Sunday

---

2   Muselmann, A slang term among concentration camp prisoners for ones who were suffering extreme starvation and exhaustion, and who were resigned to death.

back in Łódź. He ran through our shop and begged my father to let him out through the back door, which my father did. The cop was from Przytyk, a little town in Poland where a year before the war there was a pogrom on the Jews. He came to Łódź and was stationed in our district. My father detested this cop who always wore his medals in the lapel of his jacket. Also before the war, my mother ran out of bread and sardines on a weekend, a Sunday. In Poland on Sunday you weren't allowed to sell, buy, or do anything. That cop caught my mother trying to get some bread and my father came out. They had words and he let her go.

> "... under a lucky star, I met somebody who owed my father a favor."

Irvin had two brothers. One had married an acquaintance of ours and the other, he [presumably, also a prisoner] is the one who explained to me about the crematorium and things. Desperate, I walked over to Irvin and said, "Do you recognize me?" He said yes and told me he was a *Sonderkommando*. That means one who is taking people to and from. They were prisoners, Jews, who were forced to take the bodies out of the gas chambers, get their gold teeth out, and then put the bodies into the ovens. Afterward they removed their ashes. It was work the Germans didn't want to do. These workers always ended up in the crematoriums themselves. Germans didn't want them to live to tell their story. They did that with stool pigeons too and others who collaborated with them.

By then it had turned cold. We were huddled six or eight people together, and he asked can I help you. I said to Irvin that they are grabbing me to work every day and I'm starving. He got me a job in the cleaning plant where we washed and cleaned uniforms for the Germans. Instead of getting the watery soup with potato peelings that you had to eat so fast that it burned your mouth before it ran through your hat, in this place you worked hard, but you got a heavy soup, even a double portion of soup, so I could share with my brother. Besides cleaning uniforms, I also shined shoes. The time in the laundry gave me time to build myself up, and my brother too before he went to Görlitz, and get some strength. After about two weeks I was chased out of there and I never saw Irvin again.

— — — — —

You were not a human being, you were not a man, you were a nothing, just a number. That number you had to remember. When they called your number at roll call, you'd better be there every day, in time. The Germans were punctual was the reputation. One hundred percent punctuality—it is just a myth. They are punctual when it comes to the fatherland or to roll call. But they are not punctual when it is for somebody that is not a German. When not working, we were often waiting, not knowing.

If you did not come to formation or you did not show up in the morning at Appell, or something was wrong, they went looking for you. Every morning, back and forth, God forbid if you were missing. If you were missing, the whole camp was turned upside down. Everyone had to stay outside for as many hours as were necessary until the missing person was found.

Getting into the fall, the Germans took pleasure in abusing us more with extra beatings and keeping us outside in the cold for many hours because the Jewish holidays were approaching. I had six teeth knocked out, and then it was the High Holidays. Another incident was when they put everybody on Appell and that day pulled out people's gold teeth if you had any, going about it of course in a brutal fashion with added beatings. They pulled out my two gold teeth. Always before the holidays the Germans gave us something to remember. Afterward we were given a quarter loaf of bread. It took about five to six hours in the morning.

Telling this story is a shortening of the time. At the time, one day seemed like a year of living, because to us, in our minds, it was never going to end. Here's an example of day-by-day conditions, one day. We would be sent out through the guard gate to work on a truck on a certain day. We worked. One October day the truck got bogged down in the mud. An SS woman and SS men were on duty to watch us. They had German Shepherd dogs, and these dogs, if you did not do what you were supposed to do or move fast enough when given an order, these dogs were trained to go for the throat or between a man's legs. We worked, even after being beaten up. Trying to get the truck out of the mud hole, we worked for maybe three hours, and during that time we were lashed with whips off and on.

We were always so very dirty. At Auschwitz, with taking a bath or cleaning, any cleaning, there was only one place for it that you could sneak in. There was not a prisoner who did not have his body eaten up by lice. You had to be very candid about it, the conditions that you went around with. You scratched all night and all day. You could not help yourself. The only relief you got was to wash your shirt, and in order to do that you had to sneak into a place, where if you were caught they beat the heck out of you.

You ran in and washed your shirt in cold water. You did not have any soap. But most of the time you snuck in and nobody saw you and you put the cold shirt, as unbelievable as it sounds, on your back and we got six or eight guys in a stall, and one puts his back to the other until the shirts dried, rubbing on each other.

I remember going into the women's camp once, a most horrible sight. Their heads were shaved and they wore blue-and-white-striped dresses. There were some political prisoners there. When the soup was handed out, you had to stay in line. They brought a big bucket of soup and one man measured it out. When these women were finished eating their meager portions and the bucket was empty, you could see ten or fifteen of them putting their heads down and licking off the sides of the buckets, deep buckets that carried around thirty gallons of soup, for the leftovers. They were like us, put together with the criminal prisoners. There was one political prisoner who stood watch over the other political prisoners because he was a German. There was also an SS woman who watched the women work at that time.

> "When these women were finished eating their meager portions and the bucket was empty, you could see ten or fifteen of them putting their heads down and licking off the sides of the buckets . . . for the leftovers."

Right in the beginning we saw pregnant women being catered to, and we did not understand why they would kill kids and keep women impregnated and still feed them. We found out later through the grapevine that experiments were performed on these women, after which they were done away with. There were also experiments done with young boys, castration and stuff like that.

Today if I am asked, and a lot of foolish people ask, "How could you survive?" I say, "I can't explain it, the same as you cannot explain a miracle." I don't know the word or how to say it, but it's surprising how strong a person can be after so much—beatings, degradation, more than you think you can take with no end in sight—and still be alive and at the same time hanging on to the last hair and wanting to survive. But we did. We wanted to survive!

Sometimes I get angry, or else have to laugh, at the superficial way Jews divide. One goes to a Polish *shul* [synagogue], one goes to a Hungarian shul, one goes to a Romanian or German shul. We all divide, in say, fifteen parties. But the Germans didn't care. They didn't ask you which shul or how devout a Jew or how good of a professional you were or how humanitarian or how rich you were. You were just a Jew. I saw the absurdity of fighting about all these factions and divisions. It's better to stick together. We had to stick together. There is nobody but nobody looking out for you. Look what happened!

What happened to us in the war has been compared to other times when there was conflagration between civilian populations and governments where the oppressed people felt a desire to rise up against the masters. Usually the slaves or the subjugated people fought for freedom or economic betterment. This was not so in our case. Here the Germans wanted to totally annihilate a people because of their religious beliefs or their perceived inferiority. For instance, there were the Slavs who the Nazis thought of as the dumbest and lowliest, good for nothing except as slaves to serve the masters. The Aryan race did not think that it was they who were the titans, barbarians from the tenth century.

> "It was a thoughtful plan for mass killings that used the Germans' strength and resources . . . all done with German precision, and nothing stood in their way."

Their plan for eradication was well thought out and methodical. Now we could see it in Auschwitz, in our nation, our peoples. It was a thoughtful plan for mass killings that used the Germans' strength and resources, any means to improve the lot of the Aryan nation. It was all done with German precision, and nothing stood in their way.

— — — — —

Everyone in Block #11 was a skeleton. I knew five people there. Two were my father's friends, Mr. Klaussner and his son, and the other three were boys I had worked with in the ghetto metal factory. One was Moniek who lived through the war and whom I stayed close to. We all knew where people in Block #11 went, without a doubt. Right across the barracks we saw what happened every day to others on their way to the gas chambers. It was only a matter of time, and we got nothing to eat except a potato a day. But we were lucky. At that time they didn't have enough room in the gas chambers because too many transports were coming in from Hungary and Theresienstadt.

We always had pieces of wood or scraps of iron or metal that we polished on the stones for a knife, when we did not have anything to do. As soon as we got into that block, between ourselves, we were talking, the prisoners were, in the backyard. It was summer and hot. The five of us started talking and made up our minds. We were young and had nothing to lose. We started cutting into the bricks on the far end of the building where the alley was and took out ten or twelve bricks. We worked, often in the night, each taking turns and hiding, keeping one on top of the other, very compact so that nobody could see what we were doing because everybody was starting to yammer. We used pieces of tin to shovel. They were scared. They were afraid something would happen to them if we get out. But we quietly kept on working on those bricks. We hid each other with a blanket in the corner of the block and took turns digging.

> "We hid each other with a blanket in the corner of the block and took turns digging."

Finally, we knocked out the bricks and ran across, one by one, to Block #12 where we hid. We knew that when the selection came around, or morning count, that the Germans would see that five people were missing. Sure enough, at the next Appell all the prisoners from the Birkenau camp were brought out, and a search was on to find us. They were going from block to block, and we hid in the toilets, trying to maneuver so that they would not find us. There were a few hundred people in Block #12, people from age sixty to children twelve to fifteen, all men. But we couldn't get in any places because we had to be on the list of a block.

We realized we had to give up or just go back to Block #11. But then, we had an idea about Willie, leader of Block #12, whom we knew well. He was still a Kapo, still running the block. One night when he was drunk, he had come into Block #11 and told us he was a communist. He took off his shirt and showed us the scars on his body—his rear, his back—the results of the many lashings and beatings he had gotten years before in Dachau. We had heard him say more than once that he hated them all.

Klaussner and I knew then and there that we had one chance to confide in somebody, that we might have a chance to save ourselves. At that point it didn't matter. Either way, we were in the lion's den so we took a chance on Willie. We walked over in the morning and told him about our escape. He gave us two portions of soup, some cooked potatoes, and overcoats, and said he'd see what he could do to help us. He told us to keep quiet, to stay in the barracks. He was going to report that we were in there doing some cleaning or some other work for him. We knew that businessmen from industries like IG Farben often came to Birkenau and Auschwitz to buy slaves for the factories in Germany. The three of us young guys begged Willie to put us on one of those transports. He said he would try to make the arrangement. True enough, when the manufacturers came about a week later, we were picked to go to Braunschweig, Germany [750 km (465 miles) northwest of Auschwitz].

That's what Willie did for us. He said if we could escape from Block #11, we were worth saving—at least for a while. The chances of getting out of Auschwitz were one in a million. I was in Auschwitz from August 1944 till November 1944.

— — — —

Before loading us on the transport, they told us that where we were going we would have the best of everything and some believed it. It was a dangerous journey that lasted seven days and seven nights. We were not allowed to take extra clothing and were given only a light coat to wear. It was bitterest cold, below zero. We had very little food. We started to suck the lining of the thin coats that we had been given. Many died on the trains. We weren't allowed to go to a bathroom. The guards on the outside of the trains, laughing, sometimes told us to use the straw. You know what for. It's a zoo, you are a dog.

> "... they told us that where we were going we would have the best of everything and some believed it."

The worst thing that happened was the machine guns and the strafing by Allied bombers. The pilots didn't know it was a prisoner transport; the trains weren't marked. More than half of the prisoners died.

After several days riding around in open cattle cars and surviving on a jar of beets shared by twenty people, we arrived at Wattenstädt [a Neuengamme subcamp] in Braunschweig in below-zero winter cold. There was the normal routine of beatings during the first hours. Everybody had to go through the cordon. Then we were notified of the Appell location. They have to count you, as if you amount to something. You are a dog. You are nothing. But they still have to count heads.

On the Appell ground, the *Lager* [camp] leader was an SS colonel. He was about five foot two inches tall. His aide was a civilian criminal. He made a speech and told us that he was the Hangman of Neuengamme and that the

450 boys who had come in on the previous transport were all dead. It was their blood, he said, that built the houses we will live in. He has presided over the hangings of thousands of people. His pleasure is hanging. For any infraction, your punishment is hanging. This colonel used to tell everybody, if you have a complaint come to me. Some of them went with a complaint to him. They were never seen again.

After three or four days, we were picked up at about 4:00 in the morning. Then, about two hundred of us were picked out for the Büssing factory, a factory that made trucks. We were ordered to work there. They started a routine, waking us up at four or five. For Appell, God help you if you were not in line, standing straight and absolutely to perfection. When it was over, you were already exhausted. But we had to walk, as we later found out, about ten kilometers every morning to the factory. It was a huge place. All of us in the transport were working in the departments, or halls, such as #619 or #210. The rest were staying in the camps and working at other things.

I worked on Hall #620 at a lathe. There were many, many nationalities working in that hall. I worked under a German master who was lame; one foot was shorter than the other. His greatest line was when he got drunk. Every Sunday he came, I guess, after church and took out Hitler's picture from his pocket, showed it to us, and told us this is the guy who will eliminate the Jews. He tells us, "This is the guy who really wants to liquidate you off this planet, isn't he?" He used to laugh hysterically, walk around, get a couple of drinks for himself, and make fun of us or kick us with the good leg. Then he'd take out the picture again from his breast pocket and show it to you.

When we came back in the evenings, instead of food, the first two weeks we got beatings. They kicked us in the stomach because the Americans started to bomb an area nearby. At one time we heard a raid and prayed that the Allies would come down and bomb them and us too, but it happened that they bombed a factory about three kilometers away. Our block leader came in and tortured us throughout a whole night for that, with beatings and everything.

". . . in the evenings, instead of food, the first two weeks we got beatings. They kicked us in the stomach because the Americans started to bomb an area nearby."

He said, "Your *gonifs* [scoundrels], your brothers, your comrades are bombing our towns." They even hanged three people in the backyard for that.

They told us that our brothers, the Americans and the English, are bombing their cities for nothing. It was our fault. We started the war and by the time they finish with us there will be nobody alive.

I mentioned before the businessmen coming from Germany to take prisoners back to work as slave laborers in their factories. In the same way, the commissions came. Like the Red Cross commission is coming from Switzerland. The Germans are preparing to give out blankets. We clean the barracks and make up the best soup. This is going on to show off that we are treated in the most humane way, and they are the nicest people in the world there. Their voices change. They talk in a different tone and behave in a different manner. Of course, the minute the commission leaves, the blankets are taken away, along with whatever was left of the food. We get a good beating for the afternoon and that is how these crazy maniacs worked. And the world, all the world, of all these people, no help.

— — — — —

It was winter, and after a month without shoes and no coats except thin little blue jackets and pants, most of us got very weak. But still we had to go and work, and one evening while standing in the soup line I got hit over the head and lost consciousness. When I got up I was in a room where they put all the people who weren't capable of going to work—the *Revier* [infirmary].

> *"From that time on I had a lot of trouble with my head. Some times afterward and even now I feel the results of these many beatings."*

I was there a few days and they kicked me out and sent me back to the factory to work. From that time on, I had a lot of trouble with my head. Some times afterward and even now I feel the results of these many beatings.

Sometimes the Dutch or French that worked with us, they were political prisoners, or other foreign workers, snuck in a little bit of food in the bottom of the places, where I used to work, to eat. We got very little food, one soup a day and ten grams of bread. We were actual skeletons and they started calling us Muselmänner.

In morning Appell they gave us a lecture. First they said, "We will take a leg or a muscle, you'll fall down, and you are dead." We were all the time scared to death—that's how it was. "You'll never get out of this place alive," they would say, shouting at us. The torture went on until one day they told us they were going to be bombed, that the Americans are coming close. We heard the planes coming all the time and knew something was going on, but we did not know how close they were.

After two months of walking to and from the factory every day, I got frostbite. Others, too. We would try to find rags to bind our upper legs. With rags around our legs, they dragged us through the town to that factory. When I went back to that town after the war to see and talk to some of the people, they always say they didn't see a darn thing. They saw us walking every, every day in the morning in the blue [clothes] . . . but how could you miss a Muselmann, a skeleton? You walked thousands of feet, marched and walked, and they kept on saying they did not see us.

> *"With rags around our legs, they dragged us through the town to that factory."*

When I could no longer walk, I was transferred to a Lazarett because of frozen toes. After a day there, the frozen parts of my toes were cut off. I got out of the Lazarett when a Red Cross man nipped, treated, my small toe on the right foot. Even in my condition I was going through all kinds of horrible treatment. Before I got out of the Lazarett, a Jewish doctor from Kraków befriended me and we stuck together until we were shipped out in March.

In March 1945, they took us for a walk and then to a train that would take us to Ravensbrück [290 km (180 miles) northeast of Braunschweig]. We knew things were happening; we often heard gunfire and hoped the Allies were getting nearer. The same evening we were transported, and after a few days arrived in Ravensbrück. We come down from the cattle trains under the watchful eyes of the SA, and of course the beatings began, the screaming, the yelling, and a few fell dead right off the transport. We were pushed from the cars with rifles, and many were killed.

Getting off the transport wagons to Ravensbrück I fell down. It was the middle of the night. They said the camp is for women—we found a couple of nail files and such lying around in the blocks—but since it is not empty we would have to wait. We had to go back all the way into the cars to try some other camp. I was so dead almost that two friends of mine from Łódź carried me out for a kilometer or two. We finally got into the camp.

Barracks were like all the other camps, except Auschwitz, no comparison. At Auschwitz you lie on the floor and there were from 450 to 600 people in a barracks, and one sat into the other one's legs and that's how you slept for all the months you were there. Here you had a bunk bed on plain wood, no mattresses or cushions, of course, but a bunk bed. We only got a drop of water and a slice of bread in Ravensbrück. We did not do anything until April 1945, just being watched and beaten up from time to time.

We also got a peculiar haircut. A man was standing on the one side; he tried to clean us up and shave us on one side and then went to the other side of the face and did that side. After that the block leader came up and told us that he was going to make a *Läuse Strasse* [lice street]. He took a clipper, went through the center of everybody's head, and cut about two inches from the back all the way to the front.

One friend, whom I knew from Auschwitz, Eckstein was his name, about thirty years old and from my town, when he came to Auschwitz he weighed about two hundred pounds, and five foot ten inches tall. He was a beautiful athlete, a nice guy. He had another brother who was an athlete, an amateur gold-medal boxing champ. Here, when I came in, he lay down on the lower bunk and the blood is starting to spill from his mouth. He is dead.

Every day at noon sharp we got chased to the cellars under the fence. There was a beep and signals, and they used whistles to get us down to the cellars. They called it for protection. Lies, of course. It was for the Germans. They stood high up on the steps. We were chased down with clubs and cursing. The first day we thought we were going to drown. We could not understand. There was water downstairs up to your neck and to the chin. We found out that these cellars were kept as torture chambers, and we were just happy that we didn't drown. They were covered in such a way that nobody could see them from the outside.

With air raids, it wasn't for our own protection that they took us to bunkers. We had to go because they could not leave us alone in the halls and wherever we were; otherwise, they would not be able to count heads, so they had to take us along with them. It was for their protection of life, not for ours.

— — — — —

Ravensbrück had a selection again. That means staying outside for hours while the SS colonel looked us over, for some were going to be moving out from the camp. We hear a lot of bombings from far away. We had to clear the camp. We later learned that the Allies were coming closer. By that time thousands upon thousands of Jews were brought in on the trains and all the shipments. Most are dead. There had been about sixteen trainloads. There were now two cars left. After all this time I felt often like I'd rather be dead than go home. The agony. The frustration. Not only being tired and sick with frozen legs, but constantly hungry. All those years we were dreaming about a loaf of hot steaming bread. Mention the plainest food, and it sounded like the most beautiful luxury in the world.

Again we had to march to the trains. It was around 3:00 or 4:00 a.m., again with the same brutality. A few of us got shot. Some were beaten up. We were so used to the clubbing that some of us would even run out for a little piece of cigarette or something that the guards threw away, to pick them up, or if we saw in the road any kind of peelings of a potato or something like that. We even got out of line in order to grab a leaf. We were not afraid of being beaten or shot anymore. We were like animals, used to beatings. You cannot describe. By that time we were already used to beatings.

We were taken by trains to Wöbbelin [145 km (90 miles) west of Ravensbrück], near the town of Ludwigslust, in April 1945. There, broken up, really being ninety percent dead, I would say, they threw us down on the floor. It seemed like a large farm with barns. When we came in there, there were already three hundred people including American flyers who had lost limbs. We were lying on the floor, in sand and hay, of a big barn with no doors. You could feel the spring weather. All they handed out was a half-cup of water if you could catch it and we were in the worst mess by that time. Nobody thought we would actually survive. We were without food and had almost no water. Almost all were dead. I was there from the end of April to May 2, 1945, when we were liberated by American troops.

> "After all this time I felt often like I'd rather be dead than go home. The agony. The frustration. Not only being tired and sick with frozen legs, but constantly hungry. All those years we were dreaming about a loaf of hot steaming bread. Mention the plainest food, and it sounded like the most beautiful luxury in the world."

4. "If I Survive and Live . . ."
1945

1945 *Adolf Hitler's death by suicide on April 30, 1945, marks the end of Nazi Germany. The major Allies divide Germany into zones of occupation—American, British, French, and Soviet—for purposes of administration. The need to care for the millions of displaced persons (DPs) is overwhelming and immediate. Initially, Allied military forces improvise housing and support as best they can, but the United Nations Relief and Rehabilitation Administration (UNRRA) takes on oversight of the refugee population in October 1945, though the military continues to serve in a cooperative capacity. Conditions for DPs remain difficult and uncertain, even as relief agencies and hospitals work hard to address their needs. Mieczyslaw is liberated. But, alone and weakened beyond the ability to stand and barely hanging on to his life, he is unaware of any of this. He is simply in need of water, food, and medical attention. It comes—in the kind and expert attention of nurses and others, and in rations.*

For related documentation, see appendices pages 210 (map with camp locations), 231.

Photo: Weak and dying survivors are evacuated from the Wöbbelin concentration camp to an American field hospital where they will receive medical attention. (From US Holocaust Memorial Museum, courtesy of Arnold Bauer Barach.)

It started on May 2. We knew that because the guards talked about what date it was and were running around stripping off their epaulets. We started hearing artillery fire and saw the SS officers, and other Germans who used to watch us, ripping the chevrons from their uniforms and running. All of a sudden we heard a lot of noise and shooting. We later found out that it was the US Army's 82nd Airborne Division.[1] They had crossed the Elbe River to stop the Russian troops from entering Denmark. Then they moved rapidly to Ludwigslust, thirty-six miles in one day. They had to meet the Russians to establish a line through Ludwigslust. In the afternoon, the Americans walked in. They brought trucks and took people who couldn't move at all to a field hospital. I was one of them.

My attestation from people in charge says the 82nd Airborne Division, whose representative was Lt. Gen. James M. Gavin, set up two airplane hangars near Ludwigslust where they put up beds. It had a galley on the top.

---

1   An airborne infantry division that played a key role in the Allied victory and was the first to reach and liberate the Wöbbelin concentration camp. Horrified, the troops found about one thousand inmates dead, and many near death. The US Army ordered the townspeople in nearby Ludwigslust to visit the camp and bury the dead. In 1982, Melvin sent a thank you letter to Lt. Gen. Gavin for saving his life, and he received a much-treasured response (see page 231).

They used ambulances to move us to the hangars. I had been living a few days already on the sand of an unfinished barracks. When they took me to the hangar, I became unconscious. I think I was unconscious three-quarters of the time in that hangar.

I recollect a nurse from the American Red Cross and a doctor talking, and I didn't understand what about. I was given a few transfusions and vitamins. I was told later, as I recovered a little bit, that I was X-rayed and an American doctor, a captain, took my history.

The first thing they did was give us hot or cold water and a one-inch slice of bread. The rescued kept on screaming and running, dead as we were. Through translation, they said it would be a while before we were allowed to consume any significant amount of food. We would have to gradually get used to eating. I was not allowed to smoke and later learned why. It was because I had open [infectious] TB. They kept the lights on day and night for about, I would say, two weeks.

I was given many, many transfusions. I remember getting them from an American nurse, a redhead, a wonderful person who was so often there. Off and on, I must have gone into a coma or something, and I know one thing—every time I opened my eyes she was there. They brought pajamas and dressings. They changed us two or three times a night. After a week or so they took X-rays of me and said I had a collapsed lung. Of course, it has to be realized that we were like ninety-year-old people, with everything gone. They washed us, changed our clothes—so much care we received. They were absolutely marvelous, those nurses. During that time I started to hope.

> "They washed us, changed our clothes—so much care we received. They were absolutely marvelous, those nurses. During that time I started to hope."

The Americans were holding German prisoners in that hangar. They put red crosses on their backs so we knew who they were. They were used as laborers in order to help us, the refugees, or whatever you call the people from concentration camps. One American, he told me he was Greek, came over and through translation gave me a shaving kit. But I couldn't shave; I couldn't move my arms. I was too weak to shave or do much of anything. It was a beautiful gesture though. He hugged me and kissed me. They were marvelous, these people.

— — — — —

At the beginning, after being liberated, I could not walk around, just move in bed, and I could not have more than some liquid and very little food. If I asked for bread I always got the explanation—only one piece of bread a day until my system could get used to eating. Later I got hot soup and other things, like compotes, to build me up. After we came around a little bit, they told us that they had to move us to Schwerin [30 km (19 miles) north of Wöbbelin], which the English occupied, because they had better facilities. All the while they huddled us and cuddled us. From the two or three hundred that were brought in to the airplane hangar, only seventy-five of us were still alive.

> *"From the two or three hundred that were brought in . . . only seventy-five of us were still alive."*

The journey in the Red Cross ambulance took a few hours. I remember one American, I think a lieutenant, was with us—me and two others. Everything you had in your stomach went up. It was agonizing. You thought you were dead. They held you down by the hands in order that you don't injure yourself or get into a fit, but they kept on assuring us that it had to be done because they had better facilities.

I was in very bad shape, so instead of sending me to the hospital, they took me into a lady's house, a private home, and told her to take good care of me and they would come back to check in with her. It was a German household, and I don't know why they divided us—me and others who were the weakest—into different households. Maybe for better care? But this lady really tried to cook for me and take care of me. I do not know about the food, which was canned. Either the Americans left it or she had it hidden.

— — — — —

I might have been there a week. Then some Red Cross packages were brought to me. Also a Polish officer in the English Army visited. He explained that the Russians had taken over the territory, and we had a choice, to stay there or go with the English. It was in the middle of the night and I was terribly sick. I didn't know what had happened there and didn't understand politics or the divisions. The area must have been like a corridor between the Russians, English, and Americans. I was sick and half asleep but decided to go to the English Zone. I didn't want to stay with the Russians because I did not want to be under another dictatorship.

I was with less power and strength, and with a fever, but some people helped me into the truck, which crossed the border into the English Zone.

They brought us to a town called Schwarzenbek [80 km (50 miles) west of Schwerin] for a rest, and from there I was picked up and brought to nearby Geesthacht. That was September 19, 1945 [date?].

We started hearing about UNRRA [UN Relief and Rehabilitation Administration], part of the United Nations Relief Organization. An English officer who brought me into a German hospital, called Edmundstahl and in Geesthacht, assured me that it was a better facility and had TB specialists. I have a certificate signed by General L. L. Briggs, then commanding officer of #22 DPACCS [Displaced Person Assembly Center Control Staff], and certifying that I was in his hospital in a severely weakened state due to advanced TB.

Officials at the German hospital explained to the English doctor, a UNRRA officer, that they had performed a pneumothorax treatment [insertion of a hollow needle between ribs to suction out excess air] on my left side for my collapsed lung, which was dangerous because my heart was very weak and my pulse fast. I had a big cavern. Professor Hans Richter and Dr. Engelman performed the treatment on me, through the top. Richter was a professor and supervised six clinics, and the other assisted him. All six clinics performed this operation.

The pneumothorax treatment was performed at first every day, then every second day, then every third and fifth day, then every week, then every two weeks, then every month, and so on, and that kept on going. It was an agonizing feeling, always that needle. You were lying on the table, and of course you could not breathe. But you had to survive, and so after two months they also sent me out with a nurse to take a thirty-second cold shower, then back to bed with some warm food. That was the treatment.

> "But you had to survive, and so after two months they also sent me out with a nurse to take a thirty-second cold shower, then back to bed with some warm food. That was the treatment."

I was the only Jewish patient in that hospital, so the head nurse, Veronica, a Volksdeutsche, was in charge of my care. I had been very sick and weak, but after about six months I regained a little bit of strength. I was there until December 5, 1945.

Then they sent me over to another place, which became known as the biggest and best hospital, and where they put me on cold massages in the morning, and I got all kinds of treatments. After a while, they permitted me to walk, but at first no more than fifteen minutes per day. Early on, my day consisted of getting up at 7:00 a.m. with some cereal, then putting my robe and shoes on and going for a two-minute cold shower, then coming back, all with the help of a nurse. In the daytime we lay in the veranda in the fresh air with earphones listening to music and covered up with blankets. The hospital was in the forest, a very beautiful forest. We were out there for two or three hours, and then the walking for only fifteen minutes, and then back to your room and into the bed.

— — — — —

In Geesthacht I met another Jewish boy, Szmulik, and a girl by the name of Lilka Rockman that my friend, the boy, loved dearly. We were the only Jews. We found out there was a Polish camp, so we decided to look for it. This was during a time when I was out walking more than I should have.

After about two and a half hours, the three of us found the camp, which consisted of barracks. The earth is parched, no green in it. It must have been a military or civilian jail with inmates, or maybe it was housing civilian workers. We walked in and were shown to the leader's hut. We told him who we are. He is startled and runs out in the middle of the big place and screams, "Jews, Jews!" All the Poles come up, hundreds of them, and kneel down and start making the sign of the cross themselves. They thought all the Jews had been killed. They come over to us, touch us. Are we really alive? They don't believe any Jews are alive. We stay and talk. We tell them where we came from. Some hug us.

> *"All the Poles come up, hundreds of them, and kneel down and start making the sign of the cross themselves. They thought all the Jews had been killed. They come over to us, touch us. Are we really alive?"*

We tell them we are in a hospital, and some of them come to see us. They bring two bags of food—food with packaging we hadn't seen in a long time—and make us honorary members of the camp, issue us passes, also food coupons. My pass was #1849, issued on August 23, 1945. They are terribly excited, and beg and plead with us to come back. After about two weeks we go back one more time, but we are thinking about the American Zone with better and more humane treatment and decide not to go back anymore.

— — — — —

These hospitals had so many buildings they might have contained at least two to three thousand people. They had the newest facilities plus all the modern instruments and everything. They told me time and again not to walk around, to walk no more than half hour to an hour a day. After a while with the half-hour limit, that was the new limit, but I didn't believe in that. I thought, *If I'm going to die, I'm going to die. I want to start walking.* It's no use living if you cannot walk so I start sneaking out and walking around for two hours and sometimes walking up hills. One day I thought my whole inside was falling out. I came back and had to be put to bed for about three weeks without doing nothing except being fed.

At that time I also had a nurse called Ursula. It was unbelievable here. I cannot imagine that this would happen, but she actually helped me bathe. She handled me like a child and kept on cleaning me. The sister of the nurse was an anti-Semitic. She could not understand why they bring in Jewish refugees instead of keeping German soldiers.

I had an incident with a Polish patient across the hall from me. He told me openly, when I was still in agony, that he belonged to the anti-Semitic fascist party in Poland. One morning I got up and he called me "Jew." I couldn't take it. I took a hot soup and threw it at him, and I do not know with what strength. It burned his face. That was one thing I thought: *I will never be able to take any more of the taunting and name-calling. If I survive and live, that would be the end. It is better going down with dignity as a man with a weapon in your hand, dying for honor instead of giving in to hooligans.*

One day, my friend and I met up with a tall and husky fellow. By talking a little German we found out he was a Dutch Jew and had been in Auschwitz. We strolled through a little town and found a bookstore that had *Der Stürmer* [a weekly, anti-Semitic tabloid], and also swastikas in the windows. Browsing through the bookstore, we see all that hate literature and started an argument with the shopkeeper.

The next day in the hospital, we are called on the floor by an English officer, with a Dutch translator, who asked us why we gave that person a rough time. We explained that the war is over, yet they still have that hate literature displayed. He says there is nothing he can do about it and we are bewildered. We do not understand. But, all this combined, I made up my mind to get away from these people and go to the American Zone. We tell the officer that with what little influence we have, we will do something about it ourselves, especially the Dutchman will. By the way, this Dutch boy was about twenty-eight or thirty years old and could not speak Jewish. He could only speak a few words of German and was absolutely beside himself. He wanted to bomb the whole town.

We went back and tore up the store in the evening, with what strength I don't know, but we did. We were enraged and made a mess of the store, busting doors and windows. The next day the English military picked us up and took us to see a major who kept on pushing his foot towards our feet like he was angry. The woman interpreter translated that we were going to have problems. We said we would make plenty of trouble, and he couldn't send us back to Auschwitz. That broke the camel's back with the English.

Another time, traveling about, there was only me and one other Jewish boy in the whole town, and there was not much we could do about it. Incidents, like going to the post office and hearing, "Who are you people? You don't speak good German. You have an accent." And me saying, "Well . . . ." Me saying, "Ich bin ein Jude," meaning, "I am a Jew." One girl, only about twenty years old, does not know what that is. She thought, as a Jew, I should have horns, like said in some cities with their anti-Semitic propaganda. I am thinking, *This is supposed to be one of the most civilized countries, even after the war?*

― ― ― ― ―

After the war, some Germans were really shook up. Rightly so. They thought that we Jews were well enough and that we would, outside, or going into their homes, castrate them or do something to their women, the same murderous, horrendous things they did to us. Possibly other nationalities who were victims of the Nazis did. We actually saw some of that, but the Jews, we went mostly by what we were taught at home and according to the Hebrew Bible. I don't know if these people took it as a sign of weakness, but after a while we proved we were not cowards. We had to stand up and be counted. We did it in many ways. We also told them, "We are not the same Jews that you pushed around." We proved by deed that when times are quiet, we can take care of ourselves, and we proved the old fable that a Jew, even a kid, cannot become a farmer, a soldier, or anything we wanted, did not apply anymore. No more. Like the communists in Poland before the war who used to sing songs that the Jews cannot be a farmer or a soldier, cannot be an artist or a musician.

After the atrocities the inhumane Germans had committed against us, it was agonizing having to go back to the German police station to get certification that you are a good *Bürger*, citizen. Isn't this an irony of fate? And, in just a few years. Also, you would have to get a certificate that you are competent to work, could support yourself, and would not fall as a burden to Germany —or the American government, if you emigrated. Ahead of me was much to do.

5. My Will Was Strong
1946–1949

1946–1949 *Mieczyslaw has been nursed back to a modicum of health, but he is far from able to return to normal life and faces many problems. His home is gone, his family is missing, and he is too weak and sick to provide for himself. He travels across zones administered by the Allies to different DP (displaced persons) camps and hospitals for medical care and in search of any family or friends who may have survived. A Polish Jew residing in Germany in the care of British and American medical personnel, he is just beginning to understand the complexities of a postwar Europe filled with displaced individuals. Throughout the continent, supplies are limited to the meager rations provided by a variety of governmental and charitable organizations. He has some welcome chance meetings and makes some friends, and he navigates the system as best he can, including getting a job. Although he appears to have few resources of his own, he gradually discovers a wealth of will, spirit, and forward-looking determination within himself.*

For related documentation, see appendices pages 210 (map of Mieczyslaw's postwar journey), 232–236.

Photo: Bayerisch-Gmain train station, near the town of Bad Reichenhall, September 18, 1949. Mieczyslaw is second from the right.

After a while gaining strength in hospitals, I wanted to find my family and asked to be permitted to go over the border into an American hospital. I hoped, with more Jewish people in the American Zone, I would find my family there. We also heard that the medical facilities were excellent on the American side. Anyhow, we applied for the American Zone and begged for the sympathetic understanding of the English to please let us go. Americans weren't stiff-necked like the English. They were more easygoing and a lot more sympathetic.

I traveled with my friend that was with me in Geesthacht, Szmulik, and his girlfriend, Lilka. We had one place to stop in the English Zone, before our journey south. We found out there was a house with Jewish refugees in Blankenese near Hamburg. We went there and I learned of two sisters, Bella and Esther, who had lived in the back of our building in Łódź, before the war. We didn't see Esther, but I saw Bella. We were very happy that we saw each other. Out of their whole family only the two sisters were left, and they were going to Israel. The next three months we continued our odyssey towards the American Zone, where Frankfurt and Munich were [525 km and 800 km (352 and 495 miles) south].

I must have been sick and disoriented when we started our journey, as we somehow wound up in Kassel, not our destination, in the American Zone. It was absolutely bombed out. We slept in a bombed-out house—me, Szmulik, and Lilka. The next day we caught a train and wagon in Würzburg, and from there we went to Aschaffenburg. We got into a military transport. They threw us out several times, but we managed to hide. One of the men in uniform was black—the first black man I'd ever seen.

— — — — —

It was in 1946 that I arrived in Munich, in the American Zone. Where we stayed was a regular camp, like a military camp. We had a little bit more freedom and more food than before. We started to get ten grams of butter a day, ten grams of sugar, and more bread. We started to live more normal lives. Some, including me, were brought to Gauting Sanatorium [25 km (15 miles) southwest of Munich]. I was permitted to stay there. At that time the guy that performed pneumothorax treatments was Dr. Kaplan, who ended up in the United States. In Gauting they continued those uncomfortable treatments on me.

After I'd been at Gauting for about three months, when I could walk around, I set off for Frankfurt am Main—a trip with Szmulik and Lilka. Going, we went to a bombed out place in Bavaria, where there had been a castle. There was nothing there, absolutely. We went to the Red Cross, and they didn't have a piece of bread for us. We had to scramble around in the dirt and every place in order to find something. Anyhow, we finally came around to Frankfurt. For the first time I felt free.

> "... and they didn't have a piece of bread for us. We had to scramble around in the dirt and every place in order to find something."

We came to a Jewish DP [displaced persons] camp. Lilka had somebody that was alive there who was already established in that camp. And I found quite a few people that knew me. I saw a girl that worked in my factory group in the Łódź ghetto and she told me her brother was a policeman in the ghetto. She was happy to see me, but I was too sick to stick around. Her name was Sasza Hartstein [?]. She was a grandchild of the chief rabbi of Łódź, blonde, blue-eyed, and I was really in love with that girl.

We were invited to a house with friends from Łódź. It's the evening, and they invite me for supper, and Lilka too, and her friends, and we sit down at the table and start eating. A gentleman knocks on the door, a young guy about twenty-eight years old, wearing a funny uniform that I never saw before. He comes in and sits down with us. We sit and eat. He has a drink. All of a sudden, after sitting about an hour and a half talking and drinking tea, he comes over to me. He says, "I recognize you. Aren't you a Goldman from Łódź?" I said, "Yes!" He says, "I am going to tell you something, but I don't want you to repeat it. Right at this table . . . it stays right here with all these people or I'm going to be in deep trouble." I say, "What's the matter?" He answers, "Let me tell you something. I work for the NKVD, the Russian secret police. I just came from Poland."

I don't know if maybe they planted him with the refugees. He tells me, "Your brother, Aron, is alive. During the war, he was working in the Buna camp [an Auschwitz slave laborer satellite camp]. He also worked in Görlitz in the coal mines. Here's the reason I know of him. He told me these things when I met him in Łódź and took him out to eat and we had a nice time, sitting around for a couple of hours. Aron went into business with Usharovich, a guy that you people used to buy metal from. They had a big place; it was like a large hardware store. Would you like to send him a letter? I will sneak it out for you, if you want, and I will notify him."

I stayed in Frankfurt a while and did not know what to do. Then, I think, *Okay*. I pursued it. I sat down and wrote Aron a note. I told him he should get out of Poland and come to the American Zone. I told him in the strongest terms, "I'll die if you don't come. We are the only survivors." The reason I wrote such a strong letter was I tried to impress on him he must get out. Nothing good would come of being there.

> "I told him he should get out of Poland . . . I told him in the strongest terms, 'I'll die if you don't come. We are the only survivors.'"

I didn't hear from my brother for about three and a half weeks. All of the sudden communications got, I wouldn't say normal, but half normal. A letter came. The letter from my brother said that this gentleman got in touch with him. He gave another name [the secrecy was necessary because Poland was under Soviet control], changed it, and asks would I like to go to Poland, come back, and we would open the place [perhaps the old factory and the family's former house]. He said he is going around, finding some things. He couldn't tell me everything. Everything is hidden, but he found some of the little rings of my mom and some other things, and would I like to come to Poland. I think this over, wanting so much to unite.

— — — — —

All together, I was at Gauting Sanitorium for about a year. There, I was often in a state of shock. At the end of 1946, I was transferred to a hospital in Schwabing [?] near Munich. They continued to perform pneumothorax for the few weeks I was there. There were a lot of American military in that Schwabing hospital. We were kept there because they didn't know what to do with us for a while. We stood on our feet. We could walk around. We had our passes. But you were nobody yet. You weren't a citizen from any country. You didn't know what to do. You didn't know what anybody else would do with you. You were hanging in the air, in between.

It was decided that since I was on my feet a little bit, it would be a good idea to transfer me to Bad Wörishofen [85 km (55 miles) west of Munich, and south of Augsburg]. It was a cure place where people from all over the world came to heal their feet in a special kind of water. The hospital I was sent to was called Sonnenhof; it was a chronic hospital. The second day I met a person I had known before the war as Miss Potok. When I asked her, she said yes, her brother had been friends with my father in the ghetto. Her husband, Dr. Berman, was chief doctor and director of the hospital. She introduced me to him and told him who I was. He right away began to treat me, though he couldn't take care of my lung problem. I was given a small glass of red wine every day to build me up.

Dr. Berman sent me to another place for care, Kneippianum Sanatorium, in the same town. It was a German hospital requisitioned by the UNRRA [United Nations Relief and Rehabilitation Administration] through the army, for refugees, or DPs, especially TB patients. They had the equipment. There, I would be more independent and have better food and a little bit more freedom to write and read. I was there until 1948, still under medical care and on a special diet. Also, they took care of my feet [with frostbite damage], which got a little bit better.

There were 250 or 300 beds in that hospital, for grown-ups or kids. It was a Lazarett, a field hospital for officers. It was a beautiful building, immaculate with good equipment. Lots of hoopla, too. The hospital was three blocks long and very wide, with large open spaces and a beautiful big backyard. The rooms were kept absolutely beautiful, spotlessly clean. It was a paradise after

Auschwitz. This was the best time, in this place, that I spent yet, in all the years since childhood.

It was run by about twenty-five Catholic nuns and five or six doctors. The hospital was named for Father Kneippianum, who was a Catholic priest and the main doctor. The mother superior was Sister Fernanda. In addition to the nuns, private nurses came in, and also one German doctor, a surgeon. Later on, other doctors were added.

I was cared for by chief Dr. Krotowski, who later went to Israel, and also Dr. Filipowicz and Dr. Cieszykowski. I got chest X-rays, and I still got a pneumothorax according to the schedule. With these pneumos, which had been started soon after liberation, first I was getting them quite often, every day at the beginning, then every six months, later. All together, I got these pneumos for almost two and a half years. Then one day they tried to give it to me, and did not do it anymore. They had asked me in Gauting, and also here, would I give permission for an operation on my ribs, but I didn't allow it. They explained to me that they couldn't do the treatment that day or in the future because I needed the operation. I still made up my mind that I would not let them do it. I thought that I was crippled enough without the operation.

I became strengthened, gained a little more weight. Up from the eighty-some pounds I came in with, my weight was now 115 pounds. There was also more sympathy, more caring people. It started to be like what you would call normal; it wasn't normal, but you could walk, you could eat lunch and then supper. You were woken up in the morning. You were given something to eat. You come in, you had a big hall. And, from 1:00 to 3:00 every day the patients had to take a rest called *"Liegekur"* [rest cure].

> "It started to be like what you would call normal; it wasn't normal, but you could walk, you could eat lunch and then supper. You were woken up in the morning."

– – – – –

Back to my brother, who wanted to know if I would come to Poland. I wrote him, "How will I ever go back to Poland? I don't want to be under the Russians. No, I don't want to go back to Poland. There is nothing there. There is enough blood spilled. I am not even going to stay in Germany." I said, "Pack up, business or no, and come to me. Come to Germany! You come." I was feeling more settled, especially with working a bit at Kneippianum.

It went on like that for about three and a half months. Finally, after all the talk and all the writing and pleading and begging, Aron finally comes to Germany. He was healthy and was assigned to a camp in Heidenheim [115 km (70 miles) north], where he became a camp policeman. It was a Jewish camp with about two thousand heads. He became very friendly with some of the people; one in particular, a guy, was crazy about him. He was an older fellow and stuck around him. I come once in a while to that camp, and Aron also came to visit me at Kneippianum. Since I had distribution of food, I helped him out, to give him some comfort.

When you are fifteen or sixteen years of age and never touched a girl, that's okay, typical. But then, I think of when you are seventeen years old. In your head, like every teenage male in creation, he sees the world through a certain haze, a fog that colors everything. He wants to be with girls. All friendly. But, he does not know what to say, where to put his eyes, his hands. This all I missed, with the war. It's a problem, being early twenties, liberated, and no experience. And no advice from a father, like as a boy when he told me about being a good person and teaching me about money. How am I supposed to behave? I had never really dated.

Can you understand what I had mentally to overcome? In the first place I could not have a date because I was in mental pain remembering all the things that had happened to my family. I went through a time of what maybe looked like penance, and then after about two years of liberation, I had a platonic relationship with a girl. I made a date with a girl about eight years after the outbreak of the war. My first date. I had been robbed of my best years as a youth, also my schooling, and my family. Everything. I had been beaten up as a human, but I felt the time was not to despair but to have hope. My hope had grown since the Allies' rescue, especially since the Americans had helped me.

> *"A book is written in words and it has pages and it can describe suffering, humiliation, torture, and even thinking about committing suicide. But, it is only so many words and pages."*

A book is written in words and it has pages and it can describe suffering, humiliation, torture, and even thinking about committing suicide. But, it is only so many words and pages. Can you realize what it is to live every day with fear, with these sufferings and thoughts for five years? The beast did a good job. Not only did they murder six million Jews and about in total twenty-five million human beings, but even the ones who survive. Each and every one had something done to him or her physically or mentally, or both, that until they die they will never forget. They will remember pieces of it every day. I still try to live with myself now, so many years later.

— — — — —

Despite the horrible war years, before and even during the war, I had been able to gain some valuable skills and experience. And so I was elected as an officer on a committee that helped run the Kneippianum hospital, the civilian side. This included procuring food and clothing for the kids, listening to their complaints, and in general trying to improve things for them. Most of the small kids were either half Jewish or Gentile. However, ninety-five percent of the grown-ups older than fifteen were Jewish.

I held meetings. Other men were elected to be on the committee. One was Simeonoff; he had been a lieutenant colonel in the Russian Army. He was a tall guy, about six foot two inches. He had been wounded on the front lines and was supposed to watch out for me, like my bodyguard. The committee consisted of me as head, another man by the name of Teitelbaum who was also my bodyguard—he was six foot four, another named Bernstein, and also a Pole who was later repatriated to Poland.

As head of the committee, I represented UNRRA and also helped the JDC [American Jewish Joint Distribution Committee]. The capital of the *Kreis* [district] for Bad Wörishofen was Mindelheim, the largest city close to it. I got paid as an employee of the hospital, according to documents. I have a card, #2613, certifying this from the city council. I can't tell you how wonderful it felt to be involved in the beautiful act of helping the other people in the hospital, especially the three friends that are now residing in New Jersey and also others that survived.

> "I can't tell you how wonderful it felt to be involved in the beautiful act of helping the other people in the hospital."

I helped bring in food if necessary from Munich, about a three-hour ride away. I was given a handicap classification, but still worked hard, and every two or three weeks we hired a coal truck, the only transportation we could get. We went to Munich mostly, a German driver and I, every two to four weeks, and loaded a wagon with food packages, either from the military, the UNRRA, or the JDC. At the hospital, staff was hired. They and some other helpers distributed the food we brought, equally from the packages and cans.

We organized clothing the same way. There was winter clothing for everyone and lightweight outfits for warm weather. That stuff was hard to come by; once I even stole shoes for the kids. I also took care of procedures in the office. I was authorized by the chief doctor to represent the hospital in all matters to get medicine, food, and clothing. My special pass authorized me to take care of all matters with any authority. French, English, German, or American had to help me when I needed it. For example, sometimes I would have to go for penicillin in the middle of the night. Total personnel was about sixty-five, including the office.

> "In Kneippianum, I learned about the business of talking to kids, and I think they were crazy about me."

In Kneippianum, I learned about the business of talking to kids, and I think they were crazy about me. Their faces would light up when they saw me. The doctors only had time for patients and were responsible for medicine, so my committee actually ran the hospital. I had to make sure there were enough doctors. We didn't have a German doctor, so I hired one who was a surgeon. I had to have him just in case. His name was Dr. Koppel [?].

Like anyplace else, there were many problems. There was infighting and politics that I learned later go on in a committee, but I ran that hospital with a strong arm. It was clean and neat. We, first thing, made the hospital as beautiful as possible for everybody with both nuns and hired staff. I was told thousands of times, in meetings, from the patients, and people in town that it was the nicest kept and the most organized institution. People even came from the outside to get advice from us, the so-called refugees.

I was on call all of the time with full hours of duty, day and night. You had a responsibility. For a young man, I had a big responsibility at the time, all the while going around in my own physical agony and still under doctors' care myself. No other patient had this responsibility except for me, taking care of the hospital as a whole. The duties were many and sometimes more than I could take; the stress and the strain were terrible, but you had an obligation to survive and help others do likewise. There were kids who had endured a lot—Jewish boys who had been castrated and Jewish girls who had been raped.

I was only twenty-four years old, and I felt like I did the best job of my life. We had rooms with three lights—red, blue, and white. The red light was an emergency. If it was blue, I was needed to talk to a patient, something had happened. If it was white, I could sleep. Emergencies occurred when a kid got phlegmon. I might have to go in the middle of the night with a doctor for penicillin that was sometimes not available. We had to hustle, haggle, and connive—to do anything to get it. We did that, in order for a kid I remember to survive. Dr. Panich administered them, and we rescued the boy.

I felt my biggest responsibility towards the kids. We organized about a hundred pieces of furniture outside and made the kids lie down between 1:00 and 3:00, which was the custom in this part of the country. We hired people, such as the girl Hadassah, who spoke Hebrew and started teaching it. We got a record player and some French records for kids and played them in one room. We set up a game room for them. We tried to do our best to make life pleasant for these kids.

Also, to sweeten the lives of the kids, and the grown-ups too, I hired three musicians from town, and we were feeding them, and paying them about ten marks a month. Six days a week the musicians came at lunchtime, most of the time, and suppertime to play music for us while we were eating in the main dining hall, which we had fixed up. Everybody came down to lunch or supper to hear them.

> "Also, to sweeten the lives of the kids, and the grown-ups too, I hired three musicians from town..."

Kneippianum was in a town of about five thousand people and with a beautiful forest. It was a place for cures, and people came from all over the world to dip their feet in the salt water. I had some beautiful times in that town itself. Once I was stronger and had made some friends, I would take walks outside the hospital. But there were miserable times as well when my work seemed overwhelming.

We, the adults, sometimes went to Café Flora in town, where we ate and talked. There were students and several nationalities, and politics and local problems were discussed. Since I was now a member of the town council, at some times I was involved with problems. Like if someone had smuggled and had been picked up. If those people were picked up and had a record, they couldn't get a visa out of the country, so we had to make sure to take care of them. If the careers of the smugglers were ruined, they wouldn't be able to leave the country.

There was a young Polish lady, around thirty, working for the American government in Mindelheim. She was a stenographer and typist, and a helper to the person with a problem. And, she took care of these things for me. Of course, the saying was always that the DPs—displaced persons—were the smugglers, but how could a person, penniless and dependent on a package coming all the way from the United States or Canada, be a smuggler? You got the package and what if you didn't give the Germans money or didn't exchange for something. That is what some of these people did. You trade a piece of chocolate and get a pair of gloves.

I performed all these functions while I was being treated and sometimes being very ill. But in good times, I might take a UNRRA wagon or car and a few people for a short holiday to France or Italy. Italy appealed to me the most because the people were more humane than anyone I knew in Europe, except those in the Scandinavian countries. The Italians shared with you, even their last meal; not so in the other so-called Western countries, or for that matter the Eastern ones.

— — — — —

After much time, nearly a year, I started begging Aron to come and stick around with me, together, because we are the survivors from the whole family. Finally, he decided to come for more than a visit. At that time, besides living in Kneippianum, I also had another room in town before I was transferred to a farmer's place. There I was on the second floor of a nice little place. I figured I needed some rest place, to run away to. I gave some food to the farmer and I lived there. So then Aron came. He was first on his own. Now what is he going to do? He was not too broken up. They had taken care of him. He was free of the Russians, but still in all, he was in a bit better shape than I was. He had a fast heartbeat or something, but he could walk around. If he ate normal, he could live.

He had to do something. I had to get him into the hospital and get him in with some of the guys that were walking around. These guys did accomplish something. They did some work and other things and made a few bucks. I hope and I think he was very happy. Then he moved in with me in that farmer's house and we shared everything. We used to shop a little bit besides going to the hospital. Whenever I had a weekend, I used to spend it with Aron. It was a beautiful time.

> "Whenever I had a weekend, I used to spend it with Aron. It was a beautiful time. We were together all the time..."

We were together all the time until he went to America. He had applied—went through the doctors and the American Jewish Joint Distribution Committee, took out the papers, got the visa. Since we were metal workers and we knew everything about metals, they picked the city of Pittsburgh for him because it is a metal or steel town. He went in 1949. After he was settled, he wrote me that he had met and married a girl, Evy Elling. As of now [late 1970s], he has two children, a boy and girl, and they have a nice house. He is in the insurance business.

— — — — —

At the hospital, I had friends working for me downstairs. One young gentleman used to eavesdrop on the nuns. After about two years, the nuns started complaining about the refugees occupying the building. Can you imagine, such a concern, after taking away all the goods, robbing the Jews of everything, furs and diamonds and other things they had accumulated over hundreds of years. It was supposed to be their motherly duty to help us out and care for us humanely, but they started complaining and writing letters, making long distance calls to the bishop and I think even to Rome.

My friend translated what they were saying and I got very angry. They had half of a plantation where they raised pigs and all kinds of food. I went in one time and asked Sister Fernanda to please provide for the kids. They needed some of the food. No, how could we get it, she said, so I went with a few boys in the evening and took food from the field, and that was that. I mean that was all you could do. I was not waiting like we had to in the liberation when you couldn't get a potato, when it took five or six months for the UNRRA to come in and finally give somebody a piece of bread or a package. I was not letting the kids down. They were kids, only five or six years old, mixed kids, all kinds of kids, and I was not about to let them down, to go around hungry—so we organized and we took it in, and we fed them, that's all.

After a while I was advised that by some luck or some pushing, or whatever they did, that Kneippianum was being made a hospital, and it should be made for children. They had succeeded in talking everybody into it, that this should be a place more for treatment than long term healing. Some were very scared, and they had a reason to be. For the grown-ups, we, the ones over twenty, had to be moved. Moved, with the help of the JDC and the UNRRA, either to a hospital in the same town or Sonthofen, or for the patients that felt better, to a private home, like a convalescent home called Josepheim that was held and kept up by the UNRRA.

– – – – –

I was transferred to nearby Sonnenhof, the chronic hospital where I had been before and recognized Mrs. Berman. My doctor was Dr. Morgenstern, and Dr. Berman was still the hospital chief. He was a gentleman in his sixties, and I learned that before the war he was the Lithuanian king's doctor. The doctor's wife was about thirty-five. Her brother had been my father's best friend. With our personal connection from before, she came up and we became friends. Almost immediately, I had to submit to having some teeth pulled because they had not been taken care of for a long while.

Some of the teeth had been pulled out and others broken while in Auschwitz. I bled for a whole night after the extractions. I was weak. They had to pack my gums, and a nurse was assigned to me, a German nurse, who stayed with me a whole night. She poured all the love into me as a patient. I found out she had been in love with another Jewish patient there in that hospital for about two years, a man who was terribly sick. I think he had lost a leg. She wanted to marry him and he wanted to marry her, and I think they eventually got married and settled in Israel.

> "A nurse was assigned to me, a German nurse, who stayed with me a whole night. She poured all the love into me as a patient."

In this hospital I was still under a diet and wasn't allowed to walk around a lot or do any work. We started receiving rations. We were treated pretty well. From time to time we even got a little bit of red wine, but one time, a commission of English doctors and some others came and started talking about how we were well enough to have our rations cut, including how many cigarettes we were allowed. Like, we got three or four cigarettes, bringing it down to one cigarette. We had to share with the Germans, they said. We got mad and organized and chased them out of the hospital. It was too much to take. These people did not understand a darn thing. Social workers and other functionaries thought they knew everything. They came in and tried to solve our problems, and we had many, not only physical, but mental also. Unless they had spent time in Auschwitz, they wouldn't understand us in a hundred years. How could they?

I was there about a month, but they couldn't keep me there because it was a chronic hospital, but not able to provide proper care for my TB. I was referred to the area's chief doctor, at headquarters in Augsburg. Then I went through a commission, and they decided to make an experiment with me. They called me in and talked to me about a place and said I should go. I would feel better, they said. They didn't want to take the responsibility of my care on themselves, and as they explained it, the move would be to a rehabilitation center, what I needed.

After so many years of suffering and trying all kinds of treatments, they walked with me, and asked me to accept the change, saying the place would be a very nice place. I would have good food and better opportunity to try to become productive so that I could even work for an hour. I was advised that it would probably be Bayerisch-Gmain near Bad Reichenhall. After long nights and days of consultations with friends, I decided I would go. In 1948, I was shipped to Bayerisch-Gmain Rehabilitation Center [225 km (140 miles) east]. I have papers signed by Dr. A. Piller.

— — — — —

I was not disappointed in that place. It is beautiful, right in the mountains—the Bavarian Alps. It is only about ten kilometers from Bad Reichenhall to the main town, and then to the Austrian border it was only a matter of about two and a half kilometers walking. It is a really beautiful place, with fresh air, mountains, and only a while away from Berchtesgaden, where his name should never be mentioned: the Führer. He used to vacation there. The rehab center was like a summer house, about one hundred feet away from skiing.

It was for that time the best facility. It had one hundred beds. In the morning we would wake up and have a regular bath. We had food three or four times daily, a beautiful diet for that time in comparison to the general public. We had butter and sugar and most necessities. Life was almost what you would call normal, except we did not have any income except what we could come up with and we felt helpless about that. So we couldn't go out and buy anything including cigarettes. At one point, I still had a few marks saved up, so we went to the symphony.

Remember, I lost my youth at sixteen locked into a ghetto, then death camps, and got out in my early twenties. I could not yet make it as a normal person doing normal activities. It took me a long while until I got the courage, plus the will and a drop of better health, to dream of going out on a date. I hadn't lost some of the apprehension of going and coming. Eventually, I did have the courage to go out. The worst way, even walking a block, took

> "I was determined to walk and to live as normal as the people on the outside. Everything was wrong inside my body. That was the consolation—outside, if you dressed, nobody knew what was bothering you or how sick you were."

me approximately two and a half hours. I was determined to walk and to live as normal as the people on the outside. Everything was wrong inside my body. That was the consolation—outside, if you dressed, nobody knew what was bothering you or how sick you were. At least we lived, and we tried to recover our health.

The time we spent in the rehabilitation was not too bad. I had freedom of walking and going any place I wanted, for the first time actually. We were under doctors' supervision, and we got all the medical attention we needed. The director of that place was a German Jew named Auerbach. We had the following doctors taking care of us: Dr. Kaplan, Dr. Cieszykowski, Dr. Filipowicz, Dr. Krotowski, and a Swedish doctor whose name I don't remember. Dr. Cieszykowski had moved over to this rehabilitation center. We were examined every two weeks and X-rayed, and three times a week medical doctors checked us over. The director of nurses, a lady of Lithuanian descent, was the mother of the house.

— — — — —

Though I was under constant medical care, nobody would tell us what was wrong with us or how we could get healthy. I wanted to find out, outside the hospital, what exactly was my diagnosis. Some of us decided to go to Bad Reichenhall and get examined. It was a group of three doctors. In November 1949, I went through a commission there, and was given an *Invaliden* [invalid] pass in Berchtesgaden from a Dr. I. A. Erben, who signed a paper #529/49 and another #1130/16 Bayern that I was seventy percent handicapped, with fifty-five percent on my lungs, ten percent on my feet, and five percent on my teeth. I have documents attesting to this.

In German, I am called a *Behinderter* [disabled person]. That's my condition, it means I could not walk or sit. It meant I would never walk alone and I needed constant help. I have documents for this. Of course, I didn't think too much about the pass because the doctors told me originally that I will never be able to work physically, and that there is no difference had they given me an eighty percent or ninety percent. Dr. Cieszykowski, at the rehab center gave me the same as in Reichenhall, seventy percent.

With such a condition, and although the doctor did not promise I would get better, thank God, within a few months at the center, I could go out and play soccer ball. My will was strong. Either you jump off a bridge, or you are going to live and think about your parents, what they told you—that somebody in the family has to survive. Since I lived, I made a decision. I had the will. I fought with myself about it. I could play soccer ball for about ten minutes. That was the limit that I could play. There was determination and drive. I did not want to live a life being dependent, having somebody handing me a cup of tea. I thought, *Either I'm going to walk or I'm going to die.* I thought either/or. I think it was also my youth. I was young.

> "*I thought,* Either I'm going to walk or I'm going to die. *I thought either/or.*"

Stronger, we took walks around the forest, talked to the population, tried to find out reasons why, when, and for what reason, why they did it. We used to go into a coffeehouse. We saw a lot of American soldiers. The frauleins now were not particular who they went out with. Believe me, for one pack of cigarettes, they went out for a whole night with the soldiers. The "Aryan race"—all of the sudden the Aryans changed. They didn't have too much food or anything. Not only with the food and things, but otherwise—their ways seemed like they were helpless. It wasn't the big heroes in time of the war that they told you about.

6. I Was Going to Make It
late 1949 – late 1970s

- - - - -

Late 1949–late 1970s *After five years in the bedlam of postwar Europe, Mieczyslaw knows that there is no home for him here. Poland's boundaries have been redrawn. Many areas are now under Soviet rule, and some places, including Łódź, are unfriendly to Jews. The political winds are so variable, it seems there is no place on the continent that offers a stable future. Since the United States and other Allies are slow to take in refugees—especially Jews—many will spend years being shuttled around various "temporary" camps. Rumors abound. Nevertheless, Mieczyslaw holds a hopeful outlook, and he seeks out training, recognizing it could support his next move, whatever that might be. In 1948, Mieczyslaw finally has some improved prospects for emigration when Israel is founded, attracting many Jews to a new national homeland. In the United States, President Truman signs the Displaced Persons Act, with its increased quotas for immigrants who have lost their homes. At the close of the decade, Mieczyslaw decides—America it will be! At last, after overcoming significant bureaucratic obstacles, he arrives in Pittsburgh on the last day of 1950. He is now Melvin, with many physical disabilities and the challenges of a new country with an unknown language. But he has overcome seemingly insurmountable odds before. He knows how to do this.*

For related documentation, see appendices pages 210 (map of Mieczyslaw's postwar journey), 211 (map of Squirrel Hill, PA), 237–286.

Photo: Melvin Goldman in Pittsburgh, early 1950s, on Denniston Avenue.

Often I thought, *At least we lived.* Survived. During this time, while we were trying to continue recovering our health, I got around a bit. From time to time, we took a car and went into France. It took us a few weeks. Once I spent about seven weeks in Bad Saulgau [315 km (195 miles) west of Bad Reichenhall] at a place where you learned how to survive and live even though you didn't have a lot of money. Also, in this rehabilitation center, the JDC and the UNRRA set up an ORT[1] school to retrain or reorient anybody who was able to attend to learn a new trade for a future.

In that place, I was in fine mechanics and metal work. The rehabilitation center had hired a German gentleman to teach us mechanical trades for ORT. He was very good. He was very nice, amicable. He had been interned I think in Dachau. He taught us theory and was patient with us. I guess he had to be, with people who didn't at that time care about what happens in the future as long as they had food to eat and everybody left them be. I attended his classes and enjoyed them. There were not many who attended there.

---

1   World ORT (Association for the Promotion of Skilled Trades, in Russian) is a non-profit Jewish organization supporting education and training worldwide. After the war, ORT established programs in seventy-eight DP camps in Germany, serving nearly 85,000 refugees. It was founded in St. Petersburg, Russia, in 1880.

Another reason for attending and learning the trade was you got a paper stating that you were capable of performing a task or had a profession, which made it a lot easier to go through the commission for any country. If I wanted to emigrate, I had to have a trade and be strong. And I had to make contacts and apply. Some of the old did not have the stamina to go through all of that rigamarole and they stayed behind. But I moved ahead with training, with doctors' examinations and thinking about the different countries. For instance, Canada wanted only certain people, tailors and shoemakers; Australia had the quota system, only so many of a nationality and also mainly workers, no businessmen.

It's strange how all the countries made up rules. Really, it is humorous sometimes: after being imprisoned for five years by the Nazis, you had to go through a commission of about fifteen doctors and take tests in order to see if you are fit to be accepted in a particular country. It was ironic that in order to be accepted, we had to have a trade and be healthy and happy—all this, after surviving the Holocaust. We wondered, *Were these other countries full of perfect specimens themselves?* And, we consoled ourselves.

I had to prove that I was capable of working at least four hours a day. I did metal sculptures, the kind of metal work I had done in the ghetto. I finally got the certification that I could work four hours a day and that I was reliable. They notified the council and I had an appointment. I was also shown papers with names of organizations to see if I belonged to them. They asked questions and finally gave me a slip. I passed, because my father had been an independent entrepreneur and I didn't belong to any of the organizations listed.

> "I finally got the certification that I could work four hours a day and that I was reliable."

- - - - -

My brother Aron and I had discussed it before a lot of times: where to go. We had thought that either we should go to the United States or Israel. When Aron was applying to leave, the Jewish state was established only a little while back [May 1948], and I didn't know what was going to happen. I was scared at that time. We heard rumors. I kept on thinking, *My God, Aron is young enough to be drafted into the Israeli Army. I don't want him to go. Not long ago he was only like seventeen or eighteen, through the most terrible of experiences. Now, early twenties, for him to have to fight after all that he went through in the war. I don't want to lose him—we are the only two souls alive from our whole family, except the ones that were overseas.*

With my influence, Aron had agreed: we decided on going to the United States. That's where we set our sights, and he went first, in 1949. He was there now. I, though, still here, thought of my options. You would hear things, like there was a Jewish business, Fisher Scientific in Switzerland. But, my thoughts turned to family. Uncle Joel, our father's brother, wanted me to come to Israel where he was. When I was ten years old [~1933], he had moved there—Palestine at the time. I recall my father preparing clothes, suits, and giving him 1000 *meva* [?], cigarettes, and about a few hundred złotys for him to take on his journey. But I thought going to Israel right now, with its recent statehood, I could not be what you call a pioneer. I thought, *I'm done; impossible. I'm worn out, not in great health, I'm not looking for or ready to take on such a challenge.*

I considered Argentina because we had family there too—my aunt, uncle, and cousins who left Poland when I was a child. And, I had an address for them. The Argentinean consul gave me a hard time and asked me all kinds of questions, and I had to run around six or seven times to their consulate. I did not realize that so many Nazis had run away to Argentina. They asked if I am a Catholic and I said, "No. I'm not a Catholic. I'm a Jew." One of the officials asked me to sign on as a Catholic and said when I get to Argentina to do what I want. I guess he had compassion. I told him, "Forget it. After what I went through, I am not selling out." I was so enraged that they had asked me that question.

That's how the world started to turn on me, and I didn't know what to do with myself. I got terribly mad. I used to go around and talk to everybody. I felt like bombing out that consulate. Finally, I made up my mind it was high time to go through the American consulate and the whole schmear. America it would be. It was now up to the doctors and commission, and also authorities, for all legal papers. Plus, help from aid groups.

> "I made up my mind it was high time to go through the American consulate and the whole schmear."

That all took some doing, with months of frustration and standing in lines. I already had the invalid pass and verifications for being seventy percent handicapped from the year before. And, through the months I was in contact with the United Service for New Americans [USNA] and the Hebrew

Immigrant Aid Society [HIAS].[2] It was on October 24, 1950, that the JDC [Joint Distribution Committee] notified me and gave me a number in preparation for immigration—#93744. My sponsor was the Jewish Social Service, Pittsburgh, to go as a tinsmith or box maker, signed by a Gladys Roth.

The aid agencies grade and allocate newcomers for specific cities or regions based on employability. That is, applicants' skills plus the opportunities for work. Since I came from people in the metal business, this is how I ended up going to Pittsburgh, a steel town. Also, I had my brother there. I waited to be called to the American consul. There, again you go through a question period and finally you are told it is okay. Then you are awaiting the time to be called to actually leave.

– – – – –

With Aron across the sea, I was alone. Again, no family. But, I went on my trips. I was in Italy, which I especially liked, and in France and Austria. I remember I went to Austria with some of the boys and stayed at the Hotel Winkler a couple of days. I had a nice time there. We went almost to Vienna, and to Salzburg [20 km (12.5 miles) northeast of Bad Reichenhall] where I spent a lot of time. I was there about twenty-five times and went to the festivals, to Mozart's place, and looked around and visited many places. We went to the clubs and the catacombs and saw the museums. One day, all of a sudden I saw a Ceder cousin. She was at that time about twenty-five. We hugged and kissed and had a nice time for about four days. She now [1970s] lives in Israel, and I correspond with her. She had been in the Israeli Army.

I had a friend that was an East Berliner, a beautiful girl, and one day I met her with other friends in Bad Reichenhall. We were always a group of three or four. There was my friend Moniek [probably the same one mentioned twice earlier], who ended up in Sweden, and another one who married a German girl whose father had a textile mill. We stayed over until twelve or one in the morning. All of a sudden, everybody tried to go after my friend. I don't know why. And my friend, the East Berliner, goes over to that German

---

2   The USNA was formed in 1946, specifically to help Jewish survivors of the camps. The HIAS began work in 1884, in response to the exodus of Jews from persecution in Imperial Russia. Before and during World War II, HIAS aided Jews fleeing Europe. During the aftermath of the war, the organization helped more than 150,000 displaced Jews emigrate to new homes. Today, the HIAS operates in twelve countries, and in the Jewish tradition of *tikkun olam* (repair the world) provides a wide range of services without regard for religion, nationality, or ethnic background.

girl, and said she would like to talk to me, sit down and really talk. We did, and I started taking this East Berlin girl out. She was a beautiful girl, a nice girl. She brought a dog and then another dog, two German Shepherd dogs; I helped her out. We used to go for walks and all.

One day, after going out about three months, all of a sudden, she is telling me one evening that she has to go and visit her parents in the eastern zone of Berlin. So I helped her out and we talked about it. Suddenly, she says she has to leave. That's the date, she has the pets, she has to go. I warned her about East Berlin. I was there before for about six weeks. We went over there when we were right nearby, after Ludwigslust, and I felt better and everything. I told her, "Forget about it. It's bad. It's terrible. I ran away from it." She says, "No. I have to go see my mom and dad. I did not see them for three or four years." I said, "Well, go ahead." She went and I never saw her after that. I inquired and looked for that girl and learned nothing.

> "She went and I never saw her after that. I inquired and looked for that girl and learned nothing."

— — — — —

One freezing November day in 1950, we were told, "You take your belongings, whatever you have, and you will soon go to Wildflecken near Bremerhaven [950 km (590 miles) north of Bad Reichenhall] to wait for transportation to the USA." *Wildflecken* means "wild spot," and it was. We were accommodated in barracks, huts without heat, and had very few rations, since we were supposed to move out, but it took about three weeks. Freezing weather, snow up to three feet high. We were about four hundred persons. We had to help out in the camp and do all kinds of things.

Finally, the day came where we were called to the ship. It was the *General Taylor*,[3] an old troop transport ship with bunks, all to accommodate the passengers. We were all right after that. Each one got a bed, and each had this and that. It was rocky. We had been officially told that we weren't allowed to bring food or anything on board, but we heard that crossing the Atlantic in the wintertime is bad, that we should take onions or sardines; that would help with seasickness, but it didn't. I brought sardines and whiskey. The food was good, if we could eat.

---

3   The USS *General Harry Taylor* (AP-145) was built as a transport, with few weapons and a maximum of close, austere living facilities. Besides her US Navy crew of 350, the *Taylor* accommodated over three thousand troops — and later, immigrant refugees.

On the ship we performed all kinds of work. We helped paint, scrub the deck, and other labor jobs, but we did not mind. We were frozen but happy. We went in lifeboats, since we had to drill for emergencies. We also had an emergency. A hole fell on the deck. We had to be a few hours in the water.[4] I never liked the water. A saying went around, supposedly from a doctor, "Whoever gets sick gets thrown overboard." We actually believed that and were terribly scared. Because of the leak, our journey ended up taking about fourteen days instead of eight.

We were on the ship Christmas night. The crew had a party, but the boat was rocking, and only a few of us could manage to eat or dance. We didn't have much. We had no money and not much luggage, no special possessions, but deep down we knew we were going to a country that wanted us, where people will help us. The mood was happy, very happy. At last, one day we looked out and saw the Statue of Liberty.[5] Man, woman, or child, you realize, after all the things you have gone through, you have finally reached the United States of America.

> "... deep down we knew we were going to a country that wanted us, where people will help us. The mood was happy, very happy."

— — — — —

America. I came alone, no language. I had nothing but hope and a vision in my heart. Most of us were drained from the voyage, but there was the processing and Customs, which took almost half a day. If you had anything of value, like a camera, silver, or an extra watch, etc., you had to declare it. Then we were taken into New York City. At Penn Station I was told by representatives from organizations such as USNA that my train to Pittsburgh would arrive in two or three hours. Meanwhile during that two hours, I was overwhelmed with the traffic, and the bustle and the hustle.

I went out to look up at the street. I could not speak English. About what I saw in the display windows and buildings— I can say that after being all over

---

4 These are Melvin's tape-recorded words. His written records noted, "Something happened to the hull. We were in the middle of the Atlantic in rafts." It is open to question whether the emergency necessitated evacuation. It is clear, however, from Melvin's recollections, that the journey was longer than expected because of the emergency.

5 Perhaps the most iconic and fitting symbol of the United States, "Liberty Enlightening the World" has held her torch three hundred feet into the air since 1886. Mieczyslaw Goldman was one of more than twelve million immigrants to enter America through Ellis Island, under her gaze. For over sixty years, from 1892 until 1954, it was the nation's busiest immigration inspection station.

Europe, I never saw so much splendor as I saw in that short time. There was only enough money for a lemonade at the station, but I was not depressed or worried. Even though in Europe I'd had a private room, was assured of food, and knew the languages, I thanked God that I was out of there. Even though I did not have a healthy body, I felt this was the place where I was going to make it.

My train to Pittsburgh arrived around midnight. Once on the train, a lady walked over to me after I was seated and asked me if I would like to have a cushion for my head. She paid the porter twenty cents, and I thanked her in Jewish. I think she understood because she smiled, and I asked her for her name and telephone. She kept up a conversation in English that I could not understand. Later when I was in Pittsburgh, I called her, paid my debt, and we became friends. She was middle-aged, married with two kids, and had a shop in Pittsburgh.

On the morning of December 31, 1950, we arrived in Pittsburgh, nearly four hundred miles to the west. It was snowing. That was the winter of the big snow—almost seven feet high. I walked off the train, put down my suitcases. I could not open my mouth and say a word, even though I spoke several languages. I would point to something. They would tell me where to go to the bathroom and wash my face. I started out like a kid crawling. I thought, *It's like I would be born here. It's like I'd landed here, and with a big drop of humility.*

> "I walked off the train, put down my suitcases. I could not open my mouth and say a word even though I spoke several languages."

At the railroad station you wait for a couple of hours, until someone sends someone for you. A person from Travelers Aid first met me. They filled out my cards, took care of my bag, and made calls for me. My brother had been living in Pittsburgh for two years. He is adjusting to things. He could not come to meet me. He is working in a job, and his wife is working in a job.

The Jewish Federation sent a girl, a young lady by the name of Weinstein, to meet me. She was around twenty years old. She asked me something in English. I cannot speak English—just Polish and German; and, other languages I understand. But, I don't speak English. Only a few words. Finally through hees and haws, and back and forth, she asks me how much money I had. I take it out of my pocket. Two dimes, twenty cents, it's all I had.

> "Through hees and haws, and back and forth, she asks me how much money I had. I take it out of my pocket. Two dimes, twenty cents, it's all I had."

She is trying to explain to me how to take a street car. We communicate with hand signs, and this alone takes about half hour. I go to the baggage storage for my things. I had a camera I brought and some little things for the sister-in-law I have never met. For her, a brush, silver, plus a tray or something like that. For my brother, the watch on my hand. I figured I would give him that. Finally, I will go and take the street-car. Weinstein writes it out. But after a long time, I'm thinking, *Am I taking the wrong streetcar instead of going to the part of town where my brother lives?* I am. I go downtown and had to go back and walk to reach my destination.

Of course, Aron was very happy to see me again, after his leaving Germany. I met his wife, Evy, who didn't speak Jewish at all, and his father-in-law who at that time worked at the Young Men's and Women's Hebrew Association, YMWHA,[6] where Aron and Evy had met. The father-in-law, Mr. Elling, had married Ethel, who had been a nurse to his previous wife. With Ethel, he then had another daughter, Nancy.

Aron didn't have an extra room so I slept on a couch. For the first few days I rested up. But then, my brother gave me some boots, and he and his wife took me shopping—they asked me if I wanted to go. In the stores and on the streets I could not understand a word, which made me feel like a stranger. I felt like I am cut off from the whole world, that I am the biggest idiot that ever came ashore. Unless it's happened to you, nobody can understand the feeling. You walk around among people talking a language you don't understand one word of except "okay" and "all right." You are dragging around with them in the snow shopping and getting acquainted with the new city.

I was in a daze. I didn't know the language and I didn't know the city or American customs. I might have been alone since everybody went to work except for Aron's mother-in-law, Ethel, who became my friend. I met some

---

6   In the late nineteenth century, as Jewish refugees from Imperial Russia and elsewhere began arriving in great numbers, YMHAs and YWHAs were organized in major American cities. Besides serving the needs of immigrants, these developed into centers of Jewish community life, and included spiritual, educational, and recreational programs. In Pittsburgh, the separate men's and women's organizations merged in 1912 to form the YMWHA (the "Y"). By 1920, it had nearly two thousand members and had outgrown its space. With donations from the Jewish community, a new building, in Pittsburgh's Oakland neighborhood, was completed and dedicated in 1926. This was the Y Melvin remembers here.

of Aron's relatives, too. A few weeks after my arrival, my brother got some of his wife's relatives together. One lived in Munhall, a little south of Pittsburgh. They came up and made potato pancakes, a nice supper, like a little party, and tried to make it a nice evening. It was the weekend, and they did not have to go to work.

I met several people and enjoyed it, except that I sat at the table like a dummy, not understanding much. There was talk of going to work—a normal life. One couple, for working, it was him to a metal company and her to a department store. It was inspiring. Another person worked for the US government. It was the lady, not the man. They were married. Even with feeling alone, I was happy and encouraged to be in the country. I knew I was in what you would call the Golden Land.

I got over the hardships, all of them, but for months I was like a lost soul. I walked around not knowing what to do or how to behave. How do you go to a drugstore, or how do you go down to a place and ask for an ordinary cold drink? Besides that, I had no money other than the few cents my brother loaned me. It was absolutely frustrating. I asked myself a lot of questions, but I didn't have any answers. Still I thought to myself, *I will persevere, I will hold out, I will work like a decent, honest person.*

My desire was to do everything possible to be a good citizen, to be a nice person, the same as my family raised me. I will do the best I can, and with God's help I will amount to something. I will be a human being like anybody else. Thinking about plans, I thought to myself, *Schooling is the most important thing*. It always had been when I was young, and I figured now that I had been cut off from school so young, lost everything, and went through all those horrible things, it was time to go back to school.

> "I asked myself a lot of questions, but I didn't have any answers. Still I thought to myself, I will persevere, I will hold out, I will work like a decent, honest person."

I enrolled at a school for newcomers. There were thirty students in the class, an amalgamation of all kinds of nationalities—Chinese, Italians, Germans, Poles, Jews. For several months, I walked in the morning for three miles to the old school building on Forbes Avenue and three miles back, to learn English. We had a beautiful teacher, Mrs. Fruendt, who went out of her way to do the right thing. She took special pains to make every individual student

> *"Mrs. Fruendt taught us many things. She pointed out the beauty and the good points of this country and kept on saying we would work and reap the fruits of our adopted country. And it came true."*

feel comfortable, to forget our hurts and sadness, our isolation. She explained that we had to assimilate into this society.

Mrs. Fruendt taught us many things. She pointed out the beauty and the good points of this country and kept on saying we would work and reap the fruits of our adopted country. And it came true. The way she used the language has stayed with me all of this time. I remained friends with Mrs. Fruendt for many years, long after I left that school and learned English, and even later when she was in an old-age home.

— — — — —

At my beginning in Pittsburgh, I stayed with my brother for some months. I was so lucky; his mother-in-law became my friend. She was very kind to me. So encouraging. That beautiful lady! I will never forget Ethel. She was a Christian woman. She probably is the only person who invited me for a hot cup of tea in the course of about two years. She made sure Friday nights I came down to the table to eat big meals with the family. She would fight the whole world for me. There are not enough words of appreciation for this nice person. I will never forget it. She had a young daughter, Nancy, and from time to time with the meager little pennies I got from working, we would do things together. We were friends.

After about three months in school, trudging back and forth, I befriended some people, including a Jewish guy at school, Eugene. We walked to and from school together. He was a nice guy and we started hanging around together after school, going to the park for a walk. We shared a nostalgia for the past. We saw a few films, got acquainted with American music, and looked for records. We bought some Jewish records even. Money, though, was tight. I was really starting to think about getting a job.

Eugene persuaded me to apply for a job at the place he had been working for about six or seven months, pointing out that, even though the pay wasn't good but wasn't bad either, the job would help me get acquainted with things and would help me learn what is necessary to know. The job was almost like peddling—selling from place to place. It was an uptown home supply company that sold televisions and beds, stuff like that. We earned about thirty dollars a week, plus commissions.

Before I got on the job, he calls me up the Sunday before I started to work and asked if I wanted to go out with him to the Hill District. I was real green and didn't know what the Hill District was [an area plagued by deterioration and neglect]. I say okay, so at nine I met him and we walked up that hill. He tells me that there are a lot of black people there. There are also some white people and white businesses around.

We go up to a second-floor apartment, and he knocks on the door. After he knocked a couple of times, a woman opens the door, stark naked, about 250 pounds. I lost my breath. I didn't know what to do. I never saw anything like that. It would be impossible to describe how I felt. I was unable to speak. She ushered us in and here is a little boy who runs over to Eugene, pulling him by the pants and saying to him, "Is you my daddy? Is you my daddy?" I couldn't understand the whole thing. I knew a little bit, only a few words of English at that time. I walked away. Eugene did his transaction and collection. I couldn't sleep a whole night and walked around for two days like in a daze. I'd never experienced anything like that.

There were so many funny things going on around me that overwhelmed me, and serious things too. For one, after I got the job, as two young European fellows, Eugene and I were mistreated. And, I remember, Eugene and I sold a woman a Frigidaire and a television, and split the commissions. We heard two days later that the Frigidaire fell through the lady's floor. No one had checked to see if her house could handle the heavy appliances. That's how bad it could be. Yet, I have some good memories of our working together. Later, Eugene and I even tried to get into business together. Then, when he was still young, years later, in his forties, he dropped dead of a heart attack. I was terribly shook up about it. And life went on.

— — — —

My beautiful teacher at the Forbes Avenue school, Mrs. Fruendt, one day she said I had to go to another school, having finished basic English. I didn't lose my accent from those studies. I knew I never would, since I immigrated in my mid, late twenties. You don't lose that unless you come over as a young child. But I wanted to continue learning. Later I got acquainted with a school director, Mr. Passamaneck [?], a beautiful person. He loved me and encouraged me with my schooling. In the years ahead, I went to high school in the evenings and then to college while working constantly and still learning. And now [late 1970s], after being in America for twenty-nine years, and my daughter in college, I'm still going to school, still taking courses, and doing everything possible to educate myself.

With some basic English skills, I went down to the employment office. This was the early fifties. I stayed two or three full days explaining my circumstances and filling out applications. This was one of the many funny things that happened to me. Would you believe it, in nearly thirty years I never got called? That's how much they needed me! But I constantly went out and tried to meet people and do something productive.

> "I constantly went out and tried to meet people and do something productive."

After coming to the United States under the auspices of the JDC, and arriving in Pittsburgh on December 31, 1950, I still was for more than two years not allowed to do any work [formal job] given my poor health. I was being treated in the Montefiore Hospital under the supervision of Dr. Theodore Rubel, who once told me I would recover a little bit, but that in the meantime I had to watch out because mentally and physically the Nazis broke me. I had first seen Dr. Rubel on January 5, 1951. Early on, I was visiting the hospital a few times a week, and later once a week. The Jewish Family Service then had to help me, and because of my health the only thing they could do with me was to send me to school. I enrolled at Duff's–Iron City College to take bookkeeping and accounting. In other words, I laid some groundwork so I would know what I am doing. From October 1951 to August 1952, I was in Duff's, but also working to support myself, although officially under medical supervision and not capable of earning a living because of my condition.

Having completed ten months of school, Mrs. Nellie Gray there sent me to May Stern & Co. [furniture company] for a job in September 1952. Once I left there, I couldn't find a job in Pittsburgh so went to Chicago. I first worked at Rosetti & Rosetti in 1953. It was an importer of beautiful china [handpainted, from occupied Japan]. I typed customs papers for the Customs office and I used to go to Customs and present the papers. After that, I worked for Cuneo Press, 1953–1954, where I was very well treated.

─ ─ ─ ─ ─

Before going to Chicago, in 1952 I had met a young woman in Pittsburgh named Mildred Zerelstein. She had come to visit me while I was in Chicago, and even though we both didn't have anything, we eventually got married in Pittsburgh on March 6, 1954. We moved to a studio apartment in Pittsburgh on Bayard Street where we would share the room and the bathroom with about six students. We lived as poor as you can get.

My wife had a job, but I was still looking. I walked up, two or three times a week, to Schenley High School and picked the toughest teacher, Mr. Wiegand. I took English and spelling, American history, and some math and algebra, just to refresh myself and know what I am doing. Later, I met Mr. Wiegand at the Y. I had a lot going on. Besides studies, I was still working part time, peddling—watches and costume jewelry.

> "I took English and spelling, American history, and some math and algebra, just to refresh myself and know what I am doing. . . . Besides studies, I was still working part time, peddling—watches and costume jewelry."

My first full-time job, at a store in uptown Pittsburgh, was a beautiful job, a hard job. I put out twice as much effort. I knew that the man, in order to hire me, has to make money, so I worked like a dog. I put in sometimes ten or twelve hours and even went in on Sundays and Decoration Day to prove to him that I was capable of doing the job, which he realized after a while. He had another store in town that wasn't doing well. It was near a department store, which maybe took away business. He thought about selling it, so we went in and we had a big sale that was successful. He made out good on the sale and he pats me on the back.

I was reporting as an alien. And, looking to become a citizen, I registered with Selective Service local board #19 on May 7, 1954. While I worked for that man, I went to get some of the citizen application papers. Then the gentleman got sick, and I had to find another job. I began working at Home Supply Company, in sales—peddling housewares—and in collections. Also in 1954, the Y hired me as a part-time auditor, even though I couldn't speak good English. This job at the Y paid about seventy-eight dollars a week and helped me out through school.

— — — — —

I liked engineering when I was a young boy. Mildred and I didn't have the means for me to go to a regular college so I went to Duff's–Iron City College's Pittsburgh Technical Institute for industrial management engineering. I was at Duff's from August 1954 to July 1955. By the way, on May 20, 1955, in a class of thirty-seven students at Duff's, even though I couldn't speak good English, I was nominated as class secretary. This came in handy for the future. I figured it was more education; I will be able to accomplish something, make a good living, and make everybody including myself happy.

After finishing, I got a job with a jewelry company where I opened the store, did the window displays, mopped the floors, and did the sales. The owner was a fellow younger than me who didn't know anything and didn't care where I came from. He was a slimy guy, always conniving, never smiled. Even when I worked on the Fourth of July for nothing, all I got was a beef sandwich. Not a nice word. The only time I got a few extra dollars was from November 28 until December 25. I put in twelve to fifteen hours a day.

In November 1954, I got sick. Dr. Rubel in Pittsburgh, my doctor since coming to Pittsburgh, gave the written opinion that I had permanently lost seventy-five percent of my working capacity. However, I kept on pushing myself to become somebody. Around that time, I then had a sales job with a man named Paul Chernew. He trusted me and I did a good job for him, so he told me. He did not succeed in his business, and I lost my job. He wanted me to go on the road with him and stay forever. I couldn't see me doing that for life. I worked with him from 1955 to 1957.

- - - - -

On September 5, 1955, I got a copy of my birth certificate from Poland. I was often gathering up and filling out papers. Such efforts were particularly important and special early in 1956. Every newcomer to this country has to file papers in January. After that, there is a process that has to be followed in order to become a citizen. You fill out several sets of papers along the way. You also have to study, to learn certain things about America. The third papers for citizenship are then filed.

Then one nice day in 1956, it happened, what I had looked forward to. The greatest joy! I went to the federal building to be sworn in as a US citizen. My wife, along with Ethel, came to the ceremony and witnessed for me. At that time I was working for Paul Chernew, who was very understanding, a nice person, a gentleman. I was very happy. For five days I wore the new suit, my holiday suit, to celebrate because inside me I was jubilant. I felt like a new person. That is the only suit I cleaned three times in one week. I had a lot of hope. In the years of my life here, my first time to be called

> *". . . to be called an American citizen. I was joining a privileged class, like a special club not everyone can belong to. It is like experiencing a sudden luck to become a member."*

an American citizen. I was joining a privileged class, like a special club not everyone can belong to. It is like experiencing a sudden luck to become a member.

Things were progressing. My education had been moving along, and I did very well, as I had back in Poland. I had report cards from American schools, and even in 1958 I got a paper from the Polish government testifying that I had been an A-1 student in the public schools. Also, my list of people in the United States who would testify to my character, skills, work ethic, and knowledge was growing. I always had references: Dr. T. Rubel; M. B. Gefsky, assistant vice president, Washington Bank; A. J. Auerbach, executive director, YMWHA; Mrs. H. Fruendt, my teacher and friend at Forbes School; J. Roy Jackson, guidance director, PTI; and Paul Chernew, employer from 1955 to 1957. As a working man, I worked hard and always loved to give somebody his due. And I never told anybody to do something I couldn't do or I wouldn't be able to do.

> "The next goal I set for myself was to become independent. I look forward to going into business. I love the idea."

- - - - -

All through the years, even now while I'm middle-aged, business interested me. I was drawn to going into business, working on my own. And so the next goal I set for myself was to become independent. I look forward to going into business. I love the idea. It appealed to me to have a shop, a factory, or something, but I did not have enough capital. I must keep working, and saving.

After leaving work with Paul Chernew, I worked for Globe Trading until 1961. I hated the job and the man who owned it, but I kept on thinking about going into business, which meant I needed money. While working at Globe Trading I went in twice on the side with a few hundred dollars, part-time selling and collecting household goods. I went in with a friend. It didn't go well; working full time I just could not keep up with the second job. I lost. And I lost a second time because the guy at Globe was dishonest. At Globe I worked hard, but it was for naught.

We had been renting a second-floor apartment at 1410 S. Negley. Then, our housing situation improved. I had just bought a half-double house [1320 S. Negley] at the urging of my wife. I quit the Globe job and remodeled the third floor of our home. With the help of friends, I fixed up the floor and steps and made a display of my meager inventory, starting off with wallets and accessories. I

> "Why should I go out and sell for somebody else? Finally after ten years... I was able to open the door to my own business. I took a chance. I thought, This is the opportunity, this is the country, I'm going to try to do it."

started off with five hundred dollars that I saved up after many years, and I went into business.

Aware of the freedom and everything else I had to proceed as I wanted to, I thanked God I had come to this country. I thought, *I'm going to try to do the right things*. I thought of all different scenarios. I don't know now how I actually did it, because how can you invite people onto a third floor to sell them things, but I tried my best. I put out my best, and people, I think, realized that I am really serious and I am trying to do a job and trying to survive and make a life for myself. I worked hard at it, but meanwhile I had to work other jobs to bring in an income.

At that time, when I went into business, I used to go out to the coal mines to peddle where it was terribly hot, ninety or one hundred degrees. Sometimes in the winter, I went out and tried to do for myself what I had been doing for somebody else—hitting the pavement hard. Why should I go out and sell for somebody else? Finally after ten years in the United States I was able to open the door to my own business. I took a chance. I thought, *This is the opportunity, this is the country, I'm going to try to do it*.

There was a friend who felt a kinship with me and helped me out. Thanks to him I could stick with and grow my business. He came here before the war and was older than me. He came from a little town near Łódź called Zgierz. We met where I had worked on Fifth Avenue in Pittsburgh. His two older brothers—one a wealthy man in real estate, the other is now [late 1970s] in Israel—had brought him to America before the war. He was already established, had a store with a partner. He couldn't sit in the store so he made me an offer to go on the road. He had ladies' stockings and pants. I had pin lever watches and other merchandise. I built up a little trade and kept on putting the money back into my business. That was 1961.

— — — — —

My neighbors on our street reported me to the city for doing business from my home, so I had to move the business and rent a small second-floor place on Murray Avenue. It was there about one year, and then we moved the business to 5803 Darlington Road, on the corner of Murray. The name of the company was Lee Trading Co., named for my daughter, Lee Diane, who was born in spring 1958 when we lived at 1410 S. Negley Ave. My daughter was a delight and brought something into my life after I had lost almost everybody.

I still went out to peddle and kept improving my business. By this time I had established my credit and was working sometimes twelve to fourteen hours a day. I vowed to myself to never go around hungry. I would support my family in a nice way. It took everything I had to make a go of it. I slowly improved my inventory by focusing more on fine jewelry. I learned the ins and outs of doing business in America. The language instruction and my extra schooling came in handy.

I went to New York City for a course in diamond setting. I also bought art objects from various places, such as Capodimonte porcelain from Naples, and bought fine china, glassware, and artistic pieces from all over the world (Germany, Austria, Hungary, etc.). Meanwhile, I kept reading and learning. It was after about ten years, the early seventies, when I started to succeed. I can't describe the handicaps that were put in my way. But I persevered and did it only my way.

> *"It was . . . the early seventies, when I started to succeed. I can't describe the handicaps that were put in my way. But I persevered and did it only my way."*

Thank God I made a go of it. I overcame many obstacles, but in all the years of business I never sued anybody, never fired anybody, and always tried to be a *mensch* [person of high integrity]. I thanked God for my life and always remembered the family I had lost. Because of the trials I went through, I think I became a better human being. In America, bit by bit, things got better and better. I started off living on a second floor where the rain came through the roof. Then I shared a bathroom with students, then I bought a half-double house. And through it all, there was my wife then my daughter—my family, our family.

─ ─ ─ ─ ─

It takes guts to survive. Every Jewish man, woman, and child sometime in his life must come to grips with this issue. Some are overwhelmed by the battle and give up. Others with a kind of mystical *mazel* [luck] manage to cope. Inquisitions, pogroms, the Holocaust have taken their toll, but whether the struggle is greater or lesser, all of us bear the psychic scars. Even the most sheltered and luckiest among us carry the genetic scars of surviving persecutions passed down from generation to generation from those who fought the good fight on our behalf. Because they won, we are here.

7. Looking Back . . . Looking Forward
Melvin, in his mid-fifties, reflects
- - - - -

The end of the war in 1945 *does not mean the end of the story for survivors of the camps; they must live with their experiences for the rest of their lives. As they move forward, the challenge before them is to let go of bitterness enough to look with hope to the future, even as they hold on to the memories of their suffering. Melvin is able to, on his own, summon the courage to recall and tape record his darkest hours. He does so, long before there were established avenues for processing the trauma of the war in all its brutality. He is remarkable in this, and he is fortunate in that he is able to resettle in one of the thriving Jewish communities found in every large American city and begin a new life. By most measures of well-being, such as income, home ownership, and involvement in social institutions, he finds success—like the many Holocaust survivors who achieve success in their new home. These immigrants even have a higher birthrate than the Jews who are already here, a clear sign that they have faith in their future as Americans. In this concluding chapter of Part I, reflections from different parts of Melvin's tapes demonstrate his faith in his future, and the horrifying past from which it arose.*

For related documentation, see appendix pages 230, 250.

Photo: Left, a Star of David cloth badge from the Łódź ghetto, and right, the cover of a booklet Melvin received as part of his US citizenship journey. (On left, from US Holocaust Memorial Museum Collection, gift of Malwina "Inka" Gerson Allen.)

"Commanded to Remember . . . Forbidden to Despair"
- - - - -

The Holocaust was monstrous and terrible. Some have tried to convey the magnitude of horrors of the many, and the heroism of the few. It lies outside of speech and reason, because Hitler's war against European Jews from 1933 to 1945 is beyond speech and reason. It requires attention and reflection. The Holocaust forces us to realize that within the human situation, systematic evil is a horrible reality.

- - - - -

I learned in Poland that they put all kinds of different classifications on you. If you are a commie in Poland, or an anti-Nazi in Germany, you become a political prisoner. All of a sudden I am a Jew, sixteen years old, and I am a political prisoner, just like all of these others, only because I'm a Jew. Now isn't that an evil distortion of logic? If my whole family had not been annihilated by these goons and beasts, it would be laughable.

- - - - -

They were the biggest perpetrators of lies and propaganda the world has ever known. They are conniving. Because of indoctrination, at home a kid turned stool pigeon on a father and mother, and I know what happens to them.

─ ─ ─ ─ ─

Their barbarism is unheard of. Look what they did in Germany, look what they did to the world. They occupied Poland, Germany, Austria. They occupied Hungary and Romania. They occupied part of Russia, also Italy, France, Belgium, and the Netherlands. In all these countries they liquidated most of the Jews, almost ninety percent of them. All Germans, SS, SA, when they came to occupy territory, were all six foot tall, but in the camps all of them were like five foot six. They tried to show off their superman stock for the outside world, but really they were a bunch of cowards inside. The saying around now is that a German is like a dog. Maybe I'm too rash on it, but there is no rashness, there is not enough viciousness that these people did to us to say it. The reason they are like a dog, if you were around and a dog bites you, if you stand up to him and stay still, he will never do a thing and that's exactly what reminds me of a German.

─ ─ ─ ─ ─

The Germans had a lot of flunkies. I didn't see that many in Auschwitz, but in Braunschweig and Wattenstädt and Wöbbelin and Ludwigslust we started to see the Ukranian hooligans and the Latvians. They were helping the Germans, and the Germans made them do all the dirty work. They were even worse than some of the Germans. And there were the Austrians. The Austrians were the worst. They were the ones that were hating the most. They were the ones who talked with that funny accent. You could tell right away it was an Austrian. These are the beasts that took over and learned. They were like the students, learning from the teachers, and they tried to do better than the teachers did.

> *"I will also mention the Jewish heroes, the underground and the ones in the prison camps. Their example forces us to recognize the depth of human fortitude."*

─ ─ ─ ─ ─

I will also mention the Jewish heroes, the underground and the ones in the prison camps. Their example forces us to recognize the depth of human fortitude. Hear their song of defiance in the midst of hopelessness: "This [our] song is written not with lead but with blood. It is not the song of birds upon the wing, but of people upon whom the walls came crashing down, who sang it weapon in hand. Do not ever say that you go the last road. Leaden skies may hide the blue of day, yet the hour we have longed for has arrived. Our footsteps confirm: We are here!"

– – – – –

Those in power should fight hatred, not in a simplified way that's detrimental to the well being of their subjects or the people of the other countries. It should be with dedication and sacrifice. A great responsibility lies on the shoulders of the religious leaders; racists too, that teach bigotry and can't assimilate that humankind went through enough, especially some religions.

– – – – –

I heard a speech after the war from a person who was a leader of the Protestant church. He had been in camps and survived. He wrote a book about it. The speech went like this: When the Gypsies were being brought into Camp Birkenau-Auschwitz, a delegation of Gypsies went to a holy man and asked him to please intervene on their behalf. He said, "I'm not a Gypsy." Then they started to liquidate some of the Jews, and the Jewish rabbi from Berlin went to see him, and he said, "I'm not a Jew." When they started killing off Catholics, the pontiff sent a representative to Germany to talk to him, and he said, "I'm not a Catholic." Then the holy man was taken to Buchenwald, and he said, "Now I can do nothing."[1] That is how it goes. Does that teach you a lesson?

– – – – –

About church leaders and the rise of the German Confessing Church, under the leadership of Niemöller. There were stalwart examples of faith in mankind, God's creation. Actions of Dietrich Bonhoeffer and August von Galen, Bishop of Münster, challenge us to commit ourselves to the struggle of human dignity and worth. This, while the overt and blatant manifestation of the Third Reich, under the leadership of Hitler, reminds us of the ways in which evil can be organized and perpetuated by human organizations that are supposed to be existing for the public good. Also, we are reminded of the variety of ways in which human beings respond to systematic evil—systemic evil—and of the multifaceted

> "About church leaders... There were stalwart examples of faith in mankind, God's creation."

---

1 This well-known allegory, which exists in many forms, was formulated by Martin Niemöller, a German Lutheran pastor who opposed the Nazis. It is possible that Melvin heard Niemöller himself retell this parable.

escape mechanisms that are contrived to evade responsibility. The deplorable reality, however, is that some persons who became aware of Hitler's solution to the Jewish problem were intimidated, subdued by such knowledge. After the war, some of these finally found courage to announce what happened, and their own guilt in letting it happen.[2] A late reconciliation after eighteen million human beings were killed, don't you think?

— — — — —

I say to the American Jews: You were asleep when we needed you! We paid the dearest price with life, property, and well-being. I hope and pray that it will never happen again. I hope you stay on guard now and forever, and let nobody deny it or let it happen again.

— — — — —

I want to point out that some improvement came about in technological terms, like a person flying from London to the United States can be here in a couple of hours. We also made strides in other fields, medical advances, but as of yet, in human terms I do not think that nations or people have learned about the past. The present hatred and not caring hurt me, since I hoped that after World War II, and the loss of over sixty million lives, the world would wake up. We send a few people to the United Nations, and want these few to reconcile four billion people? Why can you not be nice to your neighbor next door or across the street? I hope and pray it is not too late now.

— — — — —

I say the fires of Buchenwald will still burn and the tragedy of Auschwitz still cries out for reprieve. In "The Commanding Voice of Auschwitz," Emil Fackenheim presents this challenge:

> "What does the Voice of Auschwitz command? Jews are forbidden to hand Hitler posthumous victories. They are commanded to survive as Jews, lest the Jewish people perish. They are commanded to remember the victims of Auschwitz lest their memory perish. They are forbidden to despair of man and his world, and to escape into either cynicism or otherworldliness, lest they cooperate in delivering the world over to the forces of Auschwitz. Finally, they are forbidden to despair of the God of Israel, lest Judaism perish. A secularist

---

2   Melvin may be referring to the "Stuttgart Declaration of Guilt," a 1945 document in which the council of the Evangelical Church in Germany confessed that they had failed to strongly oppose the Third Reich.

Jew cannot make himself believe by a mere act of will, nor can he be commanded to do so.... And a religious Jew who has stayed with his God may be forced into new, possibly revolutionary relationships with Him. One possibility, however, is wholly unthinkable. A Jew may not respond to Hitler's attempt to destroy Judaism by himself cooperating in its destruction. In ancient times, the unthinkable Jewish sin was idolatry. Today, it is to respond to Hitler by doing his work."[3]

This challenge is not for Jews alone, but for all people to affirm God's presence in the world and His love for all humankind.

A Country with Hope for Everybody

And now, about America, the land of the free! America is the best country! To Americans born here it might sound like a cliché, but it's the truth and I should know. I was twenty-eight years old when I came here. I had wandered around the countries of Europe, seen all the beautiful things and the old cultures, and I found nothing as wonderful as this land. I know, some people have their gripes. No matter. I have my own impressions. I'll always remember the Americans liberating me. Becoming an American was the most noble thing that has happened to me. Even now, twenty-eight years later, I still get goose bumps when I hear that song being sung: "God Bless America!"

> *"I'll always remember the Americans liberating me. Becoming an American was the most noble thing that has happened to me."*

I kept on going to school in the evening and didn't miss. I was determined to assimilate. You have to try to make the language work for you. This was the most important thing. Learn English, absorb everything, read up on everything. I kept on reading. It was funny, I had my own way of reading the newspaper. I used a blue and red pencil to underline things I didn't understand. I'd go back many times to the dictionary. I would sometimes read it in front of a mirror. I would say, "I have to beat this, figure this out. I have to learn

---

3 From *God's Presence in History: Jewish Affirmations and Philosophical Reflections*, 1972. Fackenheim escaped from the Sachsenhausen concentration camp, and had a distinguished career as a rabbi and philosopher. He noted that Judaism recognizes 613 *mitzvot* (commandments) from God and wrote this passage as the 614th.

this language. I have to be easy with it, the same as an American. I will still have the accent, but I have to read and write and understand English well. This is my country, my adopted country. I will do everything a citizen is supposed to do." And I kept on reading. You have to really try to be an American.

— — — — —

In my first years, trying to understand the system, I started to read a little bit of the US Constitution. The more I read, the happier I was. The history of the United States fascinated me. It wasn't like in Poland or Germany. It was intriguing—ordinary people setting up such a beautiful system, which after two hundred years still worked. The guiding principles were as true now as they were the first day they appeared on paper. The Constitution works; it is actually enforced. There are a lot of things that are maybe not fulfilled, or some laws still need to be put in, but I would say ninety percent fulfilled. Poland had a beautiful constitution. We had to read it, we had to sing their hymns, but the constitution was written on one hand and the laws were interpreted a different way. So that is why I say thank God and your stars if you were born here or came here to live in this country.

> *"I say thank God and your stars if you were born here or came here to live in this country."*

— — — — —

I shudder when I hear people in America talk about a ghetto when they mean that they live in a compact, slum neighborhood. Some of them are very, very poor, and I can understand the circumstances. I have read American history a little bit, and know what some people have gone through, but, My God, the ghetto we were in was a death camp. There were electric wires. In a ghetto in America, no one comes in to systematically beat them up. Nobody rounds them up for slave labor. Even in prison here, there is compassion for prisoners. I think I would rather be five years in a most terrible place in America than go back for one hour to the ghetto I was in.

— — — — —

I saw with my own eyes how free people are and it gladdened my heart. I remember, in my early US years, seeing people tear down election placards for one candidate or another, throwing it down and saying, "I don't like it, I'm not going to vote for him," because they didn't like the nominee or the political party. I'd never seen such a thing and couldn't imagine an average person making such a public demonstration against some big shot without worrying about the consequences. We did it a few times in Germany after the war, but we knew who they were, and what they could do to us. But here in this free society nobody is worried. When you live in this country, I would say living almost spoiled, you don't know what is actually going on in Europe. Even before the war, when a little kid went to the corner to sell something hot, something baked or something, you could see a policeman chasing him. Would you stop a policeman in Europe and have a chat? No. He feels like a god. Here a parent who can't speak the language could go to an official, along with his child to translate for him, and they would not be dismissed. It was unbelievable to me. In other so-called civilized countries, they would say that the grown-up doesn't want to communicate, or tell him to get lost.

— — — — —

I would say I'm terribly excited and happy even now. I make friends with all kinds of people from all nationalities. There is nothing like this anywhere else. And if some of them are bad, I would not say they are bad people, they were just influenced the wrong way. Not like in Europe, where people are sucked in with lies, or indoctrinated deeply to the core. Here you can sit down with a person and talk things out. It's a free society, absolutely free, in my opinion. I am not trying to preach to anybody, but, My God, do you realize what this beautiful country accomplished since I am here—in medicine, technology, betterment of human conditions?

— — — — —

I am reminded all the time about Europe. I read in American papers, and I hear on TV, about certain beautiful countries and their art and artists and their beautiful scenery. But here you have many more arts and artists, and the scenery is absolutely unbelievable in this country. And scientists! Technologically, America is so much advanced, and there is never a shortage of food. We have everything better. And on top of that, we do not have royalties. That is something to be proud of. They are dictators. Nothing I can write or feel or tell you would be sufficient to express appreciation for this country, where everything is taken for granted. Take little things, trivias, like bathrooms, and finding water. Things that are nothing here. And how about what this country is doing now for other countries. You cannot imagine the goodness that this country has. Do not expect that from any other country on earth, to repay us, because they are not Americans. And the friendliness. I mentioned the nationalism over there. Please don't mix this up with patriotism. What is laughable to me is when Americans give me their opinions about Europe while only being there on vacation a few weeks, and especially if on a tour bus or something like that. Here in America it is a vacation place, in comparison. I think one thing: *Let the Europeans keep Europe, and I'll stay here.*

— — — — —

Since I'm talking about America, I am asking myself the question—what fate kept us in Europe? Why couldn't my grandfather have emigrated to the United States, or my dad? Look what we would have been saved in degradation, loss of life, my family's hardships in the ghetto. The beautiful, beautiful family would have been here. We would have been able to donate something to this country and at the same time live in freedom like human beings.

— — — — —

This country gave me back my dignity, showed me what freedom is. Even though disabled for life, I was given an opportunity and took it. I would like here to say thanks to the generous people of the United States. And I owe other thanks. I have made some beautiful friendships through the years, and many have helped me in my tribulations. I could not thank them enough. And especially I must thank my wife for helping me all along in the ups and downs of life. Also to be thanked are the people and the organizations who have undertaken the great project on our behalf, to remember the Holocaust and its victims.

— — — — —

I would like to say that now my dream did come true. I have a family. I have a nice daughter. And I do have a business. I hope that we are all well. With all the things we went through here, sicknesses, like a normal average person, and everything else, thank God we are very happy. We have a house. I'm here now almost three decades, and I feel like it is my home. I would fight and do anything for this country and this home. And I can say one thing for sure, "I am delighted to be here as a citizen." I feel no other than as an American, that's all. It was hard work, but it was worth it.

— — — — —

I have much to say about my experiences here: the tribulations, the hardships, the learning, going to school, the work I went through. I was a lot like a pioneer. I got sick, fought for my survival and jobs, got married, had a daughter. But when I think back, it was all worth it because this is the best society, a free society. America is not a Utopia. There is plenty that needs changing. But it can change. Where else but in this beautiful country do you get the chance to improve?

— — — —

America is a country with hope for everybody. It has a future. We have to preserve the future in this country because there just isn't going to be another one ever again like it. If we don't fight for it, it could be lost. Each American everywhere should be an ambassador for this country. God bless America!

PART II

IN LEE'S WORDS

1. A Thriving Jewish Community

At Ellis Island my dad became Melvin. I don't know if he chose or was given that name. He told me that Pittsburgh was suggested to him because he had been a tinsmith back in Łódź, and Pittsburgh was an industrial city with many opportunities for working with metal. He had also worked with metal while in rehab in Germany. It would be easier to find a job. There were similarities between Łódź and Pittsburgh, both being very industrial, multicultural cities. Also, Melvin's brother Aron had been in Pittsburgh for a year, in the Squirrel Hill neighborhood, so it made sense for Melvin to settle in that city.

Squirrel Hill is located in the eastern part of Pittsburgh and has long been home to a thriving Jewish community. In the 1920s, its population grew because more people owned automobiles, making it easier to

Pittsburgh in the 1950s. Courtesy of Carnegie Library of Pittsburgh.

get to downtown Pittsburgh, by way of the Boulevard of the Allies. Most of Squirrel Hill's immigrant population was an assortment of Eastern European Jews who moved in from other neighborhoods such as the Hill District and Oakland to the west.

Squirrel Hill is bordered by two city parks, Schenley Park and Frick Park, which add to the area's appeal. The neighborhood's main commercial streets, Forbes and Murray Avenues, are lined with a variety of restaurants, specialty stores, banks, and other businesses. Pittsburgh's Jewish Community Center is also at the heart of the community. And, there are Jewish day schools and numerous synagogues representing a wide range of Jewish ideology, from Modern Orthodox to more liberal movements.

Shown here, one of many local Jewish businesses, a kosher meat and poultry shop, located at the bottom of Murray Avenue, 1966. Public Domain. From the Pittsburgh City Photographer Collection, 1901–2002, University of Pittsburgh.

It is a misconception that the population in Squirrel Hill is entirely Jewish. When I was growing up in the sixties and seventies, many people believed that it was a Jewish area and that everyone had money. There were families from a wide variety of economic situations, and the area still has some economic diversity, with a range of residents—poor, middle class, and wealthy renters and homeowners. In recent years, some have called into question the affordability of the area, noting the higher than average number of Squirrel Hill residents born outside of the area, likely working at nearby "eds and meds," the many universities and hospitals in the Pittsburgh area.

Over the years, the neighborhood has changed to reflect new demographics, and it is now more of a melting pot than previously. Today, Squirrel Hill is the most populous neighborhood in the city. It is comprised of about 27,000 people (per 2010 US Census), of whom thirty to forty percent are Jewish, and the neighborhood has retained its Jewish identity even as new ethnic restaurants, shops, and even grocery stores have opened up. The area still has a few restaurants that prepare food according to the requirements of Jewish law (kosher).

I want to mention some other places my family and I enjoyed while I was growing up in Squirrel Hill. My family still goes to some of them.

Murray Avenue's business district was simply known as "the Avenue." On Sundays, we usually made a trek down the Avenue to pick up corned beef, bagels, and some bakery items. Our favorite places were Rhoda's (which later became Kazansky's), Bageland (which was my father's favorite), and then Herman's Bakery, Rosenbloom's Bakery, Silverberg's Bakery, or the Waldorf Bakery. People came from a few hours away to shop and take this wonderful food back home for themselves and their neighbors. We often got takeout at the holidays from Rhoda's, George Aiken's, or our favorite pizza places—Napoli and Aiello's.

There were two movie theaters that we frequented—the Manor and the Squirrel Hill. There were many movies for kids on weekends and in the summer. My friends and I would often walk to the Manor for a fun afternoon. This was the big time for us. When John and I dated, we looked forward to going to the movies. When our son, Jason, was old enough, we would bring him and my mother along. The Manor is still going strong, and John, Jason, and I always enjoy going to a good movie. It is a great outing and brings back many pleasant memories.

Another store that was popular was the National Record Mart. Fortunately for me, it was downstairs from our family's jewelry store. You could play songs on their record player before you bought anything. I spent a good deal of my allowance on 45s (45 rpm records).

My parents and I—as a young adult and along with my husband, John—really liked to eat at Gullifty's Restaurant. They had a nice variety on their menu and their desserts always won awards. They even had a sandwich called the "Meshugana." *Crazy* in Yiddish! It was corned beef sandwiched with potato pancakes. We continued going there until they closed in 2013. We liked that restaurant so much that John and I had our wedding rehearsal dinner there. On the day they closed, they were very busy. A reporter from the *Pittsburgh Post-Gazette* interviewed John and me on our history and experiences there—it was bittersweet.

We also liked Bagel Nosh. Our son, Jason, now an adult, remembers this restaurant as well. The food was good, and it had a nice atmosphere. My father always enjoyed eating there. When it closed, it eventually became Chesapeake Bagel Bakery. At one time, they had a Ben & Jerry's in the restaurant.

Nowadays when we visit Squirrel Hill, we frequent eateries, bookstores, the Carnegie Library, the Record Exchange, the Manor Theater, and sometimes we just enjoy walking in one of the parks or along the many tree-lined streets. It is a great neighborhood where there is something for everyone.

2. Melvin and Mildred Meet

When Melvin Goldman first came to Pittsburgh in 1950, he lived with his brother Aron and Aron's wife, Evy, on Denniston Avenue in Squirrel Hill. At that time Melvin was still under medical care, still quite weak and suffering from a number of ailments. In addition, he lacked most of his upper teeth and had other dental issues. He was also faced with learning a new language. Without a room of his own, Dad slept on the couch, but after a while he began to feel like he was intruding. It was time to look for a place of his own, which meant finding a room to rent in someone's house. He went to look at a place on Sherbrook Street, became a renter, and there he met Mildred Zerelstein, who was also living there. They hit it off right away and began seeing each other.

Even though he was beginning to learn his way around Pittsburgh and had established some important relationships there, my father hadn't yet

My dad and mom on their wedding day, March 6, 1954.

settled on a career for himself, so when an opportunity for work in Chicago became available at Rosetti & Rosetti china company, he went. A short time later he went to work at Cuneo Press, one of the largest printers in the world at the time, doing bookkeeping work. Mildred visited him in Chicago at least once, and possibly due to her persuasive ways, he eventually returned to Pittsburgh, a little over a year later. On March 6, 1954, Melvin and Mildred were married.

My mother worked in East Liberty and downtown Pittsburgh as a secretary, bookkeeper, and stenographer at various insurance companies and a law firm, while Dad continued going to night school and working as much as he could. He had many physical limitations to try to overcome and an array of psychological issues as well. There was also a new language to become increasingly proficient in and a different culture to absorb and assimilate. My mother was very kind, loving, and supportive.

This photo of David Ben-Gurion, at a parade in his honor in New York, 1951, was found among Melvin's belongings and is presumed to have been taken by him. Ben-Gurion, known as Israel's founding father, was the country's first prime minister, serving from 1948 to 1963. Ben-Gurion was highly regarded by Jews around the world.

At the parade.

Mom's background was troubled in its own way, and her parents had their own unique stories. Like Melvin's family, they were Jewish; but, those families had left Europe years before World War II and the Holocaust. Her mother,

Elizabeth Slawkin, came to America from Russia as a young girl. Her father, David Zerelstein, was a sweet, caring man. He was a butcher by trade with a shop in Carrick, Pittsburgh. The youngest of nine children born to Sam (Gershon) and Rose Zerelstein, David became ill at a young age. He was diagnosed with an aneurism and died at age thirty-eight when my mother was nine years old. His cause of death was acute encephalitis and respiratory failure. Mildred, an only child, had been very close to her father, so his death was a great loss for her. Her suddenly widowed mother went on to sell the butcher shop, and several years later married Max Cohen, a man with two grown children. Max's son was married, but his daughter, still single, lived at home.

By then, young Mildred, in high school, pretty much took care of herself. She was quiet and immersed herself in books. She began working at age fifteen and took secretarial and bookkeeping classes in high school. Her first job was at a clothing shop in Squirrel Hill. After that, she found secretarial and bookkeeping jobs, which she had for many years. Soon she met my father.

3. A Personal Journey to Find His Way

It was often said that Melvin Goldman was a workaholic, but he was more than that. As soon as he arrived in Pittsburgh, he began a personal journey to find his way, to learn as much as he could, trying to improve himself. He took classes to become proficient in the English language. Then came additional schooling in engineering and bookkeeping. And while he attended school, he worked many jobs.

How did Dad survive? One word he often used was *perseverance*. When I was a kid growing up, he often told me—"Perseverance!" He had a lot of intelligence and common sense to add to the mix too.

One of my dad's early jobs was selling home goods door to door. This could be a difficult and daunting task. Dad's merchandise included melamine dishware. As I learned from him, melamine is a chemical used in the manufacture of certain products. It is characteristically durable and is used in dinnerware, some laminates, whiteboards, and many other items.

Dad used to tell me how he got his customers interested in making a purchase. He would knock on a potential customer's door, and when they would answer, he would greet them and then drop a bowl on the ground. Miraculously, it would not break, and much of the time, Dad would make a

Melvin graduates from Pittsburgh Technical Institute, 1955.

sale! What a pitch from a great salesman. And his strategy worked over and over as he plugged away.

He had determination and perseverance, yes. He put in long hours, yes. But I believe something deeper was at work. To be broken down as a young person and to have everything taken away from you both physically and emotionally, and to be separated from your family forever and live surrounded by brutality and death—all that is hard for us to fathom. It might be harder to understand the hope that grew out of his experiences. Through the entirety of his trauma, my father carried the words of his lost father with him—that at least one member of the family must live. Thus, Dad was honoring his father and his lost family. He persevered and survived.

The most amazing thing about his perseverance, which a reader might not understand from my father's own accounting of his early years in Pittsburgh, is the extreme circumstances under which he was able to accomplish what he did. Besides having very little money and being up against the language barrier, he was disabled and often sick. Dr. Theodore Rubel, treating him at the time, recognized that dauntless spirit. In 1954, months after my parents' wedding, in assessing my father's disability he wrote, "Mr. Goldman presented the picture of a physically and mentally completely broken man. He was dejected, oblivious to consolation and did not have any hope whatsoever for his future." The doctor's list of his debilitating ailments included a

> THEODORE RUBEL, M.D.
> 1722 MURRAY AVENUE
> PITTSBURGH 17, PA.
>
> November 15, 1954
>
> To Whom It May Concern:
>
> This is to certify that I have taken care of Mr. Melvin Goldman of 2354 Sherbrook St., Pittsburgh, Pa. since Jan. 5, 1951.
>
> Mr. Goldman gave a history of terrible hardship suffered in concentration camps in Europe. His history revealed, that during that time he had acquired a pulmonary tuberculosis, (Pneumothorax was done at onset of the disease), frozen feet and loss of his upper teeth by brutal force. His present complaints since his recent arrival in America were noted loss of weight, cough and dyspnea with exertion.
>
> Mr. Goldman presented the picture of a physically and mentally completely broken man. He was dejected, oblivious to any consolation and did not have any hope whatsoever for his future. He was coughing repeatedly. The physical examination of the chest revealed a collapsed rt. lung, the heart was negative bloodpressure 100/70. X-Ray pictures of the chest showed a collapsed rt. lung and an old fibrosis. Sputum was negative. The upper teeth were missing. He was able to walk without pains for 2 blocks only as a consequence of his frozen feet.
>
> The task to help him seemed insurmountable. The immediate problem was one of rehabilitation. It took me several months to convince this young man that he had a place in our community. He took a course in English language and book accounting. Because of his inherent intelligence he was able to master the English language satisfactorily and passed his examination in book accounting, but his physical defects remained in spite of intensive medical treatment the same. He is not able to take a full time job because of complete physical exhaustion after 4 hours of work in spite of a burning desire to become a successful young businessman. His cough is persisting. Repeated X-Ray examinations of the chest revealed the same damage to his lungs. Sputum was always negative. His walking capacity did not improve.
>
> In my opinion this young man has permanently lost 75% of his working capacity.
>
> Theodore Rubel M. D.

Letter from Dr. Rubel.

chronic cough, collapsed right lung and extensive lung damage, and limited ability to walk more than two blocks due to damage from severely frostbitten feet. He also had few upper teeth.

Dr. Rubel discussed prospects for rehabilitation, writing, "It took me several months to convince this young man that he had a place in our community . . . Because of his inherent intelligence, he was able to master the English language and passed his examination in book accounting, but his physical defects remain in spite of intensive medical treatment." In those early years, despite a "burning desire to become a successful young businessman," my father became "physically exhausted after four hours of work." The doctor said that Melvin Goldman had permanently lost seventy-five percent of his ability to work.

In addition to that physician's early comments, I can add that over the years and through many more doctors, Dad had several additional diagnoses—a bleeding ulcer, congestive heart failure, circulatory problems, renal ailments, a rare disorder known as Tietze syndrome (a condition of chronic pain in the chest cartilage), coronary artery disease, and very few teeth—until 1960 when he got dentures, at age thirty-seven.

4. These Were Happy Times

When my parents were first married, they lived in a small apartment in Oakland on Bayard Street. Around the time I was born, in 1958, our family rented the second floor of a house on South Negley Avenue in Squirrel Hill. The owner was a widow who was looking for additional income. This lovely lady was Ella Sunnock, and she was like an aunt to me.

"Aunt Ellie," as I called her, had a puppy named Duchess. How I loved that dog, and Duchess reciprocated. She became very protective of me. My mother recalled an incident when I was sick and the doctor made a house visit. Duchess was not happy about a stranger visiting, and it took some coaxing for her to let him examine me.

The next step for my parents was to save up for their own home. They

Mildred with Lee, April 1959.

Melvin holding Lee, August 1958.

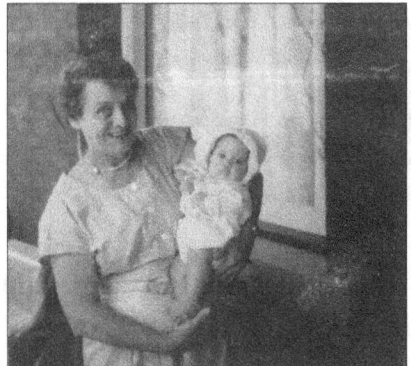

Above, young Lee with Aunt Ellie, Dad, and Duchess in Aunt Ellie's backyard, 1958. Left, top: Aunt Ellie and newborn Lee; bottom: Duchess guards Lee.

bought a duplex, also on South Negley, that we moved to in the early sixties. It was located one block away from Aunt Ellie. These were happy times. My grade school, Wightman School, was a half block away. Also, Aunt Ellie worked there, so I could see her at school as well as at her home. Her family visited on occasion, and my father became good friends with her nephew.

Aunt Ellie passed away in 1966. I was eight years old and very sad. I have such fond memories of spending time in her beautiful backyard with her, my parents, and Duchess, chasing butterflies through the garden.

In the early 1970s, another dream came true for my parents. They had been working long and hard enough to buy a house. That is, to move up from a duplex. We were all very excited. It was located on Beacon Street, within walking distance to the jewelry store my parents had recently opened, as well as the Squirrel Hill shopping district.

5. A Pearl, a Golden Totem Pole, and a Garbage Truck with Diamonds and Rubies

Melvin tried several things before he found his niche in the jewelry business. It began as a part-time venture with Dad and Mom selling costume

Melvin with German Shepherd, Match, and Lee's black dog, Cooky, 1969. The Goldmans enjoyed their dogs, but Melvin, especially, had a love of dogs and other animals.

Melvin with Lee. Above, Pittsburgh Zoo; top right: Frick Park; bottom right: a happy daddy, April 1959.

jewelry out of the third floor of our house—the South Negley duplex—just to earn some extra money. This was in the fall of 1961. It was successful and Dad enjoyed it. By the mid-sixties, with Dad in his early forties, the small jewelry business had expanded. I was getting older, and it was time to move the business out of our living space and into its own quarters, which we as a family were very excited about. It was a happy day when we opened Lee Trading Company. After briefly renting a small commercial space on Murray Avenue, we rented five rooms on the second floor of a big building in the business district of Squirrel Hill. It was on the corner of Murray Avenue and Darlington Road. Some years later, the business name was changed to G&S Jewelry. Our store faced Darlington Road but my father's office overlooked Murray Avenue above the Manor movie theater. After my parents retired, in 1988, Barnes & Noble took over their space on Murray Avenue. The bookstore occupied two floors, and the children's section was where my father's office had once been.

For my father, it wasn't enough to simply sell jewelry. Dad took as many courses as he could, and over the years he became an expert craftsman, moving on to become a designer and gemstone setter. He passed the requirements and received certification from the Gemological Institute of America. Eventually, he became well known in Pittsburgh and was often highly recommended

The jewelry store was located on the corner of Murray Avenue and Darlington Road, second floor, with its entrance on Darlington—up twenty-three stairs. The window, to the left of the "Manor" sign, looks out on Murray Avenue, circa 1970. Courtesy of Carnegie Library of Pittsburgh.

by people. Most of our business was by word of mouth. Our store had a good reputation, and that did not happen by accident. The business, something my parents had built together and co-owned, was very important to them. Therefore, much time and energy were spent planning, keeping things running smoothly, and improving the quality of our goods. Customers were treated courteously and fairly. Although one could say my father's business selling fine jewelry and goods had an excellent reputation, it was actually my parents' good traits and character that made the business prosper and kept people returning.

My dad at the end of a workday, March 1962.

Mom played an important part in all of it. She was the bookkeeper, but she also took classes to learn the trade and became a great salesperson. In addition, she was adept at jewelry setting and repairs and had extensive knowledge about stones and jewelry in general. The business had grown to include what Daddy called "fine goods." He had an eye for high-quality china, paintings, and artwork—which the store sold— but his expertise was in fine jewelry, especially diamonds.

Some of our costume jewelry included bead sets, usually colored beads with matching earrings. Church groups loved our sets. They purchased them to sell in their gift shops and also for fundraisers. I used to help box them up. It was a lot of fun. Precious gems and gold were two of Dad's specialties. He designed and sold countless engagement rings and wedding bands. People brought pictures of what they wanted, and he delivered. He had a great vision for what people liked and created many unique pieces that became timeless favorites.

A few of the specialty requests he received are unforgettable. There was a tiny garbage truck made of gold, with diamonds for headlights and rubies for taillights, to be worn on a chain as a necklace. When someone wanted a gold totem pole pendant, Daddy did not know what one looked like so he

Developing new areas of expertise was very important to my father.

went to our local library and researched it! He then designed a gold totem pole with precious gemstones.

He made countless religious medals, many with Jesus, whose tears were gemstones. Some of these medals and charms were taken by customers to be blessed by the Pope. Here was my father, trusted by many to design these personal religious items. Eventually, in the mid-seventies, my father would finish his series of gem certification classes—designing, setting, appraising, and anything and everything related to jewelry. He was specializing in engagement rings, wedding bands, and a lot of one-of-a-kind pieces. My father prided himself on his custom work. Customers could draw him a picture and he would make their wishes come true.

In the jewelry business, theft and security are a major concern. When we opened the Darlington Road store in the mid-sixties, we had a small security system installed. The door to the outside was locked, and we would look out to see who wanted to gain entrance. In April 1966, thieves broke in after business hours and used a blow torch to open our safe. They put the stolen items in four of the suitcases we had for sale—we also sold luggage—and got away. Then, just one week later, two men, armed with knives and guns, forced their way in and made my father open the safe. One of the men shoved my father and his employee onto a couch and said he would kill them if my father did not give this thief everything he asked for. My father complied, survived the nightmare, and beefed up security. This was at a time when we still had a lot of costume jewelry, and the monetary damages were not as significant as the physical and mental stress.

In December 1976, we hit a big bump in the road. Anyone who knows the retail business knows that there are several times a year to achieve your monetary goals. The big season is in November and December for Christmas and Chanukah. Business owners begin ordering goods in late summer in order to be stocked before Thanksgiving. We were deep into the season when our alarm company called to report a break-in very early one morning. There had been many false alarms over the years, but this was the real thing. I was now in college nearby and still living at home. I arrived at the store later that morning to find our world turned upside down. My parents were in Dad's office talking to a detective. Mom was doing something I'd never seen her do before: she was smoking a cigarette. Our store had been robbed by someone who knew how to disable the alarm system. They smashed most of our glass cases and grabbed everything they could. They used all of our garbage cans to haul away what they stole. And, they took their time. Our refrigerator was raided as well. Most of our fine goods, including wedding bands, rings, earrings, bracelets, chains, necklaces, watches, and charms were taken. We had some things in our safe, but most of our inventory was gone. Needless to say, we were devastated.

As was so typical with my parents, they wouldn't let this terrible incident break them. A few hours later, my father was on the phone to the many salesmen he knew in New York City, explaining the situation and making arrangements for rapid reorders. In good faith everyone came through, and after much over-nighting and restocking we somehow got through the busiest season of the year. The thieves were never caught. The police were unable to track them down and found no traces of them. In the end, they concluded that the burglars were from out of state. Between the break-in, the disastrous mess that was made, the invasion of privacy, dealing with the insurance company, and a non-stop busy season, we all felt like the wind had been taken out of our sails. My father assured us that things would go back to normal, and they did. It took time. It took a few years to really get back to normal. We got our lives back on track, adopted new policies, and made some improvements, ultimately enhancing our jewelry business. This was another time when perseverance, hope, and determination came into play.

There are many more light-hearted than heavy remembrances of our days in the jewelry business. Just before Thanksgiving, my father would give my mom and me the lecture. During the holiday season, Dad said, there was to be "no foolishness," which translated into *no unimportant discussion or extra chitchat when we were working during that busiest of seasons*. Daddy also reminded us that no one was allowed to be sick. Everyone was to focus on the business. Try telling this to a kid!

Most of the time, I enjoyed being at the store. That's where my parents were and also our many loyal customers. I would arrive after school and stay until closing, unless it got too late. My parents had lunch and dinner there while working. As I got older, I would bring back dinner from a local restaurant, and I also began waiting on customers. It was fun and gave me a great education in the retail world. I enjoyed learning about the jewelry business and made some wonderful friends along the way. I was hanging out or working at the store from elementary school all the way through to high school and into college. I continued helping out at our store, even when I began my career, until the business closed in 1988.

Generally, the store was open six days a week (closed on Sunday), closing sometime between 5:00 and 7:00 p.m., but Dad would sometimes stay longer in order to accommodate shift workers who didn't finish work until later. He would also go to the store to deal with "emergencies," such as a lost ring on the day of a wedding. He personalized his business in order to meet people's needs. From the day after Thanksgiving until Christmas Eve, we kept the store open seven days a week. Closing time depended on last-minute customers. Mom and I needed a break, and we were happy when Dad finally gave in and said it was time to leave. There was usually a restaurant open and we headed out to dinner.

Christmas Day was a time to catch our breath and just relax. We were glad to be at home. The day after Christmas was typically busy for us. Although we had very few returns, some people stopped in for ring sizings while others came to spend their Christmas money or purchase what they hadn't found in their stockings!

Melvin and Mildred Goldman at Lee Trading Company, late 1970s.

A few days after the holiday rush, we started inventory, which was all done by hand. We had a large amount of jewelry and giftware. Bless my mother for her patience. She did the majority of it. By this time it was January, and it was usually very cold in Pittsburgh. Our heat was not the greatest in our rented store. We bundled up and did our jobs, which at times seemed endless. Once we finished, my father started anticipating Valentine's Day. After that, he looked toward engagements, weddings, and other occasions.

Dad was a perfectionist, so everything in the display cases had to be in neat, straight rows. He also had a keen sense of hearing, surprising after his experiences as a youth in concentration camps. If I was curious about a certain piece of jewelry and decided to take a look, I would hear, "Who is in the cases?" It made everyone who was working hysterical with laughter.

We were a tight-knit family, perhaps drawn close because we all worked together. Dad was not one to talk or express his feelings openly, but he—probably much more so than Mom or I—was keenly aware of the importance of family closeness. And Mom deserved a gold medal for all she did: working with us in the business, but also helping Dad complete every single Holocaust compensation letter, typing his story numerous times, and taking care of our house and me. I always considered her to be the glue that held us together. She was one of my best friends and was completely loyal to Dad, especially in helping to safeguard and preserve his story—by supporting his efforts to record the horrors of the Holocaust. She deserved much credit.

When my father wasn't working, the family spent a lot of time together outdoors. We would drive to Frick Park and play soccer. Even Mom would kick the ball around. It was a family activity, but Dad was the force behind that activity. We also liked to hike the trails. My father loved nature. There were many trips as a kid to the Pittsburgh Zoo, the aviary, and one of my very favorites, Phipps Conservatory and Botanical Gardens. We visited a few times a year. I am happy to say that my husband, John, enjoys going to Phipps, and our son, Jason, has fond

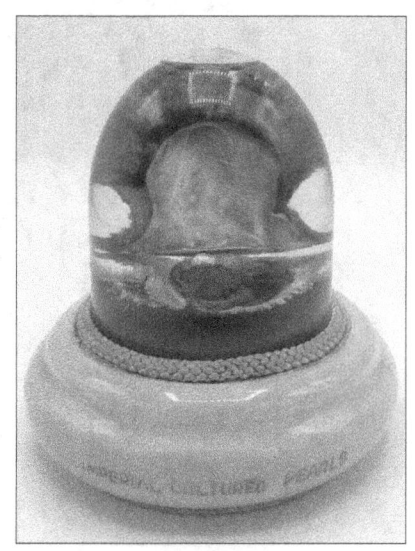

Show-and-tell: the pearl.

memories of it from his childhood. Jason never turns me down if I suggest a trip to "the flower show." Maybe partly from my jewelry store years, with my parents' influence and among so many exquisite things, I learned to appreciate beauty—whether lovely flowers or a well-crafted object on display.

It follows that, at an early age, I was tuned in to the impact of presenting stunning objects—as the following often-told family story attests. When I was in fourth grade, I had the idea of taking something unique for "show-and-tell." Dad sold cultured pearls and had in the store a beautiful display piece given to him by Imperial Cultured Pearls, a large wholesale company. The piece was an oblong glass dome filled with water; inside, a pearl rested in an open shell. It was one-of-a-kind, and that's what I wanted to present at show-and-tell. Dad said okay, and I was so excited. None of the other kids had anything like that to share with their classmates.

Wightman School was in a beautiful building that had a basement and three floors with steps of green marble. On the day of show-and-tell, I walked into school and began to climb the stairs to the second floor. Somehow, I tripped and lost my grip on the beautiful glass piece. It fell and hit the steps' hard marble. Water went pouring down the stairs while everyone stopped and stared. I was shocked and started to cry. I had destroyed this lovely object! What would my parents say? What would Daddy say? He had trusted me with this treasure. But, Dad told me not to worry or feel bad.

He called the pearl company, explained the situation, and they sent him a new display piece. Yes, he trusted me again, and this time there was no breakage. Today, I have the pearl at home on display in our curio cabinet, and I always think of Dad when I look at it.

6. He Put His Heart into Every Piece

Through the years, Dad worked hard honing his skills and making a success of his business, which he did by tailoring his products to fit his customers' needs and personalities. Ultimately, he earned a reputation as a one-of-a-kind artist. His strong following also had to do with the kind of man he was—one of good character and a friendly disposition. Such thoughts were shared by many others too.

In thinking about yesteryears and the various people who came in and out of our lives decades back, I decided to reach out to some of these people. Many simply remembered me as Melvin and Mildred's little girl. What a delightful experience reconnecting! How I enjoyed hearing the memories folks shared with me through notes, phone calls, and visits over the last few years.

Customers' reflections on their experiences with the jewelry store bring the business part of my parents' world to life in a unique way. Rose Ann Brown remembers that Dad always knew what she wanted, even when she didn't. He made earrings in a gold fleur-de-lis design for her. When he made her a large diamond ring that she thought was a little over the top, he turned it into a pendant. "My admiration for him as a talented artist is topped only by my admiration of him as a man. The Nazis tried to kill him, but his spirit was too strong. I always wished I could have asked him or Mildred more about his story but did not want to open painful wounds."

I talked with Rose Ann about how far back our families' friendship goes. Her husband, Bob, became fast friends with my father. They were both businessmen, both very adept at running all aspects of a business while keeping an eye on the economy. The two men enjoyed many conversations and respected each other's opinions. My mom kept in touch with the Browns after my dad passed away in 1996. Bob died in 2016. We still hear from Rose Ann a few times a year and get together with her from time to time. This has been a lovely friendship that stemmed from business dealings.

Their sons, Robert S. "Skip" Jr. and John, also spent time at our store, and then their wives, Karen and Audrey, respectively, came to see us as well. Skip described Dad's creations as "timeless in their beauty and brilliance." He recalls taking his wife to our home to make a purchase. "Your father showed Karen the ring, holding the box open like a clam so she could peek at it. Karen looked at it, and suddenly he shut the box like a clam closing up, which further aroused her curiosity."

Brown also knew of my dad's happiness as a US citizen, noting: "Your Dad lived the American dream every minute of his life." And, he spoke of the picture and letter Dad had hanging in his office from Lt. Gen. James Gavin of the US Army's 82nd Airborne Division. No doubt, he had heard Melvin's story about his liberation, including his admiration of the 82nd Airborne.

Skip and Karen also referred people to Dad. A good friend of theirs, Falco Muscante, was talking with them about his plans to propose to his girlfriend, Gina. Karen recommended that Falco get custom-designed engagement and wedding rings from Dad, and showed him the pieces Skip had purchased for her. Being struck by how "exquisite and of high quality" they were, Falco knew he wanted Dad to design the rings.

Falco remembers, "Melvin and Mildred welcomed Gina and me into their home and immediately treated us as if we were family. They both expressed genuine interest in us and our plans, and were not in any rush to just get down to business. Eventually, Melvin took us to his workshop and was patient with us, showing us several diamonds from which to make our selection. He was meticulous in describing the quality of each. Melvin worked with us until we were satisfied with each stone we chose. Then Melvin asked me whether I had given any thought to my wedding band. Aside from a gold band, I hadn't thought about it. Melvin showed me several men's rings, and I selected one with some distinction. I recall as we were leaving, I jokingly said to Melvin, 'Why do the ladies get all the diamonds, and the men don't get anything?'"

Dad always took pride in his work. "He was very excited to show me the rings when he was done with them. Melvin had captured every detail that we had described wanting for Gina's ring, and I could barely wait to give it to her. Melvin then said that he had a surprise for me—he had added three diamonds to my gold band, and happily said that now I had some diamonds also. I was overwhelmed by his thoughtfulness, but he had a further surprise. On the inside of each wedding band, Melvin had engraved our names and the date of our planned wedding. He had gone above and beyond what Gina and I had asked of him." This was even after Dad had closed the store and was continuing to do a little work out of their house.

Dorothy Kinner worked for my parents. "I worked at G&S Jewelry from 1983 to 1988. Melvin and Mildred Goldman were the nicest people to work with. Melvin, a proud, quiet man who didn't easily open up about his personal life, had his ways, but he was honest and didn't hold back when the truth needed to be told. He was meticulous, a master creator of custom jewelry. He put his heart into every piece he made and used only the best materials. His earlier hardships proved that anything is possible as long as you don't give up. Mildred was small in stature but had a big heart of gold. She was a good listener with a good sense of humor. Both of them were kind and generous, making me feel like part of their family. I enjoyed coming to work and seeing the new pieces Melvin had made. After thirty years I still wear a ring he made—a lady's ring with a large diamond surrounded by rows of fully cut diamonds."

Customers Ken and Pat Aites remember that Melvin was a "character" who drove a hard bargain and haggled over a price up to a point and then that was it. The finished product was always cleaned and polished to a shine. There was never any "junk" in the store. He always had lots of rings to choose from.

On Ken's first visit to the store, he was amazed at the number of steps to get to the door where Melvin would look out, unlock the deadbolt, and let you in. Then he would put the deadbolt back in position. With him being so isolated, he said that was what he had to do to stay safe. "He always shook my hand when I entered and

A pre-1965 newspaper ad for the business.

when I left. When I worked at Samson Buick and the boss asked me to take Melvin's Buick Electra 225 to his jewelry store after service, I would drive up and down Darlington Road until a spot became available because that's where Melvin always parked. Melvin always drove a Buick."

There was a small fridge in the back of the store stocked with food. Pat was always amazed at the small, saucer-sized plate of cottage cheese and veggies that Mildred would bring to Melvin. He would eat it while we sat there and chatted. Then she went to the other room to polish jewelry.

Pat Aites said Melvin had a gold bangle bracelet that he refashioned with parts from a silver and diamond watch that had belonged to Ken's family. He told her she could wear it with jeans or a dress, and that, if she needed money, it would get her home from anywhere in the world.

Melvin took care of Ken's and Pat's jewelry needs. They always felt welcome and could shop at the jewelry store knowing they would not be taken advantage of.

Another customer remembers "all those steps!" But, she also still has and loves the diamond necklace Dad made for her and a special necklace he made for her mother, who is now deceased.

Eighty-eight-year-old June Hayden recalled several items made by my father. Her favorite piece was a two-inch, circular disk engraved with her initials, *JH*, which she wore as a necklace. There was also a sapphire necklace and earring set, and a pair of emerald earrings he made for her daughter. She especially remembers that on the day she went to the store to pick them up, he told her he was closing the store. She was truly saddened, but like other customers who became friends, they stayed in touch. June and my mother spoke at least once during the year, and they always exchanged cards at the holidays. June and my family keep in touch as well.

I have always had an interest in cars, especially Buicks, and since 1981 have been long-distance friends with Richard Lasseter, another Buick enthusiast, from Georgia. He is now the director of Gran Sport Club of America, which has a worldwide membership. Dad was not interested in cars, but he enjoyed talking with my friends, including Richard, who stayed at our house on several occasions.

Richard described my father as a man who had respect—for family values and work ethic, and also for newcomers to the country. "In your father's day," Richard said, "it was about giving back and not just taking from the society they had accepted and which had accepted them. I saw all of this in your father's words and actions. It didn't take any length of time with Melvin to realize that he was an ethical and honest man whose life under very harrowing circumstances forged a very strong and honorable character. That's why I remember him so fondly, although our few times together were so long ago—in the early 1980s."

Richard's associations with Dad took place mostly at our breakfast table. "Most of our short talks were simple anecdotes about life in general. Later discussions with Mildred, both in person at Bowling Green, Kentucky, and over the phone, were always pleasant and uplifting. Ms. Mildred just made you feel good, and I always ended our conversation with a smile on my face."

I asked Richard if Dad ever talked to him about his experiences in Europe. Richard said he touched on it only briefly, over breakfast in the summer of 1984. "It was more of a light conversation about his experiences of having his jewelry store robbed. He talked about his disillusionment after that, wanting to believe in and help the same genre of people who had robbed him. It was all based on his experiences in the 1940s and believing that everyone deserved a chance and an education."

John Chamberlain is another friend of my family, whom I've known since the early 1980s. Like Richard, John always felt the warmth and welcome of my parents. My mother, he recalls, "was like an adopted mom to me. 'What's for dinner?' was how I would start the conversation after calling her! I was always welcomed with open arms to Melvin and Mildred's home!" John also remembers my father's quiet presence and loyalty to the car dealership where Melvin purchased his Buicks: "Although Melvin usually excused himself after we visited a while, I understood it to be because he was a pretty quiet person. I know he wouldn't go to the car dealership when it came time to trade Buicks. I remember that a salesman would bring a new Buick to the house, they would do the transaction, and the salesman would drive the old Buick back to the dealership. A man after my own heart!"

7. He Always Made Himself Available

As for me, I have my own fond memories of my father. He was a very handsome man. He was approximately five foot seven, with a thin frame. His stature and his accompanying scoliosis were likely the result of the circumstances he lived through during the Holocaust years. In the ghetto, Dad had picked up the habit of smoking and remained a heavy smoker throughout his life, until 1988 when he had severe health issues and quit cold turkey. No more smoking.

My father's hair was coal black, and both curly and wavy. It remained that way into his seventies with only his sideburns turning gray. Many people thought he dyed his hair. My father had brown eyes, and in later years he needed eyeglasses. Dad always wore a watch. He was more than punctual, always arriving early for everything. He also wore a diamond pinky ring. The ring changed over the years because his customers admired it, and many were purchased right off his hand! Each time this occurred, he made himself a new one.

As for attire, my father dressed on the formal side. My father collected ties, so he had many to choose from. His shoes were always polished and he prided himself on being meticulous. He had an aura that was distinctly European, but despite the accent, he was easy to understand. In a sense, his accented English enriched his personality and presence.

My father loved art, finely crafted items, nature, geography, history, and politics. Coming to the United States really had enriched his life. But, I think these interests had a foundation in his earlier experiences—the happy childhood; metalwork training and skills; imprisonment in the ghetto and death camps; illnesses, medical treatment, and rehabilitation; vacations in Poland before the war; and travel in Europe after the war.

He was very intelligent and had an aptitude for learning languages. Besides familiarity with Russian, Hungarian, French, and Italian, he read and spoke English (after some time in the United States) and was fluent in Yiddish, Hebrew, Polish, and German. My parents sometimes spoke Yiddish together at home or at the store, but Dad usually stuck to English.

When dressed up, Dad always wore a two- or three-piece suit and French-cuffed shirts that required cuff links. My father always looked distinguished and debonair. Here, he has a carefully folded handkerchief in his suit pocket, 1970.

He had painstakingly taught himself the intricacies of English by studying newspapers. He had to learn certain facts about the United States to become a citizen, and from there he took off, immersing himself in learning about his new country. He used school and work as outlets to keep his mind busy. Once he mastered English, Dad carried on his avid reading, just as he had done as a boy, enjoying mostly nonfiction subjects such as history and politics, past and present. He read magazines and books, mainly biography, autobiography, and the occasional novel—mostly Westerns and suspense fiction.

He also enjoyed TV, preferring news shows, PBS, dramas, soccer, and some comedy. I remember that he liked "Larry King Live" and one comedy in particular—"Seinfeld." He thought it was hilarious. My mom got Dad watching it. Some of his favorite comedians included Jackie Mason,

Daddy spent a lot of his spare time reading.

Don Rickles, Buddy Hackett, Joey Bishop, Sammy Davis Jr., Rodney Dangerfield, and Henny Youngman. As for movies, he liked Westerns, dramas, and musicals. My parents shared similar tastes in TV.

He was an enthusiastic lover of music, especially Jewish music, opera, and classical. His favorite singers/performers were Richard Tucker, Jan Peerce, Mario Lanza, Placido Domingo, Luciano Pavarotti, Jose Carreras, and Beverly Sills.

Dad wasn't much into sports. The only sport he liked was soccer, although he only played it with Mom and me occasionally. He had played a lot of soccer as a kid.

As for subjects relating to the Holocaust, Dad probably followed the trials of high-profile Nazis such as Eichmann, but he didn't attend movies or art exhibits relating to that period. He read a lot of Jewish literature and history but didn't delve into survivors' stories. He subscribed to the *Jewish Daily Forward* (a Yiddish paper from New York), the *Jewish Chronicle*, the *Jerusalem Post* (published in several languages, but I do not know which one Dad read), and a Polish newspaper. He read numerous other publications, in English and other languages as well. Some of them he got from newsstands.

The Holocaust Memorial Museum opened in Washington, DC, in 1993, three years before my father died. Although he was thrilled that such a museum had opened in the United States, and even though Aron went, Dad could not bring himself to go. He did, however, submit a fifteen-page testimony of his Holocaust experiences to the museum. Many times, my father intimated that there was so much to say about his Holocaust experiences. In that testimony, he said, "It would be impossible to fully describe here the six years from 1939 to the liberation May 5, 1945. All the tribulations, hardships, obstacles, just to keep the soul alive, in a measly few pages describing all of that. In order for that [a serious description] to happen, it would take six months just to tell the story."

Also, our family worked together to submit the names of his murdered immediate family to Yad Vashem's Victims' Names Recovery Project. Yad Vashem, the World Holocaust Remembrance Center, is a Jerusalem-based institution established in 1953 dedicated to commemoration, documentation, education, and research. Their central database of Shoah victims' names has now recorded names and details for 4.5 million out of the 6 million Jews killed by the Nazi regime. In 2014, Jason, John, and I were fortunate to have a guided tour of Yad Vashem. It was quite moving to be at a place with such an important mission, and one that related directly to our family history. Jason was in Israel for his Birthright trip, and John and I had flown over to meet up with him in Jerusalem at its completion. The three of us appreciated these memorable experiences.

In 1961, my father became a Mason, one involvement of his I do not know much about. He was sponsored by a friend and eventually became a 32nd degree Mason, meaning he was a full member of the Scottish Rite, equal to all Masons throughout the world, but having no higher stature. This is a high honor to achieve, and Dad was very proud of this accomplishment.

My parents did not do a lot of socializing. They worked five to seven days a week and cherished their time off. They took car rides to parks and restaurants, and also went out shopping. They occasionally visited with friends. Both of them were extremely likeable and could talk with anyone about anything. Dad—with a wonderful, artful sense of humor—was very friendly toward others.

Dad liked telling jokes, sometimes in Yiddish. Even if people didn't understand the words, it sounded funny and everyone laughed. After John and I married, the four of us spent lots of time together. We later added our son, Jason, and also included my mother-in-law, Elizabeth "Betty" Kikel on outings, dinners, holidays, and special occasions. She was a wonderful woman, a second mom to me. We all got along well and enjoyed each other's company.

My parents were people who wanted their privacy respected. They were careful because of the business they were in—not giving out too much personal information. My dad trusted people and believed in fairness. A handshake with another person made things valid and credible. If someone broke that trust, such as bouncing a check or backing out of a deal, the bond was broken.

After growing up with extreme scarcity, my dad sometimes purchased extra things while shopping—for instance, two cans of coffee rather than one, just in case you needed to barter in the event of a shortage in some sort of emergency. It's my understanding that this was typical among survivors.

My father was fascinated with stamps, and enjoyed collecting them from all over the world. Studying them gave him a sense of the history of various regions. He shared his interest with Mom and me. Stamp collecting was a family activity and continues to be, as I have in turn passed on my enthusiasm to John and Jason. My mother always purchased the latest US postage stamps. She looked forward to the new designs, and we discussed the artwork and themes. It is always enjoyable to see the newest stamps, and it is a wonderful connection to my parents. Today, when my family travels, we look for postal museums to tour and also purchase foreign stamps to add to our collection.

My father liked Eastern European foods such as borscht, schnitzel, and pierogies, but our diet was mainly American and Jewish. Some of our favorite Jewish foods were matzo balls and chicken soup, different types of kugel

---

Melvin-isms:

"Bang the table, the scissors jump."

"I look good on the outside, and I stink on the inside."

"I am rotten." [ill health]

"God forbid anything happens . . ."

"Don't take chances."

"You make a better door than a window."

"Jump through hoops . . ."

"Psychology is common sense."

"Common sense is not so common."

"You live to eat, or eat to live."

"What starts out difficult will eventually get easier."

"Mildred!"

"You people!"

"Your diamond will light up like a five-hundred-watt bulb."

"Competition is good."

My father was so right about this last one. An example: A fancy jewelry store was going to open about a block from us. My father was happy to see the competition. He had a very good reputation and did not worry about losing any business.

(noodle and potato casseroles), cholent (a Sabbath dish of meat, potatoes, beans, and barley), and various Jewish foods that were holiday-specific.

Today, there are many cholent recipes—Ashkenazi, Sephardic, vegetarian, and even vegan. You can use a crock-pot or slow cooker instead of the oven.

Both of my parents were very generous toward others, usually contributing in anonymous ways. They didn't feel the need to have their name associated with giving. But they often jumped in and personally helped out. In the 1970s, during an influx of Russian immigrants to Squirrel Hill, my dad helped some of them find housing and jobs, and he assisted in locating educational or training opportunities. He always made himself available if someone wanted to talk or needed something. Mom was a helper too. She received "volunteer of the year" award at the mental health agency where she volunteered and I worked. In Allegheny County, she was the first recipient of this award, and our family, as well as the agency staff and clients, were all thrilled for her. It was an award she richly deserved.

Dad had strong feelings regarding Jewish "statelessness" as it related to his life. The Jews had been stateless since the Babylonian exile of 586 BCE, resulting in their dispersion, or the Diaspora. Although they subsequently developed cultures in various countries, Jews were often considered outcasts and were sometimes purged or exiled. In many countries, they were under the ruler's supervision. Their outcast classification sometimes led them to form ghettos within larger populations.

Israel had become a state in 1948. My father was elated that there was a place for Jews to live in freedom and independence. It is my opinion that growing up under Polish anti-Semitism, my father never considered himself Polish, but rather a Jew who lived in Poland. For instance, as a boy, his soccer team consisted solely of Jewish kids. They played teams of Polish Catholics. During those years, ethnic slurs and fights were common, even though many of the kids were neighbors.

Thus, Dad was a staunch supporter of Israel; he felt that there should be a place for Jews to live freely or go to if something bad happened, such as persecution. Mom also supported Israel and what it stood for.

My father survived World War II but found himself to be a young man without a country. However, coming to the United States he felt that his dream of having and belonging to a country had finally begun. Above all,

Dad was proud to be an American. He loved this country and all that it stood for. He believed in democracy, the US Constitution, and the Bill of Rights, and he felt that America was the greatest country in the world.

Dad traveled to New York on business, New Jersey to visit friends, and the DC area to sightsee with Mom, but he had no desire to ever go back to Poland. While in rehab in Germany, he saw parts of the Alps, Austria, Italy, and France, but he never considered visiting Europe until later in life when his health was deteriorating and it was too late. Dad definitely did not, however, want to return to Poland. It brought back too many bad memories for him.

My parents were great role models with a strong influence on my life—my attitudes, political views, religion, work ethic—and how I live my day-to-day life. I was educated in the public schools where there was a mix of students. I did have Jewish friends, but my parents encouraged me to branch out, so I had friends from all ethnic and racial backgrounds. I learned from my parents to treat everyone equally.

8. They Were Looking for Answers and a Place to Start Over

– – – – –

My father knew several of the Holocaust survivors in Pittsburgh. Some were more acquaintances than friends. Some were customers at our store, and some were people Dad ran into on the Avenue—Murray.

Dad had three good friends—Powel (Paul) Goldhersz, Mayer Klay, and Abe Lewitt—who were also Holocaust survivors. Powel and Mayer lived in New Jersey, and Abe lived in New York. Even though they didn't get together often, they kept up with each other by phone. They mostly talked about what was currently happening in their lives rather than reliving the horrible experiences of the past. When I had my bat mitzvah, they came to stay with us—Powel, Mayer, and Abe. The three of them and my father were very close and loved each other. When they were together, they usually spoke English, but sometimes they would use Hebrew or Yiddish. Abe and Mayer passed away before my father. They were wonderful, caring people.

My father and Powel Goldhersz had met after the war, in 1947, at a rehabilitation facility in Germany called Kneippianum Sanatorium. Powel was working as a telephone operator. They became instant friends. Powel came

Powel Goldhersz with Melvin, 1971. Given their jewelry business, it's not surprising that my parents loved beautiful things. Here, some of our special items can be seen in the china closet.

Melvin, Mayer Klay, and Lee, 1971.

from Łódź as well but the two hadn't known each other there. Powel immigrated to New Jersey because his aunt lived there. He had his own business until retirement. He and my father remained friends up to my father's passing. I still have regular contact with Powel and his wife, Gloria. They have three grown children. He only visited our store once and told me after Dad died that he was very surprised and impressed to see the quality of Dad's work. Also, he described Dad as a very intelligent and happy person.

"Baby Abe" Lewitt, 1971.

I remember Powel's telling me how much he had liked spending time talking with my father. Apparently, Dad would tell him about talks he had with Dr. Krotowski, in the hospital at Kneippianum, who was interested in "the long sickness" (chronic problems). The doctor was very interested in Dad's explanations, because of the reading he did on the topic, but also, presumably, because my father was living it and knew of what he spoke.

9. Aron: My Father's Brother

While it has often been said here that my father "lost his whole family"—either to conditions in the ghetto or at Auschwitz—there was his brother

My father kept a suitcase in his closet that contained items he brought to America. It included clothing and personal articles, such as shaving items, toiletries, documents, and some foreign coins. There were also many photos and over one hundred postcards that he had received and had exchanged with friends while traveling around Europe after the war and in his early years in the United States.

I sat with my father one afternoon when he was in declining health, and we looked through the photos and postcards. I wanted to know the names of his friends and acquaintances. No one else could identify them. We only got through a handful because he was very tired. We never got back to it. Twenty years later, I realized that I had a treasure trove of my father's remembrances—a beautiful trail of memories, especially precious since he is gone.

The journey of these gems began when my father was in a rehabilitation hospital after the war, and it continued when he and friends began traveling around while recuperating. Eventually, they began leaving Germany and Europe. Most headed to the United States, and many kept in touch until and after getting settled.

These young people, in their early twenties, were out in the world exploring after losing everybody and everything. Many of them had no fear. They were looking for answers and a place to start over. They became each other's family.

Most of the notes, descriptions, and captions on the postcards are in Yiddish, Polish, and German. After a lengthy and tedious translation process, I organized them in albums, and, eventually, I put together a story within a story. There are also a few postcards that my mother sent to my father when they were dating. They were in English!

Aron, who also survived. Living in the same city, the two of them, Melvin and Aron, knew some of the same immigrants and Holocaust survivors who had relocated to Pittsburgh. However, for reasons I don't know or understand, my father and my uncle were not close. They reconnected in Germany briefly after the war and then reunited in Pittsburgh, but a strong adult relationship between them did not happen, although Dad always wished him the best. My father did try on several occasions to be connected, even hiring Aron at one point to work in the jewelry store with him. Aron and Evy raised a son and a daughter, Howard (deceased in 2012) and Barbara (now residing in Florida).

Uncle Aron's physical health was better than Dad's until his later years when he, too, suffered his share of illnesses. He passed away six months before my father, a death that was extremely hard on Dad. It was one of the few deaths of someone close to him in America after the war that he had to deal with. For the rest of us—Mom and I, and my husband, John—Dad's grief was difficult to watch. Jason was too young to be affected by the tragedy.

Aron held various jobs throughout the years, including selling insurance. Although our families weren't close, there were occasional family get-togethers, since we lived in the same city. At times, Aron would share a few

Aron Goldman in Germany, as an officer with UNRRA (United Nations Relief and Rehabilitation Administration), circa 1949.

Aron Goldman, August 1950, location unknown.

of his recollections of Łódź and Poland. He was fourteen years old when the ghetto was established. He described early Łódź as a beautiful city with parks and lots of recreation. Like Mieczyslaw, Aron enjoyed family vacations in the Cherry Mountains. He once described to us how the family took the train and then had help taking their suitcases by *wóz* (a little cart pulled by a horse). He had memories of catching butterflies and eating baked goods with blueberries in them sold from a baker's cart.

Łódź was important for its manufacturing, so the city was captured, rather than bombed. Aron remembered when the Germans came. Many were on motorcycles with sidecars. They had machine guns and began rounding up the Jews. They used loudspeakers and forced their way into houses, terrifying the occupants and stealing valuables. After the ghetto was established, many German Jews who lived in Łódź committed suicide by going into the tallest buildings and jumping to their deaths. The dead were picked up and taken on two-wheel carts to the cemetery.

He remembered the Goldman family staying together in the same house on Wolborska Street until August 1944. No one was permitted to practice Judaism. Sabbath candles could not be lit and holiday practices were banned, yet my father and his brother said they never forgot who they were.

In August 1944, the liquidation got underway. Aron recalled that the family packed up and was taken to the train station. They were forced onto a cattle car with no food or water. Mieczyslaw was very sick and barely survived the trip to Auschwitz. When they arrived, there were German SS, many with German Shepherds, deciding where people would go. Suitcases were tossed from the cattle cars and the SS separated men, women, and children. In doing so, naturally, families were separated. They put canes around people's necks and pulled them in different directions. Mieczyslaw and Aron went to the right, and the rest of the family went to the left, never to be seen again.

After going through the selection, Aron remembered that prisoners were disinfected and shaved. They were given a shirt or jacket and a pair of pants. They were sent to the transition block (Block 11), also known as the death block. Prisoners slept on a cement floor. It was very cramped. People were lined right up next to each other without any space between them. It was crowded and uncomfortable. At any time, the prisoners might be doused with cold water. No eyeglasses or gold teeth were allowed. Soup consisted of a small amount of kohlrabi and water. Prisoners were beaten with whips.

Aron called to mind that he and Mieczyslaw saw a cousin of theirs who was related to their mother. He had spent two years at Auschwitz and had worked in a coal mine. He only had one leg. He later flung himself onto the electrified wires and was electrocuted.

Aron was sent to Görlitz, where he did factory work after working in a coal mine. He survived a death march and was eventually liberated by the Russians in May 1945. He recalled there being a Russian Jewish general among the liberators.

After the war, Aron returned to Soviet-occupied Łódź in search of family. The city was bustling. He thought back to seeing the Goldman house and factory—both, empty. During the liquidation of the ghetto, the Germans ransacked houses and businesses in search of Jews and valuables. Aron found four walls and the remains of a chimney. From roof to basement, the family house was empty. However, Aron did recover a few of their mother's rings and Mieczyslaw's sixth grade picture hidden in the chimney.

10. Becoming Me

My father was raised as an Orthodox Jew. In Łódź, he and his family welcomed the Sabbath each week and celebrated all of the Jewish holidays. It became increasingly difficult to practice their faith after the Nazis invaded in 1939 since Jews were degraded and belittled. Some people celebrated holidays in secrecy, but if you were caught you were often beaten or simply "taken away." My father was the only one of his siblings who became bar mitzvah.

While he was recovering in hospitals after the war, young Mieczyslaw had many questions about God and religion, even though he never forgot that he was Jewish. When he came to the United States and resided with his brother and sister-in-law, he discovered that they did not practice much in the way of Judaism. My father and a few of his friends decided to go to the synagogue to celebrate Rosh Hashanah, the Jewish New Year. These young people with very little money were told they needed to pay to participate in the holiday observance. Melvin was offended by this and backed off from what he called "organized religion."

Nevertheless, my parents were married in a small Jewish wedding ceremony. Mildred's grandparents were Orthodox Jews. Her parents (David

Zerelstein and Elizabeth Slawkin Zerelstein) were not as religious. My parents observed the Jewish holidays but did not keep kosher. I attended Sunday school and Hebrew school, but after my bat mitzvah when I was thirteen, I was allowed to decide how I approached Judaism.

Over the years, I've learned that being Jewish is not just about religion. It is a culture and a lifestyle that I am proud to be a part of today. John and I raised Jason in the tradition of Reform Judaism, a branch that is more relaxed about strict religious practices and that emphasizes the evolution and questioning of issues of faith. Although he wasn't raised as a Jew, John participated in all of our observances and officially converted to Judaism before Jason's bar mitzvah. Thus, our son has two Jewish parents. Dad was deceased by then, but Mom was thrilled, and we celebrated the event.

We observe many Jewish traditions. We continue to celebrate Chanukah in much the same way as when I was growing up, even though both of my parents are deceased. Customary foods include matzo ball soup, turkey or brisket for dinner, and chocolate Chanukah gelt (chocolate coins), and we light the menorah for eight days and play the dreidel game.

We observe a small Passover seder each year with the reading of the Haggadah (Passover guide) and eat traditional foods. A favorite of mine is matzo brei—fried matzo with eggs—that my mother always made. Several other

Bat mitzvah, 1971. Lee celebrates with her parents.

Mildred and Melvin, Lee's bat mitzvah, March 26, 1971.

My mother used this recipe for cholent—a Sabbath-day dish. My father helped her with the ingredients so that it resembled his mother's.

2–3 beef marrow bones
1 lb. beef short ribs
2 cans lima beans or kidney beans
1 cup uncooked barley
3 peeled and cut potatoes

Line a roasting pan with foil. Put bones and meat on bottom of pan. Add half of beans, barley, and potatoes. Alternate the ingredients. Add some salt and pepper.

Add water so that it comes to the top. Put roasting pan on a cookie sheet to prevent spills.

Bake at 325° for 7 hours, up to 12 hours.

Check and make sure it is browning. You can raise temperature to cook faster. Add more water if necessary.

---

holidays provide celebratory outlets for enjoying traditional foods and relaxing with family—Rosh Hashanah (the Jewish new year), Sukkot (a harvest celebration), Simchat Torah (the conclusion and beginning of the annual cycle of Torah readings), and Purim (the commemoration of the saving of the Jews from Haman). We especially like Purim when the book of Esther is read. It is often done with humor, and kids and adults dress up like their favorite characters from the book of Esther.

To mark special occasions, our family plants trees in Israel through the Jewish National Fund, an organization that plants trees in forests all over Israel and sends the donor a certificate. Anyone can plant trees for any occasion no matter what denomination you are. They make a nice remembrance. And we observe Holocaust Memorial Day (Yom HaShoah), typically in April, lighting candles for our family and everyone who perished in the Holocaust.

My father was a true *mensch* (good person). He abided by what he had been taught and always gave generously to others, almost always anonymously. Jewish people believe in performing *mitzvot*. These are good deeds

- -

Directly below is a partial list of organizations Melvin corresponded with over the years, related to issues such as restitution and recovery. These are largely government agencies and non-profits from the United States and Germany. They are followed by the names of some of the many organizations his daughter, Lee, corresponded with in later years.

> Bankhaus H. Aufhäuser, München
> Comité International De La Croix-Rouge, Service International De Recherches (International Committee of the Red Cross, International Tracing Service), Arolsen Waldeck, Deutschland
> Consulate of the Federal Republic of Germany, Philadelphia, PA
> Foreign Claims Settlement Commission of the United States, Washington, DC
> German Retirement Consulting Agency, Michigan
> United Restitution Organization (URO), München and New York, NY
> World Jewish Congress, New York, NY
>
> Central Zionist Archives, Jerusalem
> Consulate General of the Republic of Poland, New York, NY
> Embassy of the United States of America, Warsaw
> International Tracing Service, Bad Arolsen, Germany
> Muzeum Stutthof, W. Sztutowie, Poland
> Panstwowe Muzeum, Oświęcim, Brzezinka, Poland
> United States Holocaust Memorial Museum, Washington, DC
> Yad Vashem, Jerusalem

- - - - -

Five notebooks, containing some of Melvin's records. Besides the correspondence related to claims and reparation, these notebooks include letters and applications related to searching for Melvin's missing family members, documentation of Melvin's time in rehabilitation facilities from 1945 to 1950, mementos, historical documents such as birth certificates, medical records, education (performance reports and certificates), and Melvin's various applications to refugee and emigration organizations. There is also correspondence to several attorneys during the claims process, as well as some of the correspondence produced by Mildred and Lee.

- -

done every day without having to be told to do them. This could be as simple as being courteous to someone or as big as donating or giving anonymously.

11. He Was Driven by Principle— To Have Things Made Right

— — — — —

Dad had many health problems. He was constantly under medical care for one physical ailment or another. Over the years, Mom was extremely patient, most of the time going with Dad to his appointments. Even when he had made a substantial recovery, there were still issues with his health and well-being. My mother described to me the nightmares he had for many years.

After the horrors suffered in his younger life, how could he not have disturbing dreams? They subsided after a while, but I can still recall his yelling out when I was a little girl. Today, Dad might have been diagnosed with PTSD. He had a particularly hard time effectively dealing with and expressing his grief. He never really had the chance to properly grieve the loss of his family, since he had to focus on his own survival for so many years. He kept his emotions inside, as he was never taught what to do with them. When Aron died, he was so overwhelmed by the loss that he nearly had a heart attack. Dad was also deeply affected by the deaths of our pets throughout the years. As a coping mechanism, he was always keeping himself busy at work and taking care of his family. We were the one reliable outlet for his displays of affection. Daddy loved me dearly, and when I was a baby he was afraid I would break. Later, with Jason, he still had some of the same fears, but was eventually able to relax more and enjoy every minute with his grandson.

Held against their will for about five years, my father and his family were forced to live in subhuman conditions that did not let up. In the ghetto there was starvation, unrelenting harsh weather, sickness, forced labor, and death. There was an atmosphere of agitation and worry, around the clock. Everyone witnessed roundups and killings. Slave labor was a way of life. My father worked in various factories under Nazi rule where the conditions were deplorable. At the Auschwitz camps, he lived with continuous fear and anxiety, and he was constantly watchful as the inevitable unexpected and unprovoked beatings and torture went on. Meanwhile, he was hungry, cold, and tired—always. Later in life, his doctors determined that most of his illnesses came from his time in the ghetto and camps.

My father felt that amends needed to be made for the numerous wrongs he and his family had been subjected to and witnessed. When he wasn't at the jewelry store, he spent many hours at home working on letters to organizations and government agencies here and abroad, tracking down documents, filling out forms, and having things translated or notarized. My mom was involved too. She provided ongoing secretarial—and moral—support for his efforts. I know that my father felt very beaten down by the whole process, but he wouldn't have done anything differently. He was driven by principle—to have things made right.

In the late 1950s, my father began applying for restitution and reparation related to the valuables stolen from his family, and to his years of imprisonment and the ensuing hardships with health and finances. The issue of his never-ending medical expenses was not insignificant. From the time of his arrival in the United States, my father was being treated for medical problems, which he could not afford to pay for. The claims process was not an easy undertaking. After many rounds of correspondence, in 1967 he was finally awarded an advance payment for compensation for some of his family's possessions in Łódź. Later, a figure was established for ongoing restitution, and my father finally began receiving a small check from the German government each month. I didn't know how much he got, other than it seemed like a small amount, a token, rather than something a person could actually live on.

The following testimony, which was part of the application to the German government, provides a compelling example of his determination and his commitment to the process:

> All this, therefore, I wrote down and can prove with statements, witnesses, and documents, which I have, that it is the absolute truth. Any papers or documents needed, or examination of myself, I will gladly submit to. In view of the facts as described and cruelties I suffered, I want from the German Government, for my body damages, what I think I am entitled to—a monthly payment which would include first, 60 percent of my salary because I can show that I am handicapped and would make, when in normal condition, 60

percent more. That means as follows: 60 percent of my rent, electricity, and gas bill, and the same percentage for movies, books, theater, and elementary things a person needs. I would also take one lump sum of money covering everything in order to establish myself here so that I could at least be capable of making a living, but under arbitration on the condition that I have the final decision as to whether to agree to this amount or not.

No doubt, perseverance had played a part in his ability to survive the camps, and those qualities certainly helped him receive at least some monetary compensation for the years he had suffered. Again, I emphasize the word *perseverance* because his correspondence, back and forth, for this eventually filled two fat three-ring notebooks. My father had to submit documentation for all treatments, including doctor visits, tests, blood work, dental treatment, medications, and all procedures. Many people would have given up, but not my father. He kept plugging along, as he would have said, until he received what he thought was fair. He could not be cured or even come close to being as healthy as he had been prior to 1940, but he believed that on a certain level he had won. After many rejections, he prevailed. He fought and won against the bureaucracy.

In addition to the monumental pile of correspondence necessary for eventual receipt of some compensation for his medical problems, Dad made similar attempts to get restitution from Poland for the family property that was, in effect, stolen by the Nazis and later stolen by the new Polish government. Dad included Aron's name in these documents. I was struck by this, in John Weiss's *Politics of Hate*: "In 1946, there were approximately 86,000 Jews in Poland . . . People who took over Jewish property would not give it back to their rightful owners. Police and local officials sided with Polish citizens and would not intervene. This led to 1,500 to 2,000 Jews being murdered as they tried to return to their former homes from 1945–1947. Many people, including small fascist groups, used the slogan 'Kill the Jews and Save Poland.'"

The Goldman family's lost property was itemized, in part, as follows: "Mother's fur (Persian lamb) coat, diamond set, pin, bracelet, necklace, earrings, men's ruby ring, household goods, appliances and clothing. Household furniture—chairs, living-room, dining-room, and bedroom suites, pictures.

Machinery, and equipment at factory at #33 Wolborska, owned by Chaim Goldman, sole proprietor. Raw materials, merchandise, supplies, and inventory at warehouse at #31 Wolborska, owned by Chaim Goldman, sole proprietor. Equipment, furniture, office equipment, merchandise, supplies, and inventory stored at #2 Cegelniana [sic], which Chaim Goldman owned in conjunction with [an equal partner]. There were also measuring devices, air purifiers, and a large debt owed to Chaim Goldman." Family property was valued at $38,610.00, a figure on official rejection paperwork received by my father in 1964 from the Foreign Claims Settlement Commission of the United States.

No compensation was paid out; my father's efforts in that case were for naught. Poland is one of the only countries that never paid restitution to survivors. Poland would not acknowledge stolen property, including businesses, factories, or valuables. The government was able to rationalize its rejection of claims by laws set forth in the International Claims Settlement Act of 1949, and the Polish Claims Agreement of 1960. My father's claim was denied because Poland had been "nationalized," and because the claimant had submitted no documentation that such property had been owned by his family. It is a shame that to date, over seventy years later, the few survivors who are left have received no compensation—or even an apology—from Poland for what was taken from them. I hope that survivors and their families can be compensated. This might finally provide them some closure.

12. A Sad Time, but Looking Forward

My parents finally decided to close the business. Dad's health was not improving, and they felt that it was time to retire. Dad was sixty-five, and Mom was fifty-nine. April of 1988 was a sad time, especially for them, but I was looking forward to my parents spending their time in other fulfilling ways. They closed the store, but Dad kept in touch with special customers and helped many of them when they needed to purchase jewelry. He also continued doing appraisals and kept up on the jewelry business in general.

Closing the store seemed like a long process. My parents let many customers know about it, so they could make final purchases. My dad had talked with me about taking over the business after I attended college, but he was in ill health and I did not think I could manage the business on my own. He was also worried for my safety as it can be a dangerous business. I was pursuing my counseling career, and I felt that my father would have less pressure if he could just retire. We had a gentleman who was a jewelry broker come in to purchase our inventory.

Dad faced growing health problems in the 1980s. Insulin controlled his diabetes, which had caused eye problems requiring laser surgery. Through that, Dad refused to miss a full day of work. He insisted on driving himself to his appointment alone and came back to work afterward. He scaled the twenty-three steps up to G&S Jewelry and got back to work. He also had Bell's palsy, which temporarily affected the right side of his face and one eye. He had to go for physical therapy. He listened to his doctors and was able to recover fully. With Dad's many ailments, he still looked good in his later years. He used to say, "I look good on the outside, but I feel rotten on the inside."

Retirement provided my parents the opportunity to spend more time relaxing with family. Here we are on an outing to Phipps Conservatory. Left to right: John, Lee, Mildred, and Melvin.

13. A Nice Backyard, a Garden, and Peacefulness

The early years after they sold the business were a time when my parents began to enjoy their retirement while staying active with various undertakings of everyday life. And then, a special event came along to keep them active.

Dad was quite pleased with my decision to marry John Kikel, confident that I would be happy and the good life he had envisioned for me would come to fruition. It has. My parents were ecstatic about the engagement and the upcoming wedding. They wanted to pitch in and help with preparations. But for Daddy, that wasn't to be as he'd hoped. He suddenly started

Left to right: Melvin, Lee, John, Elizabeth "Betty" Kikel, and Mildred, May 11, 1991.

Melvin with Jason, circa 1994.

experiencing excruciating internal pains that he said felt like being hit with a baseball bat, and that his doctor could not explain. The specialist called in for further evaluation diagnosed Dad with internal shingles. By then, it was too late for medication, so he had to ride out the illness. Thankfully, most of Dad's symptoms were gone by our wedding day, May 11, 1991.

When John and I announced that a baby was on the way, Dad was overjoyed. With quiet elation he kept a close eye on me and my prenatal care. Although not big on demonstrations of emotion, Dad stayed with us throughout my labor, doing extremely well for being nervous. It's a funny and heart-warming memory. We welcomed Jason into the world in the summer of 1992, and Dad was high above the clouds with happiness and pride. He was *kvelling*! Bubbling over.

A special bond sprang up instantly between Jason and Dad. The many good, positive emotions that Daddy had typically held in check were let out, and he was able to relax and have a wonderful time with his grandson—that is, after he got over thinking Jason would break if he picked him up! Grandfather and grandson spent many hours of quality time together. They played ball, took walks, and read. Daddy entertained Jason with his wealth of Yiddish tales that made both of them laugh like crazy. One of our best outings was when all of us went to the Pittsburgh Zoo. We rode the zoo train, and my dad beamed all day long.

After Jason was born, there was no question that my parents needed to live closer to us. They thought an apartment might be more suitable to their needs, but we found a lovely ranch home for them close to where we live now, Hampton Township. My father enjoyed his last years with a nice backyard, a garden, and peacefulness. It was a beautiful setting.

Lee and Jason visit Melvin at home, summer 1996.

Melvin and Jason, Labor Day, September 2, 1996. The last picture of Melvin, shortly before his death.

My parents truly loved spending time with their grandson. Top left: my dad and Jason on the train at the Pittsburgh Zoo; right: my dad with Jason on Halloween; and bottom: our family, left to right: John, Jason, Lee, Mildred, and Melvin. All photos, circa 1993.

14. Dad Remains with Us

My father passed away on September 26, 1996. He had not felt well for an entire year, but somehow he pushed along. He continued to function pretty well until a few weeks before his death. Dad even drove until two weeks before he died. In the last month or so, he was becoming weaker and his breathing was more labored.

John and I brought Jason over to my parents' house on a Saturday night. Jason and my dad hung out together watching TV and just generally talking, enjoying each other's company as usual. Mom called on Sunday morning to tell me dad was in the hospital. She had called the ambulance Saturday night because things were much worse. There was no longer much that could be done because his body was starting to shut down. He and Mom had already decided not to accept dialysis as a treatment option.

At the hospital he rested as comfortably as he could. He was in hospice and had been put on a ventilator. Then, on Thursday, John took Mom in to see him, and I came later in the morning with Jason. Mom stepped out of the room for a break, and I went in to see him. I believe he had hung on waiting for me to arrive. We talked briefly, and then he passed away. I cannot describe the sense of loss that I felt. Our wonderful family unit now had a very big hole in it.

We all believe Jason's presence kept him going much longer than the doctors thought possible. He lived to see Jason print his own name, thanks to Mom, who predicted he would read and write before preschool. Although just four years old when Dad passed away, Jason today has very good memories of Grandpa.

Dad's cause of death was renal failure due to diabetes. Other underlying causes that contributed to his death were congestive heart failure, hypertension, coronary artery disease, and anemia.

It's interesting that Dad died on Sukkot, one of his favorite holidays and a day on which Jewish people are not buried. Jewish tradition states that a deceased person should be buried within twenty-four hours of his or her death. There were already people having funerals on Sunday, so we had to wait until Monday. By the time Monday came, we were all cried out. We went through the motions and eventually picked up our lives where we had left off.

Dad remains with us. I know that he would be so proud of Jason and his many accomplishments. They would have had many topics to discuss, including politics, history, literature, religion, and humor. Things would not have been dull.

15. An Accomplished Woman

My mother was very bright and, over the years, had become an accomplished woman, after spending years in the jewelry business as well as completing many college courses at the University of Pittsburgh. Not long after Dad died, Mom started volunteering more of her time. She was already involved in a new program called Compeer, in which volunteers were matched with persons who had mental health needs. I worked as a rehabilitation counselor at a psychosocial rehabilitation center, in which various groups were conducted to teach living and coping skills to individuals. There were also recreational groups. When the woman who ran our arts and crafts groups retired, Mom came on board as a volunteer. She stepped in and rescued the two groups. The clients deeply appreciated her kindness and her willingness to help out.

Dad's passing left Mom much extra time to devote to volunteer work. She had begun some work at the agency before Dad's death. She volunteered at events for the clients, such as craft classes, cookouts, and Valentine's Day and St. Patrick's Day events. She did a lot of cooking. They always had a big dinner the week before Thanksgiving in which she made turkey dinners for groups of up to seventy people. As a regular at the agency, she was part of the support system that was there for the clients. When Dad was alive, he would come in about once a month. The clients enjoyed his support and involvement also.

Mom also helped out at the local library, and later on at Jason's schools, from preschool up through high school. Jason has fond memories of her bringing in her homemade potato latkes, a Chanukah staple, for his entire class each year when he was in elementary school. Mom would make enough for about seventy-five kids—all the students in Jason's grade. I'd accompany her, and we'd share the story of Chanukah, light the menorah, and teach the kids how to play dreidel. Jason was often one of the only, if not

Mother and daughter celebrate Lee's twenty-first birthday, 1979.

the only, Jewish student in his class, so it was a special, memorable occasion for all the kids. To this day, some of Jason's friends still mention to him their fond memories of "Mrs. Goldman coming in to serve latkes." One year, we were even featured on the local news!

After Dad died, Mom's friendships with others deepened. She had friends in her neighborhood and in our community. The other "moms" at Jason's high school where she volunteered loved her. She socialized with some of the people she met. Most were much younger than she was. She enjoyed being with people who were lively. Kathy was her friend from Compeer. They were close for almost thirty years, the relationship ending only when my mother passed away.

Proud Grandma with Jason at his West Virginia University honors celebration.

Mom was an ongoing, regular part of Jason's life. She worked with him from an early age, ensuring that he could read and write before he entered preschool, and stayed involved through young adulthood. Theirs was a solid, close relationship with much love and mutual respect. They enjoyed kid things and school things, discussed world events and political views and trivia, and explored gardening and Jewish culture and cooking. You name it—they got into it, and she never missed any of Jason's school activities.

For about five years before she died, Mom was sick off and on, but in those final years she had a great attitude and didn't let things get her down or hold her back. She kept on driving until she started having major trouble with her legs. Health problems did not keep her from attending Jason's activities or other family outings. If needed, we used a wheelchair because she wanted to be out with us. In her last years, she

Lee and Mildred, at a scrapbooking workshop, 11/9/11. One of the last photos Lee has of her mother. Courtesy of Linda Joseph.

often used a walker. She lived independently until April 2012, when she had undiagnosed pneumonia, lost her balance, and fell. She was not able to recover from that.

She deteriorated over two months, and passed away on June 25, 2012. She fought hard and was more concerned about John, Jason, and me, always putting us first. That was her nature. This was one of the saddest times in my life. To me, my mom was the best mother in the world. She was also one of my best friends. Besides her closeness with Jason, she considered John her son, not her son-in-law. Her death was a huge loss for us, and I still miss her every day.

16. In My Father's Footsteps

Jason was awarded an opportunity to study in Berlin in the summer of 2015. With Germany on our minds, thirty-six years after they had been recorded, I finally decided to listen to my father's Holocaust cassette tapes. Listening to fifteen hours—of often very tragic narrative—in Dad's voice that had long been silent, and imagining a family I had never known, was a moving experience for me. It had been almost twenty years since I had heard my father's voice. Between my father and Uncle Aron a handful of old photos from before the war had survived. I had often studied

The first archives building we visited in Łódź, where I found my grandfather's birth certificate.

Jason Kikel on Wolborska Street, Łódź, July 2015.

Above, 36 Franciszkańska Street in Łódź, where the clandestine ghetto library was located. My father would risk getting caught sneaking here through back alleys and streets to get books for reading late into the night.

Left, the Polish Archives in Łódź, where we were able to find a number of birth and marriage certificates.

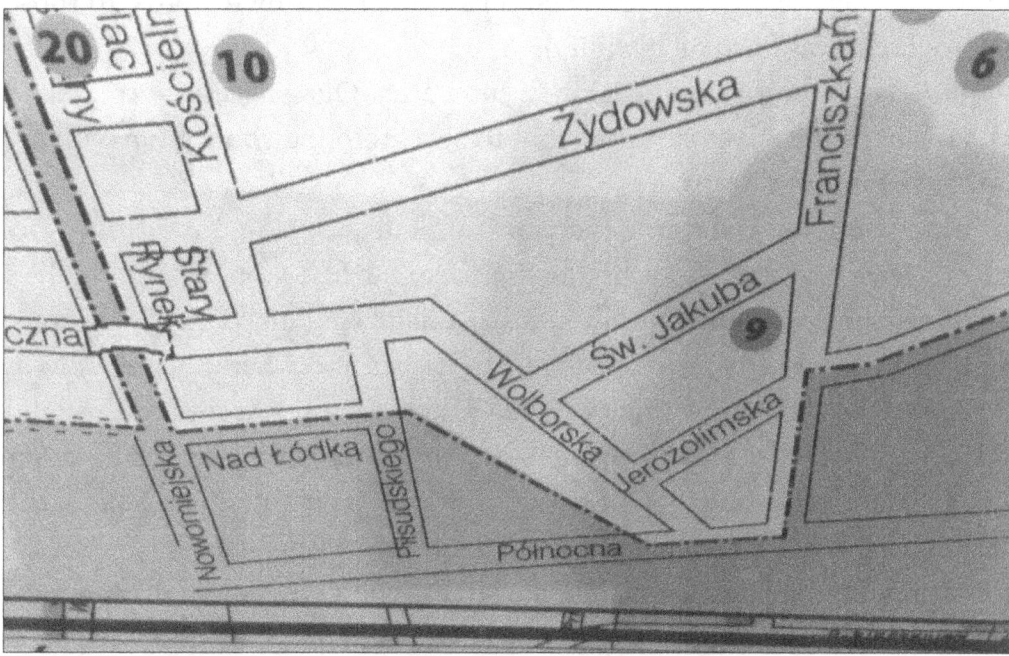

The Goldman home and Chaim's factories were once on Wolborska Street, seen here. This zoomed in photo is from Radegast train station where they had display boards with maps of the Łódź ghetto, shown in the lighter color.

The Kripo, where my grandfather and countless others were tortured by the police.

these. There was a picture of my grandmother and one of Dad with all of his six, younger, siblings. I had these, and a mostly impersonal knowledge of the Holocaust, although Dad had from time to time discussed bits and pieces of his experiences. Now, adding my father's story, in his own words, to those photographs was fresh on my mind.

John, Jason, and I visited Łódź in June 2015. Our pilgrimage to Poland was the beginning of what turned out to be a profound connection with my father and my family's past.

John, Jason, and I flew into Warsaw from Budapest. We drove from Warsaw to Łódź and parked in the town circle. Our first stop was an archives building where we found my grandfather Chaim Goldman's birth certificate and other documents showing Goldman names and where they had lived. Since my dad's maternal relatives, the Ceders, were not from Łódź, we did not do any searches related to them. In the evening, we checked into our hotel and walked along Piotrkowska Street with its many shops. This is the main street in Łódź, and Dad had fond memories of this street.

After dinner, we located Wolborska Street, where the Goldman home and Chaim's factories had once stood. The street was also where the synagogue had stood before the Nazis burned it down at the beginning of their occupation of Łódź. In place of factories, there is now a park, Park Staromiejski,

Radegast train station, now a memorial. Behind the station, there are large, concrete monuments shaped a bit like cemetery headstones, one for each of the six camps where Jews where shipped from this station.

One of the original cattle cars used to transport Jews to the death camps. This car is now a memorial at Auschwitz. A visitor has placed a wreath at its base in remembrance of those it once carried to their deaths.

Memorial stones at Auschwitz, in four different languages, in memory of the fallen victims.

with well-kept trails, flower gardens, and a pond with a fountain. We felt sad standing in the pleasant park, because it somehow magnified the absence of the old buildings and people; whereas before the war, there were over 200,000 Jews in Łódź, today there are only about 5,000. Around the corner we found Franciszkańska 36, the place my father, as a teenager, went in secret at night to borrow books to read, disregarding the Nazis' curfew.

The next day we found the Polish Archives and spent several hours requesting documents. This was a second archival building we visited, also with documentation such as birth certificates and marriage licenses. The experience was difficult with little cooperation, at first, from the archivists. After taking a number and waiting my turn, I had to request someone who spoke English. The ice was finally broken, and I saw some documents. Copies of birth and marriage certificates were sent to me over two months later.

We returned to Franciszkańska Street and took pictures of the building, #36, before entering. Inside it was chilly and dank, and seemed reminiscent of the Cold War, although it was built before World War II. It had lightbulbs without fixtures hanging in the hallways.

Then we strolled around the city. As I reflected on how many family members we lost, I felt very alone. It was strange to be standing in a peaceful, prosperous city that seventy years before had been a center of chaos, fear, and death. We stood outside the Kripo building, the "Red House" as the ghetto inhabitants had called it, where the ghetto police had carried out torture, where my grandfather had been taken and beaten up. Before and after the war it had been the parish house of St. Mary's Assumption Catholic Church. Today, it houses a business. Outside there is a plaque commemorating its use in the war. It was chilling to see that building.

We also found Radegast station, located outside the perimeter of what had been the ghetto. During the war years as many as 200,000 Jews were taken from the ghetto—either transported by wagon or force-marched—to this train station where they were deported to the death camps of Chełmno and Auschwitz. Radegast is now an official place of Holocaust remembrance. Three of the original cattle cars stand with their doors open at the station's platform. At the rear of the station, very large monuments shaped like headstones state the camps where the trains traveled: Auschwitz, Chełmno, Ravensbrück, Gross-Rosen, Sachsenhausen, and Stutthof. Memorial plaques also mention the Jews of Vienna and Luxembourg who came through Łódź on their way to the death camps.

Block 13 at Auschwitz where my dad and Aron were initially assigned. Two or three hundred prisoners were forced in the room, which was originally designed for fifty.

Block 11 at Auschwitz, where my father and Aron were later assigned. Block 11 was typically the last stop for prisoners before being sent to the gas chambers, but my father and two (?) others managed a narrow escape.

At Radegast station, there were recorded lists of people who had been deported. However, there was no mention of our family. The tracking was stopped at some point before my family's deportation in July 1944. Wolborska Street can be seen on ghetto maps, but we found no record of our family's names. I understood this was due to the fact that it was the end of the Łódź ghetto liquidation and things were hurried along. Therefore, less documenting took place. We left Łódź after two and a half days.

We drove to the beautiful city of Kraków and did some sightseeing before visiting Auschwitz the following day, by way of a prearranged bus tour. At the well-known death camp we toured with a small group. No one spoke. Our guide led us through the entrance gate where the famous sign proclaims

"ARBEIT MACHT FREI" (work makes you free). We saw the tracks where the trains came in with their cattle cars filled to capacity with people not knowing what awaited them. And I wondered, again, *How could this have happened?* We saw the unloading platform where Dr. Mengele, and others like him, made their "selections," and I of course tried to imagine my family going through that process, being separated from each other for the last time, astonished at the long odds of two of them surviving. We continued on down streets lined with the old barracks. In one building the guide showed us a large room with holes in the wooden floor that were used as toilets, describing to us the indignities and lack of privacy.

Moving on, we came to a room that displayed the old suitcases in which prisoners had hopefully carried their few possessions, with identifying names still visible on them, and the many belongings—pots and pans, clothing, housewares, eyeglasses, and other personal items. There was a case full of shoes; they take up half a barracks room—over 40,000 shoes, we were told. One room that made me particularly sad held display cases full of human hair. At that moment, it would have been impossible not to imagine the hundreds of thousands of fearful women being forced through this terrible process—unceremoniously having their heads shaved. I thought of the photo of my beautiful grandmother Bajla. How carefree and full of life she had been. Her life had ended here at only forty-four years of age, much younger than I was at the time of our trip to Poland. I tried to imagine how degraded and scared all those people must have felt not understanding what was happening to them, and especially, I wondered, *Why?*

Equally upsetting to me and my family, was that despite this room having a prominently displayed "no photos" sign, many people had their cameras out snapping away, disrespecting the people who had suffered there. By the time we came back outside to continue the tour, I felt completely numb. I remember that the weather was warm and sunny, and there were a few clouds in the sky, a normal summer day. But I had been transported back to times so unimaginable that I must have been overwhelmed, and I simply felt numb. At the same time, I was also very concerned about how John and Jason were handling the tour.

There were occasional breaks during which we all had the opportunity to reflect quietly on what had happened at this concentration camp. We walked around outside and saw the remains of the gas chambers and crematoriums.

There were informal memorials for all of the people who were murdered in Auschwitz as well as, presumably, for particular individuals and families. They were the flowers and candles that visitors brought and left here and there—on the ground, on ledges, everywhere. People suffered and were beaten on every inch of that property. The small, personal memorials were randomly placed because a prisoner could have suffered, struggled, or died anywhere.

As difficult as it was for me to tour this camp, I felt that I had a better understanding of what my father and our relatives had suffered, but I also realized there were memories my father had that he could never put into words and that would have never been erased from his mind.

Of course, my father wanted his story to be told. During his life he was focused on survival, first for himself and later for his family. After his many hours recording his story, he had put his project on the back burner, perhaps not knowing how to go about getting his story out there. But now, at this time in my life, I was able do this for him. There are so few remaining survivors. As many personal stories as possible need to be put forth. Preserved, safeguarded, and shared. It's all part of educating the world, keeping the memory alive, and ensuring that something like the Holocaust never happens again. I think of my family and all those who perished in the Holocaust every day.

Epilogue

The process of writing this book has led me in many directions. Some, like traveling to Poland and seeing where my ancestors lived, worked, and were murdered, have not been easy, but honoring my father's life and his wish to have his story remembered meant exploring every possible path. The process has also taught me that no story ever really ends. Two recent developments have kept the tragedy and joy of this book alive for me.

On October 27, 2018, I was reviewing my father's last chapter in Part I on our computer. I got an alert on my phone from *Haaretz*, an Israeli newspaper, saying there was a security incident at a US synagogue. It turned out to be a shooting at a synagogue in Pittsburgh's Squirrel Hill neighborhood, my childhood home. My son, Jason, was out of town and I immediately contacted him. He had the news on at his hotel and told me to turn on the TV. John and I were devastated when we found out a massacre had occurred at the Tree of Life synagogue. I thought back to many memories at Tree of Life throughout my life: as a student at Sunday school there, Jason attending story time as a child, my family briefly attending services there, and Rabbi Alvin Berkun officiating my father's funeral. Now, we pass by the synagogue each time we visit Squirrel Hill. I wondered, *How could this happen so close to home? Why is there so much hate and violence in this world?* It takes the same energy to do your best and be kind and respectful of others as it does to hate and spread bigotry.

Many of the Tree of Life shooting victims lived, worked, and shopped in Squirrel Hill. My father noted in his own story, "we are commanded to remember," and I know my father and mother would want us to keep alive the memories of the victims:

Joyce Fienberg	Bernice Simon
Richard Gottfried	Sylvan Simon
Rose Mallinger	Daniel Stein
Jerry Rabinowitz	Melvin Wax
Cecil Rosenthal	Irving Younger
David Rosenthal	

—

My joyful development occurred while I was working on my family tree. I had been working on it for many years, slowly—due to lack of information, a language barrier, and the incredible amount of time needed to gain every little piece of information. Don't give up when trying to put together a family tree. At some point, it can become very rewarding. You might even receive a surprise or some information that is totally astonishing, which is what happened to me, and will continue to happen, I expect. I have now found cousins living in Sweden, Israel, Illinois, Nebraska, Ohio, and New York.

As I resumed my search again, I received information, from a genealogical site, on my grandmother, Balcia Maria Ceder Goldman, and her family. I started checking names on a worldwide site, and I put this information together with an old family tree my parents had received from an Israeli cousin in 1966, as well as with archival records from the Jewish Historical Institute in Warsaw. Eventually, I found cousins I never knew about! I did further research to verify my findings, and I reached out to them. John, Jason, and I were all very excited to find some of my father's relatives who had survived the Holocaust. Our cousins were equally excited to learn of us.

A few weeks after the Tree of Life shooting, John and I met up with Jason in Amsterdam. During this trip we were able to meet two of our Swedish-born cousins. We met Lili and her husband in Amsterdam. Then, we flew to Gothenburg, Sweden, to meet Fanny and her husband. It was wonderful to spend time discussing our families, exploring museums, and celebrating Shabbat with family. With the help of my family tree, we were able to put together some more information about our extended families. We learned that their grandfather and their fathers arrived in Sweden on the White Buses, which was part of a World War II operation by the Swedish Red Cross and the Danish government. I am sad that my father did not live to learn about his cousins' survival, lives, and families in Scandinavia. We now have regular contact via email and Skype.

Many Jewish people we met in Europe on that trip felt terrible about the recent shooting at home, and they wanted to speak with us at length. So many synagogues all over the world have security constantly; sadly, it is second nature to some Jewish communities. What a shame it is when you need protection as you worship and reflect.

—

My father went through unimaginable horrors and was not bitter toward his fellow human beings. He was tolerant, accepting of others, and he treated people the way he wanted to be treated. If he could live like that after all he experienced, others can, too. His life reminds us that besides being "commanded to remember," we are "forbidden to despair."

Editor's Note

It has been a joy to help bring *Perseverance: One Holocaust Survivor's Journey from Poland to America* to the public, and a special joy to work closely with co-author Lee Kikel. Not only was she passionate and committed, but also, as she and I liked to say, she "did her homework assignments." Expertly, and with enthusiasm! And, the assignments were many. The unusual nature of this book has called for an extraordinary effort, both in the number of different tasks and the sheer hours entailed.

One arduous requirement was rendering Mr. Goldman's audiotaped memories into the most accurate possible written form. Lee brought us draft printouts, totaling nearly two hundred pages, but perfectly transcribing Mr. Goldman's words proved impossible. His English was excellent after nearly thirty years in America, but his narration and word choices were influenced by his multilingual upbringing and experiences in Europe during and after the war. At times the transcriptionist could do no more than write "sounds like . . ." for a word or phrase that was unintelligible, and presumably in Yiddish, Polish, German, or perhaps even Hebrew or English. Also, the audio quality of the tapes was sometimes uneven.

Thanks to Lee's efforts at cleaning up the drafts' muffled, unintelligible, and otherwise unknown words, Mr. Goldman's own words are preserved as faithfully as possible in Part I. Accordingly, non-English words and turns of phrase have been retained, and when possible, many of these are presented along with a bracketed translation or explanation. A few words and phrases stumped us; they are followed by "[?]," upon, at least, their first mention. We hope that Mr. Goldman comes across here as the conversationalist he was: intelligent, engaging, and articulate, with a way of speaking that reflected his extraordinary past.

Like her father, Lee has saved and treasured her family's documents—letters, postcards, photographs, official records, and more—and a select group of these provide an important part of this book. Lee says, "The most difficult part of the project was the translations. Notes, descriptions, and captions were in languages other than English. I had to contend with Yiddish, Polish, and German. I translated much of the German with the help of my son, Jason. I am thankful to have had wonderful help from experts to translate most everything. This was a very tedious process; because I could not send original photos and postcards through the mail, I photographed and scanned material, numbered everything to keep it organized, and sent the copies to translators."

All this effort led to quite a few happy moments along the way. Lee recalls that one of these grew out of her work with the family's photographs and postcards. "The end result is two albums, one with all my father's photographs and one with all of his postcards. Stories within a story. My father had wonderful friends who wrote very endearing notes to him. These were one more testimony to his great character, and something tangible that I will always cherish."

Another special challenge in editing and assembling this book was accuracy and consistency. Mr. Goldman recorded his story during pauses in his workday as a jeweler and designer. He spoke from the heart—sometimes, perhaps, without being able to collect and organize his words ahead of time. Surely, too, he was interrupted on occasion. As a result, his memories were not told in a strictly chronological, organized sequence. These tapes, though, are the largest collection of Mr. Goldman's memories, and it is on the tapes that he expresses his desire that his story be preserved in book form, so their content—arranged chronologically—has been the primary source for Part I. The taped information was supplemented, minimally, by the written testimony Mr. Goldman later presented to the US Holocaust Memorial Museum, and some of his other saved documents.

Even the best recollections can be imperfect. Understandably, there was some conflicting information among the sources. As such, assembling the wealth of divergent material into this book, especially Part I, has required some editorial decisions. The account presented here is as complete and accurate as many hours of careful, skilled, and loving attention could make it.

—

Everyone at Populore Publishing Company has been deeply touched by *Perseverance: One Holocaust Survivor's Journey from Poland to America*. We will continue to carry it in our hearts, and to be grateful for the opportunity to be part of this important work.

Rae Jean Sielen
Summer 2019

Appendices

The War in Europe, Poland, and Łódź

In the 1920s and 1930s anti-Semitism in Europe was growing, and it further intensified in Germany with the rise of Adolf Hitler. That nation had already been devastated by World War I, from 1914–1918. Not only had military campaigns damaged industry and infrastructure, but Germany had been ordered to pay reparations to the victors. Jews became a convenient scapegoat. Hitler became chancellor in 1933, popular with the German people because he put them back to work.

In defiance of the Treaty of Versailles, Hitler began developing and mobilizing a military organization that was second to none. Industrial centers and a network of roads and highways were also built. With the aid of his right-wing National Socialist German Workers' Party (Nazi Party) and the strong military, he ended democracy, was declared der Führer (the leader) of the Third Reich, and began an aggressive campaign of European expansion and conquest. The Nazis also wanted to bring about defeat of the Soviets to ensure German hegemony and to get rid of Jews and other undesirables in order to establish a pure Germanic, "master" race of people—"Aryans." In 1938, Germany annexed Austria, an action followed shortly by the occupation and conquest of Czechoslovakia. Then Hitler looked toward Poland.

In 1795, Poland had been partitioned among Germany, Austria, and Prussia, and had ceased to exist as a nation. In June 1919, the Treaty of Versailles, which reorganized Europe after World War I, forced the three occupying nations to give up much of their annexed territory, and Poland was reconstituted. The new nation, known as the Second Polish Republic, was tragically unfit for survival in the stormy climate of interbellum Europe. The war had devastated much of the physical infrastructure. German companies continued to control large portions of the few industries that still functioned. Particularly challenging was the political unrest among several large minorities—including Germans, Ukrainians, Belarusians, and Jews—who did not feel themselves part of the new country. To the east and west were the Soviet Union and Germany, the successors to Russia and Prussia, both still coveting the land they had ceded in 1918.

Germany invaded Poland from the west on September 1, 1939, marking the official beginning of World War II. The Soviet Union saw an opportunity and invaded from the east, sixteen days later. On September 28, Warsaw fell, and Poland once again effectively disappeared into chaos. The country had survived for slightly more than twenty years.

Łódź, in central Poland, was one of the largest Polish cities. It is where Mieczyslaw Goldman was born and where he was living with his family when the Nazis invaded. The city had grown rapidly at the turn of the century and again after 1918. A multicultural and industrial center of textiles and metal manufacturing, according to the 1931 census, it had a diverse population of approximately 604,000. Of these, fifty-nine percent were Poles, thirty-two percent were Jews, and nine percent were Germans. By the time of the German invasion, the Jewish population had swelled to over 200,000, many of whom were involved in industry.

Mieczyslaw was sixteen years old when the Germans came in. He remembered prewar Łódź as a beautiful city. He and his family lived in a Jewish neighborhood, which had Jewish bakeries, kosher poultry and butcher shops, and fish markets. There were numerous synagogues, and life was good. That changed on September 8, 1939, when the German unified armed forces (the Wehrmacht) invaded and took over the city, renaming it Litzmannstadt after Karl Litzmann, a German general who had won a significant military campaign in the area during World War I.

Almost immediately, the Nazis began putting restrictions on the Jewish population. Jews were only allowed to withdraw small amounts from their bank accounts. They were forced to sign their businesses over to the Germans. Piotrkowska Street, the city's main avenue, was off-limits to Jews. In 1940, a ghetto would be established in order to completely segregate, restrict, and relocate Jews.

Anti-Jewish measures, meant to inflict terror, increased. Many intellectuals were killed in a nearby forest; others were hanged in the street. In November 1939, the Germans blasted the Kościuszko Monument honoring national hero Tadeusz Kościuszko. And, they torched numerous synagogues throughout the city, including the principal Orthodox synagogue, the oldest in the city, know as the Altshtot (old city) or Stara (old) synagogue. This was on Wolborska Street, not far from Mieczyslaw's house.

On November 14, 1939, a decree was announced for Łódź, imposing a curfew and requiring all Jews to wear a cloth badge with the Star of David.

Anyone who failed to do so could be put to death. This was the first order of its kind, and other localities would soon impose their own versions of laws requiring identification and curfews for Jews. Eventually, on October 1, 1941, Reinhard Heydrich would extend this rule and decree that all Jews in the Third Reich above the age of six were to wear a badge with the Star of David.

Then, wooden and wire fences were erected around the ghetto, and in February 1940, the Nazis began resettling Jews into the ghetto. They were forced from their homes and into substandard housing in the Old City. What businesses they still controlled were seized, along with the rest of their valuables, and many Jews were shot or tortured. The ghetto area was sealed on April 30, 1940. Anyone trying to get in or out would be shot.

Łódź ghetto was the second largest in all of German-occupied Europe, after Warsaw ghetto. Łódź was a valuable asset to the Nazis, and because of the goods produced in the ghetto's factories and other industries, it was the last major ghetto to be liquidated. It housed around 150,000 Jews from around the Łódź area, fewer than the Jewish population in 1939, because about twenty-five percent were able to flee Łódź before the ghetto was established. Over time, the population would shift as more people—mostly Jews, but also some Romani people—were brought in from the rest of German-occupied Europe, while some others were deported to concentration camps.

Unlike other ghettos in Poland in which food and goods could be smuggled in from the outside world, the Łódź ghetto was so tightly secured that the inhabitants were totally dependent on German authorities for all of their needs, including food and medicine. There was a special currency, *ersatz* (substitute), as well. Many people traded their remaining belongings for the ghetto currency, thus losing everything they had. Food was rationed in very small quantities, providing a subsistence diet of barely enough nutrition to keep people able to work. Many residents suffered severe malnutrition or died of starvation. The ghetto was kept isolated from all of Europe. In addition to keeping people in or out of the ghetto, the tight security measures prevented information to flow across the fence.

The Nazis had a "perfectly designed" system in the ghetto. Hans Biebow was the head of the Nazi ghetto administration. A Jewish Council of Elders, the Judenrat, was established—imposed—to oversee the daily operations. Chief Elder Chaim Rumkowski had been head of a Jewish orphanage from

1925 to 1939 where some said his work was more self-serving than charitable. As head of the Judenrat, he was a controversial person because of the power he held. He reported directly to Biebow, who had given him full power to organize the ghetto to maintain order, confiscate Jewish assets and property, and coerce labor.

Rumkowski had proposed the ersatz, believing it would dissuade smugglers. He also created many departments and institutions to deal with the ghetto's internal affairs, all of them headed and operated by the Jewish population. This included housing for tens of thousands of people, food distribution, maintaining seven hospitals, five clinics, seven pharmacies, a sanitation corps, and the right to confiscate businesses and property that were still owned by Jews in the ghetto. The police, known as the Kriminalpolizei, or Kripo, and firemen were made up of Jews. The education system in the ghetto was the most advanced of any ghetto, with forty-seven schools. Inhabitants not assigned to any of these jobs worked in the many factories.

Many people were bothered that Rumkowski got involved in religious life. The Germans had disbanded the rabbinate in 1942, and Rumkowski took on religious duties, such as performing wedding ceremonies. It was said that he treated the Jews in the ghetto like personal belongings. At times, he would beat them. When he spoke, he was rude and arrogant. He helped transform the ghetto into an industrial base where supplies were made for the Wehrmacht. He and others mistakenly believed that the ghetto's productivity was the key to Jewish survival beyond the Holocaust. Forced labor became a way of life.

A preview of the coming deportations came in July 1941, when most patients in the ghetto's psychiatric hospital were drugged and taken away, never to be seen again. Chełmno, the first camp built by Nazis specifically for the purpose of extermination, began its gassing operations in December. Two weeks later, Nazi authorities announced that 20,000 Jews would be deported to undisclosed camps. By the end of January 1942, 10,000 Jews from Łódź were deported to Chełmno. Regular successive deportations continued through fall 1942, totaling 72,000 victims in this first wave of deportations.

Anyone not fit for work, such as children and the elderly, were to follow. The Judenrat, under the guidance of Rumkowski, made the selections. He gave a speech, "Give Me Your Children," when the Germans forced him to comply with the deportation of 20,000 children and elderly, who were sent to Chełmno. Other waves would follow until the end of the war.

Chaim Rumkowski was deported with his family on the last transport to Auschwitz. There are conflicting reports, but witnesses at the Frankfurt Auschwitz trials later testified that Rumkowski was beaten to death by the Sonderkommando inmates (those in forced labor units responsible for disposing the bodies of gassing victims) who sought revenge for his role in the selections and roundups. Or, they may have been acting on behalf of other Jews from Łódź who sought vengeance. His family was gassed with thousands of others.

Beginning August 1, 1944, underground Polish resistance fighters tried to liberate what remained of Warsaw from German occupation in what became known as the Warsaw Uprising, distinct from the Warsaw Ghetto Uprising of spring 1943. The Germans crushed the movement and intensified the liquidation of the ghettos. 25,000 Jews from Łódź were sent to Chełmno and killed, and nearly all the rest were sent to Auschwitz-Birkenau. Only a few were left behind to help clean up the ghetto. When Soviet forces entered Łódź on January 19, 1945, only 877 survivors remained, 12 of them children. Before World War II, the Jews of Łódź numbered around 233,000. Approximately 10,000 survived the Holocaust elsewhere. Among them was Mieczyslaw Goldman.

Notes

– – – –

This section is devoted to recalling Melvin Goldman's ancestors and presenting parts of his family tree. This information is included for two reasons. First, some readers may want to look here for context, as they encounter some of the names in this book. Also, Melvin's parents fervently wished that, in his words, "their family cling together, remain together." It seems fitting to present this tragically scant homage to that wish.

Genealogical information for the Goldmans and Ceders continues to grow, as new connections and discoveries are made. However, comprehensive, to-date details for all branches are not provided in this Family Trees appendix. The family trees chosen for inclusion are only those that directly relate to Melvin's story. In them can be found dates and places, when known, for birth, marriages, and death.

—

Melvin believed that, after the war, "only two souls [himself and brother Aron] were alive from the whole family except the ones that were overseas." The fact that Melvin and Lee reached out to these few relatives highlights their sense of loss, that this large and close-knit family had been nearly all murdered during the war.

Sadly, Melvin Goldman's assessment of his family's losses seems to be correct. Lee tried to confirm the fate of Melvin's parents and siblings, and found it true that nearly all had been murdered at Auschwitz. Melvin's younger sister, who would be Lee's aunt Rojza, had been transferred from Auschwitz to Camp Stutthof, on the Baltic Sea. Lee was unable to learn anything further, but always has had some hope that she was able to survive. Even among Nazi concentration and death camps, Stutthof was a horrifying place, with typhus epidemics, the gas chamber, and a slaughter of prisoners even as Soviet forces closed in to liberate the camp.

As Melvin had supposed, the remaining shreds of his large family were to be found among those who had left Poland before the country's fall in 1939. Joel Goldman, the brother of Melvin's father, had gone to Palestine before the war. As recalled in this book, Melvin's father rejected the idea of joining Joel, because life in Poland was going well. After the war, Melvin might have considered joining Joel in the new state of Israel. Joel married in Israel, and had a daughter named Rosy. After Joel passed away, Melvin kept up correspondence with Rosy for a time. Rosy has two sons, and Jason, Lee's son, intends to try to find them.

Before the war, one of Melvin's aunts on his mother's side, Chaja Sura Ceder Ekman, and her husband, Chaim Ekman, had emigrated to Argentina. There they had a son, Mario Ekman, and a daughter. Melvin says that he considered the possibility of joining them after the war. Melvin later kept in touch with them, and exchanged letters and photographs. There is a good chance Chaja Sura was the source of the photograph at the beginning of Chapter 1 in Part I.

Sarah Ceder is the cousin with whom Melvin had a chance encounter in Austria, a couple of years before he came to America. Sarah had eventually moved to Israel, and the two kept in touch through the decades. After Melvin's death, his daughter, Lee, continued the correspondence until Sarah died in 2000. In 2014, Lee, John, and Jason were able to meet Sarah's daughters—Ada, Dina, and Elisheva—while traveling in Israel. The three women didn't know much about the Ceder family, but from Sarah's family tree the relationship was clear, which strengthened the connection to this branch.

Sarah's father, Abram, was a first cousin of Melvin's mother, Bajla Maria Ceder Goldman. Part I includes Melvin's recollections of Sarah's father leaving Łódź for Palestine before the war, and then returning for his wife and kids. However, the story might be more involved and difficult, as this confusing excerpt—excluded from Part I—from Melvin's tapes suggests: "There was a Ceder cousin of my mother's that left. The only survivors was a girl, a boy and a girl. And right after the war started, and this is two months in the ghetto, they used to live on Lagiewnicka Street. My dad used to send me down there to do some odd jobs for her [the mother left behind?] in order that they could survive and make a living, that they don't lose the customers. And, I did it for them. And later on, I met that girl when I went on my trips, to Austria . . ."

Melvin's Immediate Family

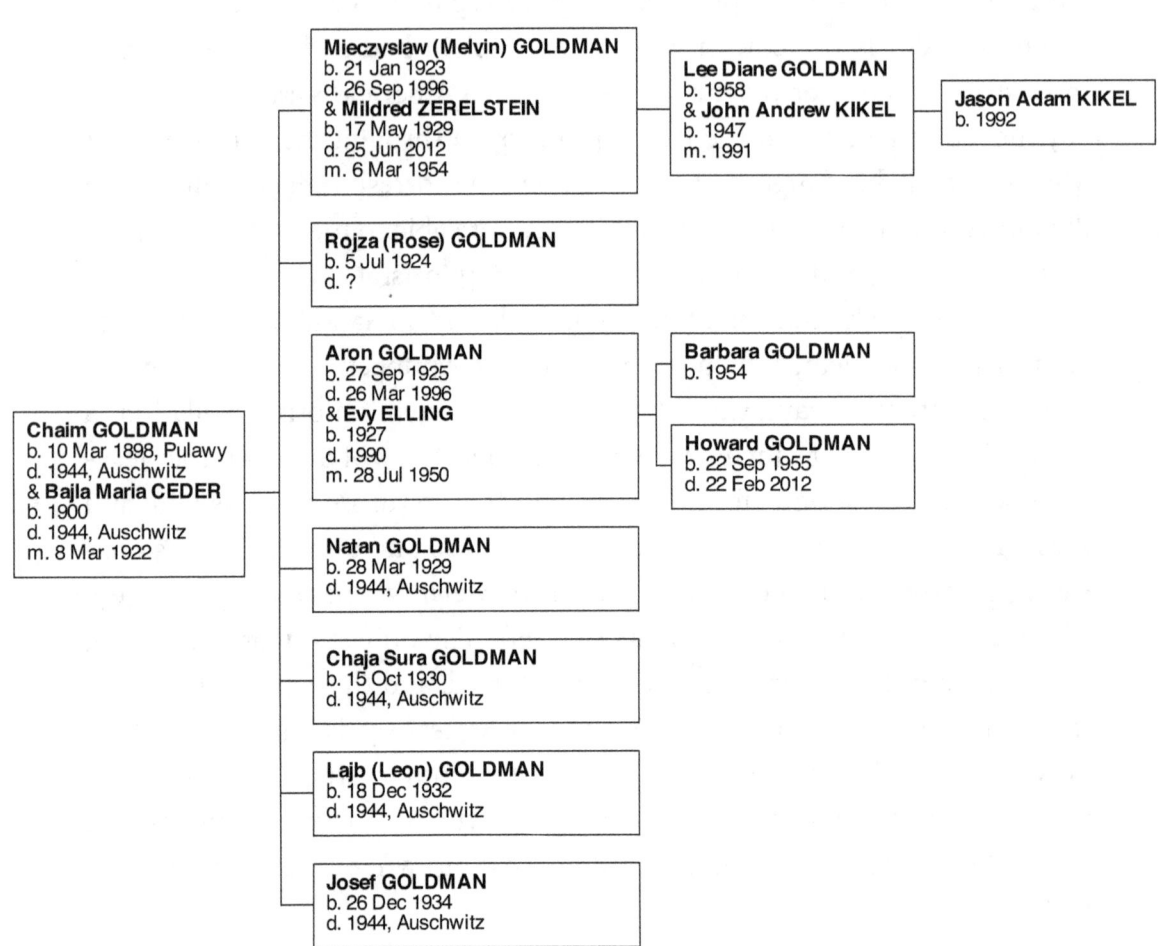

Melvin's Paternal Ancestors

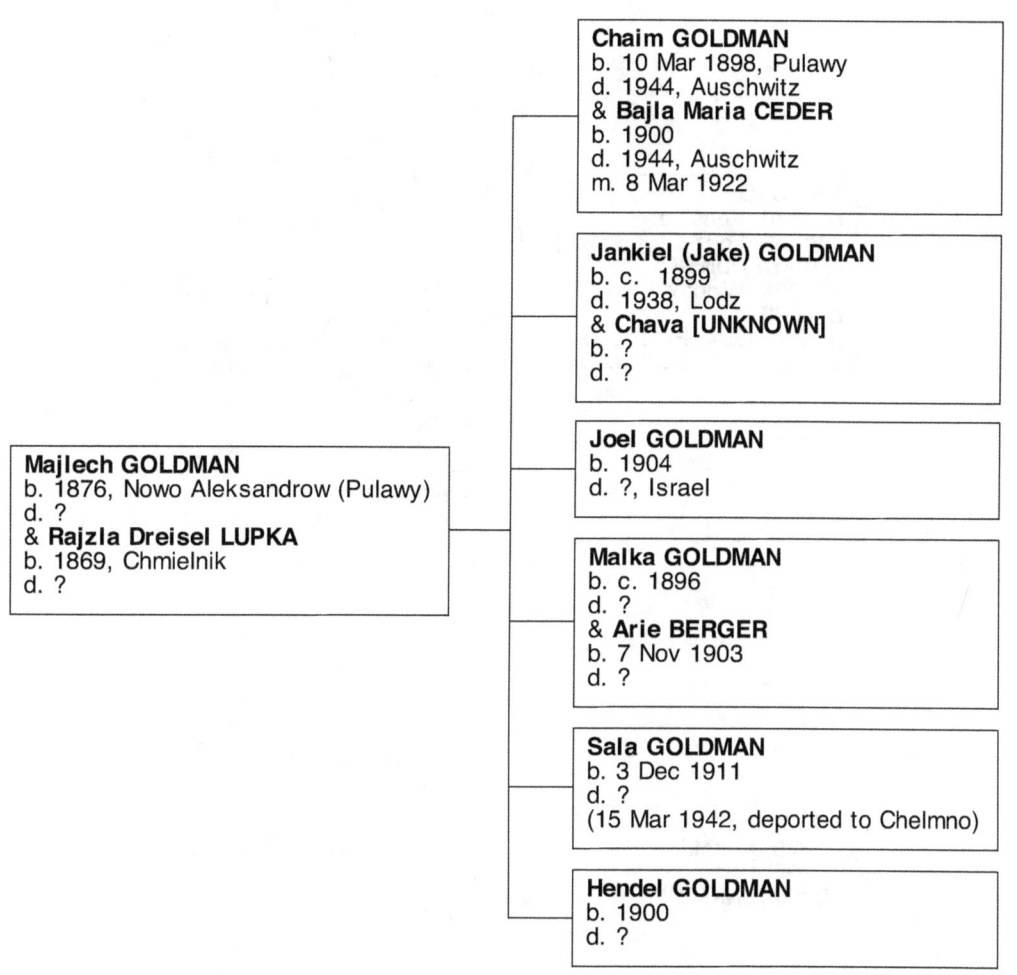

Melvin's Maternal Ancestors

- - - - -

Icek CEDER
b. 1870, Konskie
d. 1936, Lodz
& **Rojza DUNSKA**
b. 1866, Widoma
d. 1909
m. Dec 1894, Przedborz

- **Bajla Maria CEDER**
  b. 1900
  d. 1944, Auschwitz
  & **Chaim GOLDMAN**
  b. 10 Mar 1898, Pulawy
  d. 1944, Auschwitz
  m. 8 Mar 1922

- **Ruchla (Rachel) CEDER**
  b. 1900
  d. ? , Lodz
  & [Unknown] BERGER

- **Chaja (Celia) Sura CEDER**
  b. 10 Nov 1901
  d. 18 Sep 1981, Argentina
  & **Chaim David EKMAN**
  b. 1900
  d. 1987

- **Dawid Josef CEDER**
  b. 1896, Przedborz
  d. ?

Icek CEDER
b. 1870, Konskie
d. 1936, Lodz
& **Dyny [UNKNOWN]**
b. ?
d. ?
m. ?

- **Jankiel CEDER**
  b. 1916 [?]
  d. ?

- **Gitla CEDER**
  b. 1917
  d. ?

- **Abram Mortka CEDER**
  b. 1919
  d. ?

Łódź Ghetto

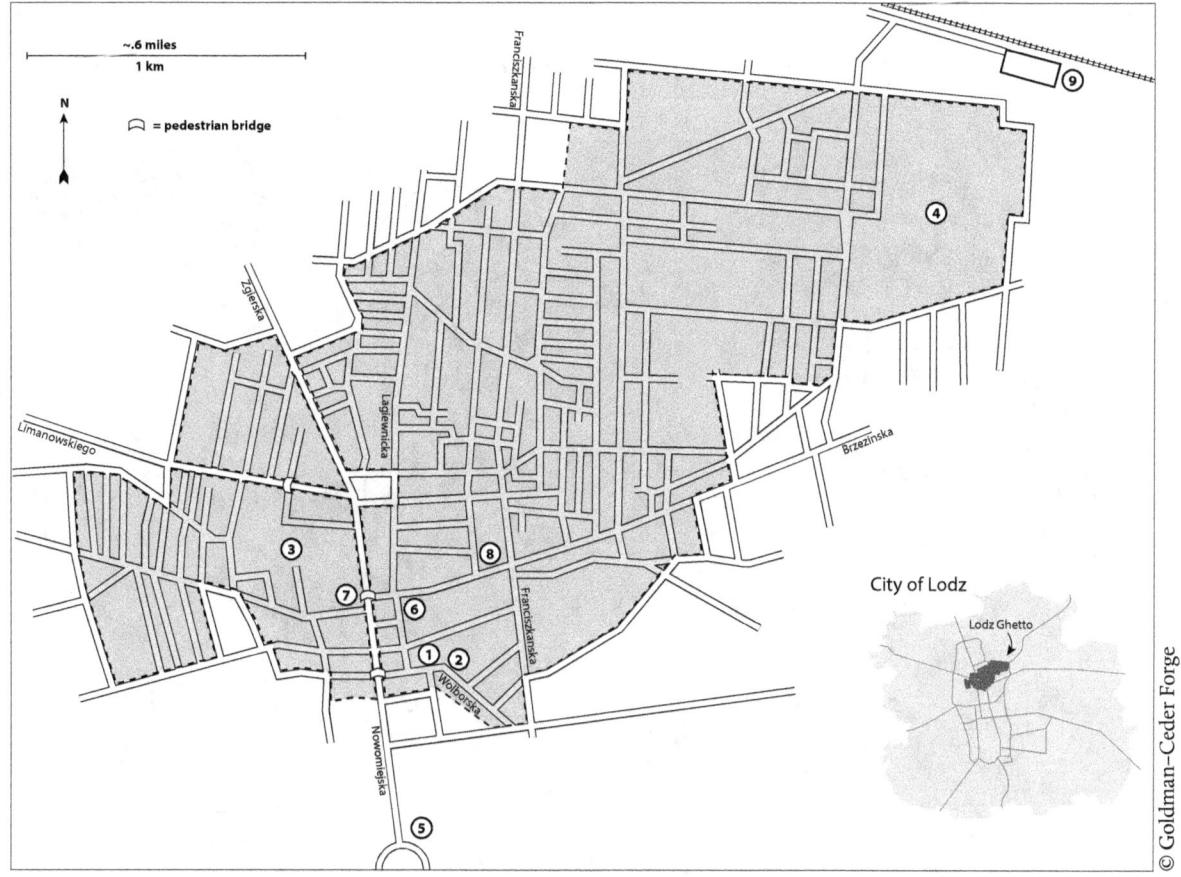

1. The Goldman residence and business. The warehouse was located at 31 Wolborska, and the factory at 33. The Goldmans lived in an apartment adjoining the factory. Chaim also co-owned a warehouse at 2 Cegielniana, 15 km (almost 10 miles) to the south.
2. The Altshtot (old city) or Stara (old) Orthodox synagogue, 20 Wolborska, destroyed November 1939.
3. Old Jewish cemetery.
4. Jewish cemetery. After the ghetto was formed, the southern end of the cemetery was used for mass burials of those who died in the ghetto.
5. Plac Wolności (Freedom Square), which contained the Kościuszko Monument, destroyed November 1939.
6. Kripo headquarters.
7. Jewish police headquarters.
8. 36 Franciszkańska, the "library."
9. Radegast train station.

Notes: In the early 1930s, the population of the city of Łódź was about 600,000. After the ghetto was established, more than 150,000 people were forced into a mere 4 square km (1.5 square miles) of the city. Ghetto maps may be found online showing other key locations such as markets, trolley lines, squares, hospitals, schools, factories, guardhouses, deportation assembly points, sites of public executions, and the children's and gypsy camps.

Melvin's Journeys in Postwar Germany

© Goldman–Ceder Forge

1. Melvin was liberated from Wöbbelin, and then transferred to Schwerin, just north of the death camp.
2. He was then sent west, ultimately to Geesthacht, near Hamburg, stopping at Schwarzenbek on the way.
3. From there, Melvin headed south to Munich, in the American Zone. While in this area, he stayed at Gauting Sanatorium and a hospital in Schwabing.
4. Next, he was transferred to Bad Wörishofen, where he stayed at Sonnenhof, a chronic hospital, and Kneippianum Sanatorium.
5. For continued recovery, Melvin went to Bad Reichenhall, where he stayed at Bayerisch-Gmain Rehabilitation Center.
6. Melvin spent about seven weeks in Bad Saulgau, where he received training for living independently.
7. Finally, Melvin headed to Bremerhaven by way of Wildflecken, where he stayed for a few weeks while waiting to leave Europe for America.

Note: The concentration camps where Melvin was interned are named and indicated with a triangle. This map depicts Allied-occupied Germany, 1945–1949.

Squirrel Hill, Pittsburgh

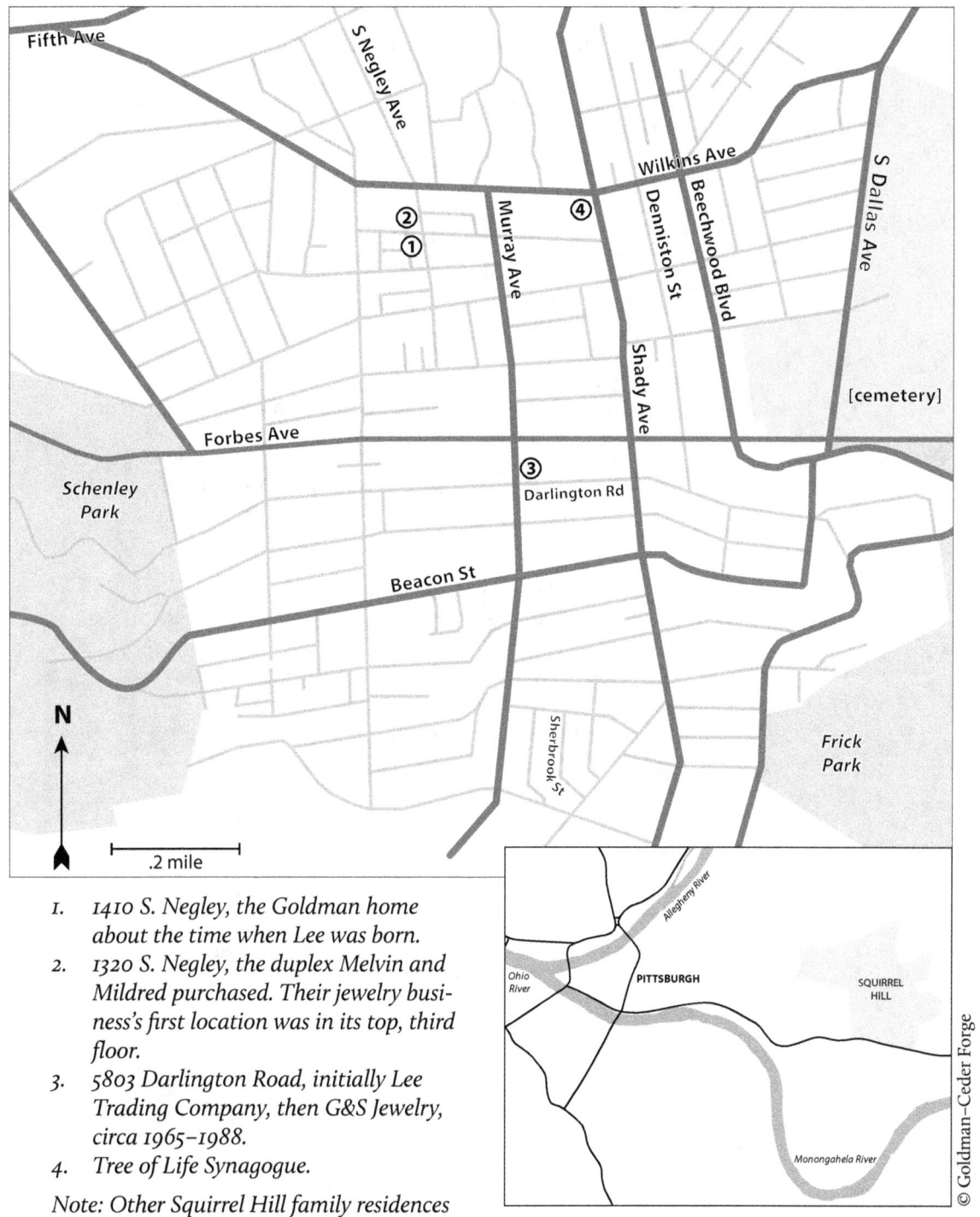

1. 1410 S. Negley, the Goldman home about the time when Lee was born.
2. 1320 S. Negley, the duplex Melvin and Mildred purchased. Their jewelry business's first location was in its top, third floor.
3. 5803 Darlington Road, initially Lee Trading Company, then G&S Jewelry, circa 1965–1988.
4. Tree of Life Synagogue.

Note: Other Squirrel Hill family residences were on Denniston, Sherbrook, and Beacon. Early in Melvin's marriage, he and Mildred briefly lived on Bayard Street in the Oakland neighborhood to the east of Squirrel Hill.

Melvin's Timeline (1923–1996)

January 21, 1923	Melvin's birth
~1935	Begins working at family factory
1936	Bar mitzvah, age 13
1939	Germany invades Poland
1940	Łódź becomes a ghetto
1944–1945	Sent to camps
1945–1950	Liberated, then in hospitals and rehab
1950	Arrives in United States, age 27
1954	Marries Mildred
1956	Becomes US citizen
1958	Daughter Lee born
1961–1988	Operates jewelry business
1960s	Starts claim applications
late 1970s	Records audiotapes, age ~55
May 11, 1991	Lee and John marry
1992	Grandson Jason born
1994	Writes USHMM testimony
September 26, 1996	Death, age 73

Melvin's Family, 1898–1939

Chaim Goldman's birth certificate, located in the archives in Łódź, Poland, and found by Lee on the family's trip to Poland in 2015.

(Melvin's Family, 1898–1939, continued)

Bajla Maria Ceder, middle, with her sisters Chaja Sura and Ruchla, circa 1920.

Ruchla Ceder, circa 1920.

(Melvin's Family, 1898–1939, continued)

Family members: Melvin's aunt Chaja Sura Ekman, Melvin's uncles, and Melvin's grandfather pictured on the right, circa 1920. Melvin's cousin Mario Ekman sent this photo to Melvin from Argentina in the 1980s with notes as shown.

(Melvin's Family, 1898–1939, continued)

Copy of marriage certificate of Chaim Goldman and Bajla Maria Ceder, married March 8, 1922. The copy, including an English translation (opposite), was issued by the Director of Register Office in Łódź in July 2015.

(Melvin's Family, 1898–1939, continued)

352

The event took place in the city of Łódź, on the 8th of April 1922, at 1 in the afternoon. The following were the witnesses: Zelman Ajzenberg, shoemaker, 49 years old and Icek Jakub Rotsztajn, weaver, 30 years old; both residing in Łódź. They have stated that on 8th of March of this year in Łódź at 7 in the evening: Chaim Goldmnan, bachelor, tinsmith, 23 years old, born and resising in Łódź, of Jewish faith, permanent resident of the city of Puławy, son of Majlech and Rajzla Goldman and Miss Bajla Maria Ceder, 22 years old, born and residing in Końskie, ofJewish faith, a permanent resident of Końskie, a daughter of Icek and Rojza Ceder got married.

The marriage was predated by three announcements at a local syngagogue on the following days: the eleventh, eighteenth and twenty fifth of February as well as at the Końskie synagogue on the twenty first, twenty eighth of January and the forth of February of the current year.

The religious wedding was given by the member of the local rabbinate Mojsze Dawid Dąb.

The newlyweds have not made any prenup agreement. The bride has enclosed the authorization of the Końskie rabbi for the religious marriage in Łódź. The bride is illiterate.

The certificate has been read, accepted and signed.

Register Office Clerk /signature/

Father /signature/   Witnesses / signatures/

The column on the right side:

No. 352

The Office of the City of Łódź

Dept. of Services and Administration

Register Office Pilsudski Avenue 100 /Postal code/ 92-326 Łódź

Seal: I do confirm the agreement of this copy with the original document of the birth certificate

IV-352/45/1923.

The copy was issued due to family genealogy. Seal: The copy has no power of the official document. Łódź, 8th of July, 2015. /signature/

The fee of 5 zloty was paid. On behalf of Director of Register Office - Inspector, Ms. Anita Pazura

(Melvin's Family, 1898–1939, continued)

In the 1980s, cousin Mario Ekman sent Melvin a bar of Miracle brand soap, and included this story in a letter: When Chaim Goldman, Melvin's father, went to Varsovie (Warsaw) for military service, Chaja Sura Ceder, Chaim's future sister-in-law, provided him with food. In appreciation, he gave her this bar of soap, which she kept for many years. Mario sent it to Melvin because it was something Melvin's father had purchased and held in his hands. The soap is now over one hundred years old, and the company is still in business.

Copy of birth certificate of Mordka Goldman, born January 21, 1923. This copy, including an English translation, was issued by the Director of Register Office in Łódź in July 2015. The certificate lists his name as Mordka, his given, Yiddish name, which he probably would have gone by at home, and with Jewish friends and groups. The Polish name Mieczyslaw or its diminutive, "Mietek," appear on various documents. Perhaps it would have been used in other, more public settings.

(Melvin's Family, 1898–1939, continued)

Mieczyslaw Goldman in sixth grade. When Aron returned to Łódź after the war, he found this photo in the chimney of the family's home, where it had been hidden. Translated from the original Polish, the back of the photo reads: "My loveliest brother, Mietek Goldman." Perhaps this was written by Aron when he gave the recovered photo to Melvin.

The children of Chaim Goldman and Bajla Maria Ceder Goldman, circa 1938. Left to right: Chaja Sura, Aron (in back), Lajb, Rojza, Mieczyslaw, Josef, Natan.

(Melvin's Family, 1898–1939, continued)

Melvin Goldman recalled fond memories of his prewar life in Łódź. Although the city was heavily industrialized, it was a pleasant home for the Goldman family, with wide avenues, lively markets, commanding architecture, and a variety of cultural and recreational offerings for its diverse and multicultural population. It's easy to look at these photos and imagine young Mieczyslaw carefree and at home in his city, doing what youngsters enjoy: wandering around, kicking a ball, running errands, playing with siblings and buddies, and exploring everything he could in his neighborhood and city.

—

Łódź was an important industrial hub. Early in life, Mieczyslaw began working alongside his father, Chaim, in the family metal-fabrication workshop, warehouse, and factory, thus becoming part of the productive life of the city. This view is from south of Wolborska Street, facing east, date unknown. (Wikimedia Commons.)

(Melvin's Family, 1898–1939, continued)

The layout of Łódź featured several impressive public squares. Freedom Square (Plac Wolności), at the north end of Piotrkowska Street, circa 1930, was one of the finest. Melvin had early pleasant memories of the square, which was a short walk south from his family's home. Central to the square is the Kościuszko Monument, which would be destroyed by the Nazis in November 1939. (Wikimedia Commons.)

The Great Synagogue (Wielka Synagoga), often called the Temple, was one of the architectural treasures of old Łódź, and served the Reform branch of Judaism. Although Mieczyslaw's family was Orthodox and worshiped elsewhere, certainly he was aware of this impressive structure. It was just south of the Goldman's neighborhood. The Nazis burned it to the ground in November 1939. (Wikimedia Commons.)

(Melvin's Family, 1898–1939, continued)

The Green Market (Zielony Rynek) area, circa 1937. Melvin recalled delivering products from the factory by horse-drawn wagon, and the Goldmans would hire a horse and buggy from the train station for the final leg of their journey to a cottage in the mountains for summer vacations. Horse-drawn wagons and buggies were a common mode of transportation. Melvin also noted that the family metal factory fabricated power stanchions. Is it possible that this photo or others in this section include something from the Goldman factory? When the ghetto was cordoned off in 1939, the Green Market section of the city was southwest of the ghetto's southern border. (Wikimedia Commons.)

Residents enjoying a fine day on Nad Łódką Street, near Wolborska Street and the Goldman home, before 1940. Melvin remembered the many open spaces in Łódź, where he and his friends would walk and play soccer. (Wikimedia Commons.)

(Melvin's Family, 1898–1939, continued)

The Altshtot Synagogue, an elaborate Moorish Revival creation at 20 Wolborska Street, not far from the Goldman home, which adjoined their factory at 33 Wolborska. Mieczyslaw's father and grandfather were members, along with the other Orthodox Jews, until the Nazis burned it down in November 1939. (Wikimedia Commons.)

(Melvin's Family, 1898–1939, continued)

Stary Rynek (old market) square, 1930. This square wasn't too far from one end of Wolborska Street, where the Goldmans lived. Wolborska was less than a mile long, so the square must have been a familiar sight to the Goldmans. Notice the streetcar tracks. Mieczyslaw ocassionally got to ride the streetcar on errands for his father, delivering or picking up jobs or materials for the factory. (Wikimedia Commons.)

A typical day at the market (the Green Market, Zielony Rynek)—fresh produce, butter, clothing, and more. Markets such as this one in Łódź were a vital part of the economy, as well as a place to mingle. (Wikimedia Commons.)

(Melvin's Family, 1898–1939, continued)

Stary Rynek (old market) square, 1936, in Mieczyslaw's neighborhood, which he remembered as a lively, close-knit community where neighbors loved to gather. (Wikimedia Commons.)

Surely, Mieczyslaw's family frequented Piotrkowska Street, the commercial and cultural heart of old Łódź. Melvin remembers taking items between his family's factory and Voss's, a friend of his father who did nickeling and silvering jobs at his factory on Piotrkowska. Also, Mieczyslaw's parents—especially his mother—loved the symphony and theater in the district, and often took him along as the oldest son. The bookstore shown here was near the southern end of the street, the opposite end from the Goldman home. The store's owners refused to sign the Volksliste and declare allegiance to Germany, so the Nazis took the store from them after the September 1939 invasion. (Wikimedia Commons.)

(Melvin's Family, 1898–1939, continued)

Elementary School No.

Łódź, Magistracka Street 6

Łódź, 20th of June, 1958

CERTIFICATION

The management of the Elementary School in Łódź certifies that Mr. Melwin Goldman, born in Łódź on 21st of January 1923, the son of Chaim and Blejla Maria, residing at Wolborska Street 33, has completed a 7-grade elementar yschool in the year 1938 with very good grades.

This certification is given in order to be submitted to the school authorities.

/seal/ /signatures/

Certificate for Mieczyslaw's completion of schooling through seven grades, with an English translation.

War Years, 1939–1945

Paper and coin currency issued by the Nazis for use by the Jews in the Łódź ghetto, which was known to the Germans as Litzmannstadt. The note's text reads, "Der Aelteste der Juden in Litzmannstadt" (The Elder of the Jews in Litzmannstadt). This was the title of Chaim Mordechai Rumkowski, who was a Polish Jew appointed by Nazi Germany to head the Council of Elders. The currency was commonly known as "rumki" and "chaimki," in reference to Rumkowski whose title is prominently shown on the notes and coins. Special ghetto postage stamps were also issued, with some denominations including a portrait of Rumkowski.

—

Identification numbers were used to track inmates in Nazi concentration camps. Initially, numbers were marked on clothing, armbands, and/or bracelets. The staggering death rate in the Auschwitz compound, however, gave rise to the practice of tattooing ID numbers on inmates. The tattoos were given via a special stamp that was made up of needles in the shape of numbers. This method was used so that the Nazis could mark incoming inmates quickly, and then keep track of their identities even after death, since their clothing was taken from them when they died. A common misconception held today is that all camps tattooed inmates, but only Auschwitz did; so many people went through Auschwitz before being sent to other camps, that the tattoo ID was present throughout all Nazi camps. Mieczyslaw, however, did not end up with a tattoo at Auschwitz.

Needless to say, Melvin didn't have personal photographs from his years in captivity. However, he managed to keep this bracelet with his ID number—KZ 64277, which he was given at one of the camps. (See the note regarding his number in the report on page 229.)

228 — Appendix 4

(War Years, 1939–1945, continued)

ITS
International Tracing Service
Service International de Recherches
Internationaler Suchdienst

ITS · Große Allee 5-9 · 34454 Bad Arolsen · Deutschland
Tel. +49 5691 629-0 · Fax +49 5691 629-501
email@its-arolsen.org · www.its-arolsen.org

Ms Lee Kikel
USA

Bad Arolsen, 26th September 2017
BB

Our Reference
(please quote)
T/D – 93 936

Your request/email
of 27th September 2015

Your request regarding your father,
Mr Mordka (Mietek) GOLDMAN, born in Lodz on 21.01.1923

Dear Ms Kikel,

We receive a very large number of requests every day and to our regret, despite all efforts, it is not possible to reply as promptly as we would have liked. We apologize for our late response and appreciate your understanding.

We can inform you today that we – based on the data you provided – have made an extensive check of the documentation available to us. Please find attached copies of all the documents found in the course of our search. An explanation of the individual documents is given in the form of a short description in the foot note.

We wish to draw your attention especially to the fact that some documents may contain sensitive or unsettling information. To help you in better understanding our information and the particularities of the enclosed documents, we also point to our general guideline (FAQ) in the attachment.

From the documents available to us we were able to draw up the following outline for the path of persecution for your father, Mr Mordka (Mietek) GOLDMAN:

Time period	Information available
August 1944	confined in KZ Auschwitz Doc.ID. 3768429

The supreme governing body of the ITS (International Tracing Service) is the ITS-International Commission. Its members represent Belgium, France, Germany, Greece, Israel, Italy, Luxembourg, the Netherlands, Poland, the United Kingdom and the United States of America.

In September 2015, Lee sent an inquiry to the International Tracing Service in Germany in the hope of obtaining clarification of the "path of persecution ... for Mr. Mordka (Mietek) Goldman" after he was taken from Łódź ghetto in 1944. Two years later, extensive documentation was emailed to her, including this summary of the various camps and hospitals in which he was housed. (continued next page)

(War Years, 1939–1945, continued)

date not mentioned	deported to KZ Neuengamme/ sub camp Watenstedt Prisoner number: 64277 *(remark: according to our findings this prisoner number has been issued in KZ Neuengamme in October/November 1944)* Doc.ID. 3768429
date not mentioned	deported to KZ Ravensbrück Prisoner number: 17826 NS prisoner category: Jew Nationality: Polish Doc.ID. 3766791, 3766879, 3768553
1st August 1945	registered in DP Camp Wentorf (= AC 1217) Doc.ID. 67194303, 67194304
10th January 1946 and at an unspecified time between the 3rd and 17th February 1946	registered in DP Hospital Gauting Doc.ID. 81984990, 81985170, 81985177, 81985178
date not mentioned	registered in DP Camp "Luers" Bad Wörishofen Doc. ID. 81965636
12th March 1946, 28th March 1946, 23rd June 1946, 14th June 1947, 25th August 1947	registered in DP Hospital Bad Wörishofen Doc.ID. 67194301, 67194302, 81965717, 81965696, 81965699, 81965703, 81965704, 86938655, 81965710, 81965713
27th June 1949	registered by the AJDC (= American Joint Distribution Committee) Emigration Service Paris for an emigration to Australia, residing: Bad Wörishofen Doc.ID. 80195724
21st August 1950	registered by the AJDC (= American Joint Distribution Committee) Emigration Service Paris for an emigration to Australia, residing: Bayer.-Gmain near Bad Reichenhall Doc.ID. 80195723
15th October 1950	left Rehabilitation Centre Bayerisch-Gmain to Munich Doc.ID. 67194305, 86938656
21st November 1950	transferred from IRO Resettlement Centre Munich to Wildflecken Doc.ID. 81752212, 81752213
12th December 1950	emigrated from Bremerhaven aboard the ship "General Taylor" to the USA Doc.ID. 81674021, 81674052

(War Years, 1939–1945, continued)

In reflecting on Jewish heroes on pages 120–121, Melvin quoted a few lines from the song "Never Say" ("Zog Nit Keyn Mol" in Yiddish). The lyrics were written in 1943 by Hirsh Glick, a young detainee in the Vilna ghetto, and set to a familiar tune. Glick was inspired to write the song by news of the Warsaw Ghetto Uprising of spring 1943, when 13,000 Jews died fighting the Germans rather than willingly board the trains to the extermination camps. In the words of one survivor, the Jews had decided "to pick the time and place of our deaths." The song quickly spread throughout the Jewish and resistance communities, and there are several translations into English, as well as other languages. The translation below, which matches Melvin's memories, is by an unknown translator. It is often sung at Holocaust remembrance gatherings.

Never Say

Never say that you are walking the final road,
Though leaden skies obscure blue days.
The hour we have been longing for will still come.
Our steps will drum — we are here!

From green palm-land to distant land of snow,
We arrive with our pain, with our sorrow,
And where a spurt of our blood has fallen,
There will sprout our strength, our courage.

The morning sun will tinge our today with gold,
And yesterday will vanish with the enemy.
But if the sun and the dawn are delayed,
Like a watchword this song will go from generation to generation.

This song is written with blood and not with lead.
It's not a song about a bird that is free.
A people, between falling walls,
Sang this song with pistols in their hands.

So never say that you are walking the final road,
Though leaden skies obscure blue days.
The hour we have been longing for will still come.
Our steps will drum — we are here!

Liberation, 1945

‒ ‒ ‒ ‒

>
> Acorn Park
> Cambridge, MA 02140
> June 24, 1982
>
> Mr. Melvin Goldman
> 5803 Darlington Road
> Pittsburgh, PA 15217
>
> Dear Mr. Goldman:
>
> Thank you for your letter of May 29. I was deeply touched and pleased to learn that you have recovered from the war experience and that you are well. You are very kind to thank me for your survival, but I think that the 82nd Airborne Division should get most of the credit. It was a divisional effort that made all of that possible.
>
> Several days before we reached your camp, we crossed the Elbe River with orders to stop the Russian troops from entering Denmark. It took us a day to get the bridgehead established and all the troops together, and then we moved as rapidly as we could toward Ludwigslust, making 36 miles in one day. We did not know that the camp was there, but we had to meet the Russians and establish our line through Ludwigslust. The camp was a great shock to all of us, as it was to everyone who saw it. Fortunately, we were able to get the use of some large airplane hangars nearby and using our ambulances, we were able to move the survivors to the hangars. I suspect that if we had delayed another day or so, many of you would have been dead.
>
> Congratulations on becoming a U.S. citizen in 1951. I am taking the liberty of sending your letter to the 82nd Airborne Division. It should get credit for the liberation of the Wobbelin-Ludwigslust camp.
>
> With best regards,
>
> James M. Gavin
> Lieutenant General, USA (Ret.)

In 1982, Melvin wrote to then-retired Lieutenant General James M. Gavin, commander of the US Army's 82nd Airborne Division, which rescued young Mieczyslaw and the other prisoners from Wöbbelin in May 1945. A framed copy of General Gavin's reply was proudly displayed in Melvin's offices for many years, first at the store, and then at home after his retirement.

Rehabilitation, 1945–1950

Above, Edmundstahl Hospital, in Geesthacht, was one of the first places Mieczyslaw received treatment. Left, Kneippianum Hospital, in Bad Wörishofen, where Mieczyslaw spent several months.

Mieczyslaw (top right) with friends in Bad Wörishofen, August 1946. Below, Mieczyslaw, Bad Wörishofen, August 1946.

(Rehabilitation, 1945–1950, continued)

Mieczyslaw (with hands on boy's shoulders) posing with friends at Kneippianum Hospital, December 1, 1947. Left, in Bad Wörishofen, May 1947.

Mieczyslaw (seated) with friend and colleague at work at Kneippianum, circa 1948. Right, Mieczyslaw with a doctor at Kneippianum Hospital, circa 1948.

(Rehabilitation, 1945–1950, continued)

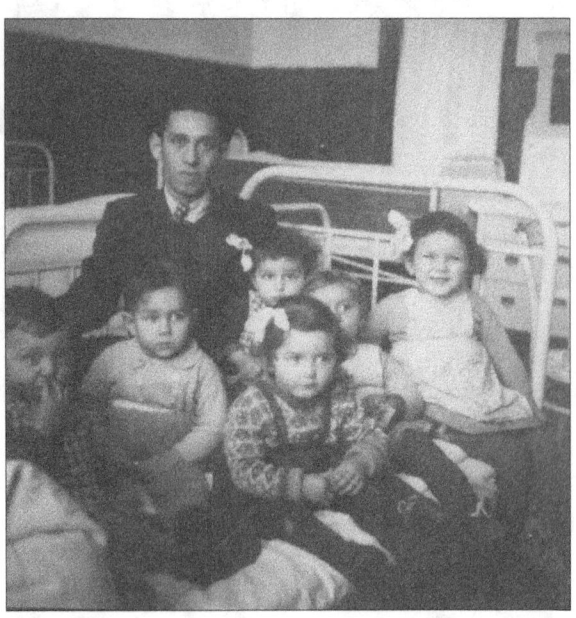

Above, Mieczyslaw (right) with friends, somewhere in Europe, circa 1948, and with children at Kneippianum Hospital, 1948.

Left, Mieczyslaw (top left) with friends, somewhere in Europe, circa 1948. Above, Mieczyslaw, probably during rehabilitation in Germany, late 1940s.

(Rehabilitation, 1945–1950, continued)

MAX SCHÖLLHORN · BAD WÖRISHOFEN

Sanitäre Installation / Bauspenglerei / Blitzschutzanlagen
Haus- u. Küchengeräte / Reparaturen u. Neuanfertigungen

Fernsprecher Nr. 285 / Postsch.-Konto München 7218 / Bank: Bayer. Hypoth.- u. Wechselbank Bad Wörishofen

Den 11. Juni 1949

Bestätigung.

Ich bestätige Herrn Miätek G o l d m a n, daß er bei mir verschiedene Arbeitsproben im Spengler-Handwerk abgelegt hat, woraus ich ersehen konnte, daß er diesen Beruf erlernt hat und auch den Anforderungen, die an einen selbständigen Gehilfen gestellt werden, entspricht.

Max Schöllhorn
Installation und Bauspenglerei
Bad Wörishofen Tel. 285

MAX SCHOLLHORN – BAD WORISHOFEN

Santation Installations / Plumbing / Lighting Protection Systems

House and Kitchen Equipment / Repairs and Renovations

11th of June, 1949

STATEMENT

I confirm that Mr. Mietek Goldman has performed various work in plumbing trade for me, hence I can state that he has learned this job and, if required, he can perform it as an independent assistant, accordingly.

Max Schölhorn

Instalaltion and Plumbing

Bad Wörishofen, Tel# 285

/signature/

After the war, still in Europe, Mieczyslaw received some tradesman training.

(Rehabilitation, 1945–1950, continued)

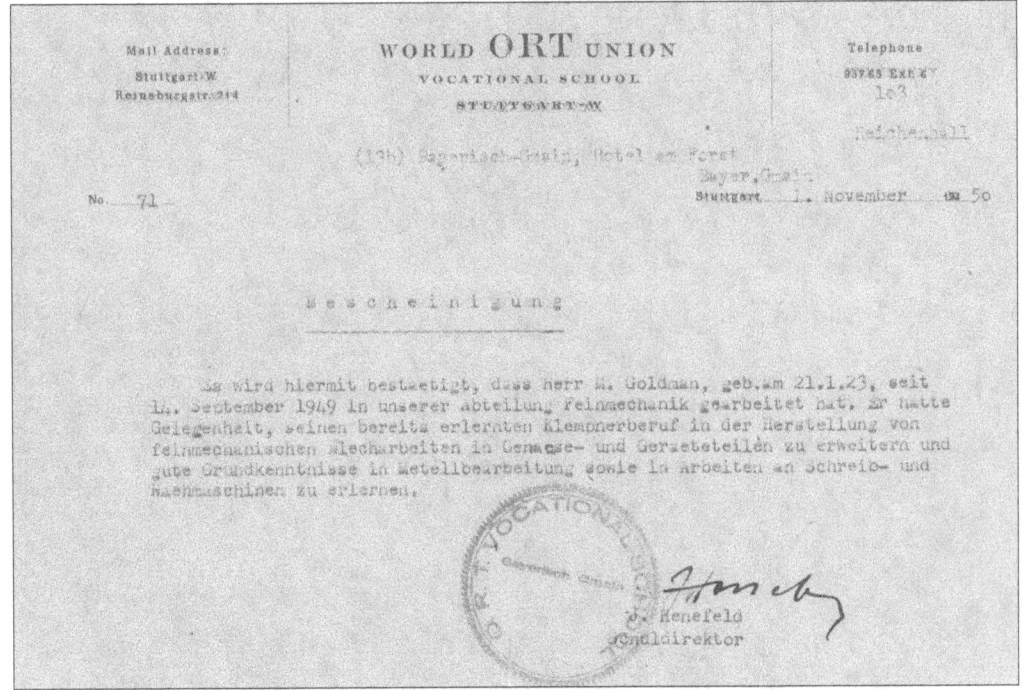

Herewith s confirms that Mr. Goldman, born on 21st of January 1923, has worked in our department of Precision Engineering since September 14th, 1949. He had the opportunity to expand his existing tinsmith skills in the production of precision sheet-metal work for equipment parts and has acquired good basic knowledge in metal-working as well as typewriting and working with a sewing machine.

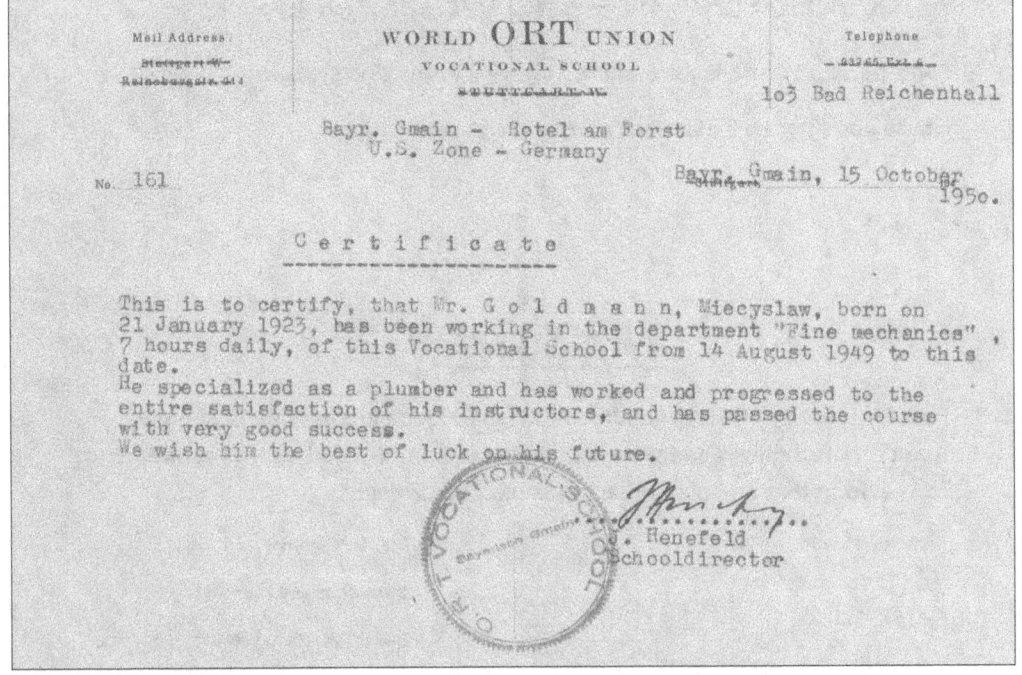

As shown here, he became proficient as a plumber and worked in the Fine Mechanics Department.

Emigration, 1950

Mieczyslaw Goldman's 1948 application for eligibility to emigrate with the Preparatory Commission for the International Refugee Organization.

(Emigration, 1950, continued)

```
              AMERICAN JOINT DISTRIBUTION COMMITTEE
                       EMIGRATION SERVICE

                                    Munich,  October 30.1950

       FOR WIEDERGUTMACHUNG PURPOSE ONLY

           This is to certify that  GOLDMAN Mietek /Mieczyslav/
       Bayerisch-Gmain
       ..................................................
       is/are registered with this Office for emigration to  USA
       ..................

           He/she/they is/are in possession of  EON.93744
       ................................ and will be leaving within
       the next  3-4 weeks  ..........

                                              [signature]
                                              Amy Zahl
                                              Director of Emigration Service
               Our reference  US.834

           No.:  107

                    FOR THE "AUSWANDERERLISTE"


           URGENT
```

The official notice from the American Joint Distribution Committee approving Mieczyslaw Goldman's emigration to the United States.

(Emigration, 1950, continued)

Baggage declaration: Mieczyslaw Goldman travels to America aboard the General Taylor *with five "total pieces of baggage."*

(Emigration, 1950, continued)

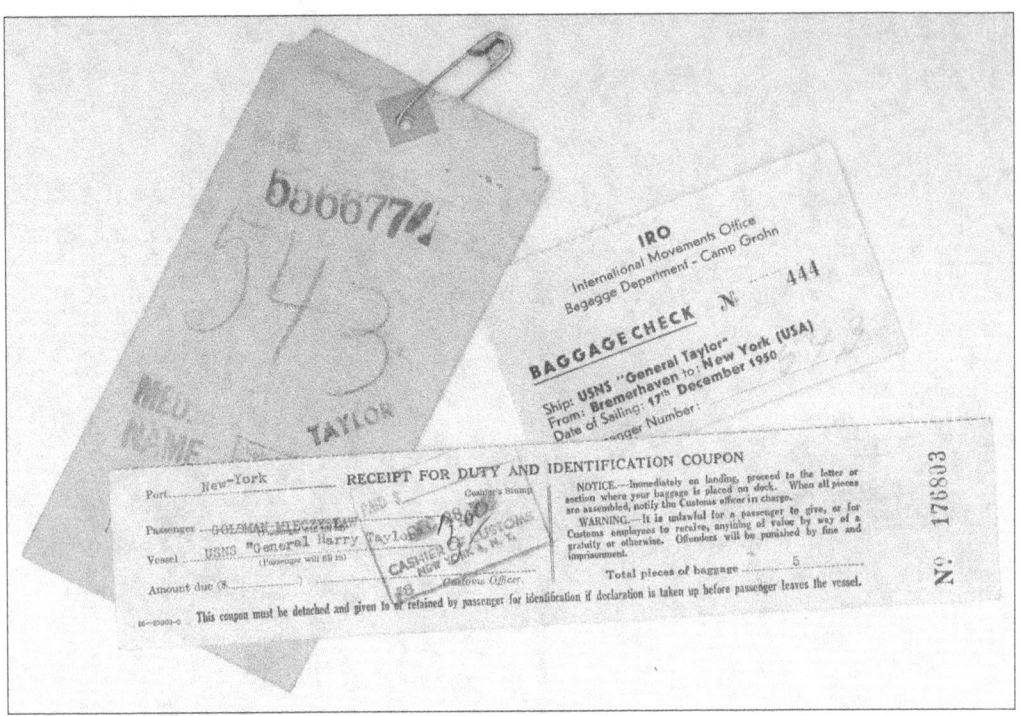

Reminders of a memorable voyage across the Atlantic.

(Emigration, 1950, continued)

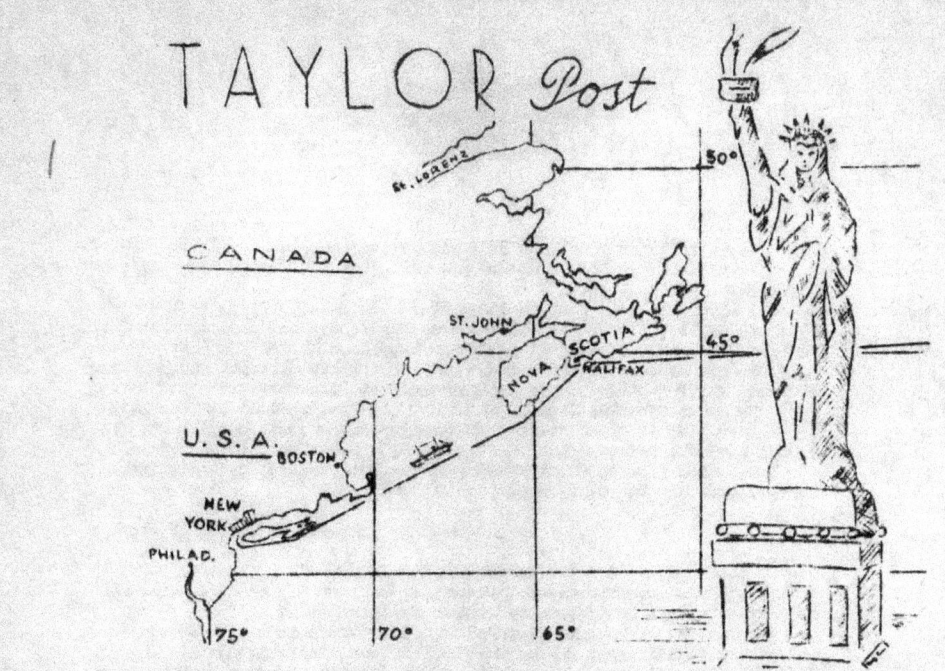

U S N S General Harry Taylor   27.12.Wednesday.1950.No.6.

S O U V E N I R   E D I T I O N   N E W   Y O R K

Now is the time to say Goodbye,

You will soon arrive in New York and the General Harry Taylor will have accomplished once more its task for the International Refugee Organisation. The Voyage may have seemed full of petty irritations and you will arrive tired and pleased that it is over but, in good health with New Hope and a New Life in front of you – your voyage will soon be forgotten but I hope those memories remaining will be happy ones. Here is wishing you all much success, happiness and Good Luck for a Brave New World – Goodbye and Bless You all.

                                          WILLIAM H U N T
                                          Escort Officer.

Nun ist die Zeit gekommen, Lebewohl zu sagen.

Sie erreichen bald New York und unseres Schiff "General Harry Taylor" hat wieder einmal seines fuer die IRO getan. Die Reise hatte manche kleine Unannehmlichkeiten und Sie kommen muede an, froh dass Sie darueber weg sind. Doch Sie sind gut gesund, haben neue Hoffnungen und neues Leben vor sich. Die Schwierigkeiten werden schnell vergessen und das Zurueckdenken darueber wird angenehm sein. Hier wuensche ich Ihnen Allen viel Erfolg, Froehlichkeit und gutes Glueck fuer ein schoenes neues Leben. Lebewohl und Gott soll Sie Alle segnen.

* * * * * * * * *

"Souvenir Edition," with an uplifting message from an escort officer: you will arrive . . . "with New Hope and a New Life in front of you." (continued next page)

(Emigration, 1950, continued)

Today has been your last full day aboard the "General Harry Taylor" tomorrow we arrive in New York and you have your first glimpse of your new homeland.

I sincerely hope that it comes up to all expectations, that you find good employment, pleasant homes and true happiness, and that the New Year is indeed the commencement of a new and happier time for you all.

Remember though that nothing comes of itself, anything worth having is worth working for, so make up your minds to work willingly and hard.

Remember too that work alone is not enough - include in your plans friendship good cooperation and neighbourlyness, - what you give out always returns, friendship is met by friendship and hate by hate.

Remember this and I am convinced the future holds much happiness for you all. May God bless you.

ANN DOUGLAS
Assist of Escort Officer

Heute war es fuer Sie der letzte Tag am Bord des "General Harry Taylor". Morgen kommen wir in New York an und Sie werden ihren ersten fluechtigen Blick auf ihre neue Heimat werfen koennen.

Ich hoffe ergebenst, dass es alle Erwartungen erfuellt werden, dass Sie gute Beschaeftigung, angenehmen Heim und ein wahres Glueck finden werden und dass das Neue Jahr fuer Sie alle wirklich zu einem Beginn einer neuen gluecklicheren Zeit sein wird.

Erinnern Sie sich daran, dass nichts von selbst kommt, etwas was einen Wert besitzt ist auch Wert dafuer zu arbeiten. Darum bewaffnen Sie Ihren Geist um bereitwillig und gut zu arbeiten.

Vergessen Sie nicht, dass Arbeit allein genuegt nicht - schliessen Sie in Ihre Plaene Freundschaft, gute Mitarbeit und Nachbarschaft. Wie Sie es tun werden so kommt es auch Ihnen zurueck. Freundschaft wird mit Freundschaft und Hass mit Hass erwiedert.

Erinnern Sie sich daran und ich bin ueberzeugt, dass die Zukunft fuer Sie mehr Glueck bringen wird. Moege Sie Gott segnen !

* * * * * * * *

TELEGRAMME

USNS GEN.H.TAYLOR : TO ALL PASSENGERS TO NEW YORK HAPPY NEW YEAR GOOD BYE AND GOOD LUCK * CAPTAIN *

USNS GEN.H.TAYLOR: FAREWELL GREETINGS AT THE END OF YOUR VOYAGE AND GOOD LUCK * TRANSPORT COMMANDER *

FUER ALLE REISENDEN NACH NEW YORK FROHLICHES NEUES JAHR GLUECK AUF UND LEBEWOHL * KAPITAIN *

SCHOENE ABSCHIEDSGRUESSE BEI DER BEENDIGUNG DER FAHRT UND VIEL GLUECK * * TRANSPORTKOMMANDANT *

NEW YORK: DIE UNO BEZOG FORMELL IHR HAUPTQUARTIER IN DEM NEUEN AUS GLAS UND MARMOR ERBAUTEN WOLKENKRATZER, DER SICH MITTEN DER STADT MANHATTAN, BEFINDET UND BEENDETE DAMIT EINE GIGANTISCHE UMSIEDLUNGSAKTION DIE IM AUGUST D.J. BEGONNEN HAT.

NEW YORK: AM DIENSTAG, DEN DRITTEN JAHRESTAG, UNGEFAEHR UM DIESELBE STUNDE DES GROSSEN UNHEILVOLLEN SCHNEESTURMS DES JAHRES 1947 SAUSTE WIEDER SCHNEE UEBER DIE GROSSSTADT. PANIKARTIGE TELEFONANRUFE WURDEN AN DIE WETTERWARTE GERICHTET, DIE JEDOCH VERSICHERTE, DASS SICH DER DIESMALIGE STURM, DER EINEN SCHNEEFALL VON 65 CM UND 20 TOTE ZUR FOLGE HATTE.

VATIKAN: PAPST PIUS VERLAENGERTE FUER DIE GESAMTE KATHOLISCHE WELT DIE FEIERLICHKEITEN DES HEILIGEN JAHRES 1950. DER PAPST TRUG DIESE AKTION

Early Pittsburgh Years, 1950s

– – – –

Melvin's 1950 train ticket from New York City to Pittsburgh, with a December 31, 1950, arrival.

(Early Pittsburgh Years, 1950s, continued)

Instructions, upon arrival in Pittsburgh, and a note that "Mr. G has had breakfast." Various groups and individuals helped Melvin with his travels—alone in a new country and unable to speak English.

(Early Pittsburgh Years, 1950s, continued)

```
                PITTSBURGH TECHNICAL INSTITUTE INC.
                         1204 PENN AVENUE
                         PITTSBURGH 22, PA.

                         ACHIEVEMENT RECORD


Name  Goldman, Melvin                    Date  July 27, 1955


Subject                                                        Grade

Introduction.................................................    E
Basic Motion Study...........................................    E
Industrial Mathematics.......................................    F
Basic Time Study.............................................    G
Charts and Graphs............................................    E
Report Writing...............................................    E
Basic Industrial Relations...................................    G
Basic Job Classification.....................................    F
Job Classification...........................................    F
Wage Plans...................................................    G
Complex Time Study...........................................    E
Blueprint Reading............................................    F
Complex Method Study.........................................    E
Incentive Systems............................................    E
Plant Layout.................................................    E
Production Control...........................................    F
Standard Cost................................................    E
Budgeting and Estimating.....................................    E
Industrial Relations.........................................    E
Industrial Psychology........................................    F
Department Organization......................................    F
Labor Laws...................................................    E
Industrial Training..........................................    G
Plant Safety.................................................    E
Plant Survey.................................................    G
Maintenance Engineering......................................    G
Quality Control..............................................    P
Product Engineering..........................................    G
Industrial Problems..........................................    G


                         System of Grading              B+

              E - Excellent           91 - 100%
              G - Good                81 -  90%
              F - Fair                71 -  80%
              P - Passing             60 -  70%
              U - Unsatisfactory      Under 60%


                                        Thomas E. Maker
                                    President and/or Director
```

Melvin was a strong student, as shown by this achievement record from Duff's Pittsburgh Technical Institute, 1955.

(Early Pittsburgh Years, 1950s, continued)

```
                    PERSONAL DATA SHEET

Name                  Melvin Goldman          Tel. No.  Mayflower 1-1927
Permanent Address     4632 Bayard Street      State     Pennsylvania
City  Pittsburgh      County    Allegheny


Date of Birth         January 21, 1923        City   Lodz, Poland
Age       32
Health    Good        Height  5'6"            Weight   135
Married   Yes


Education

High School           Magistracka 6    Poland          1930    1938
Course                Academic
Activities            Sports, boy scouts
                      pre-military training


Special Training      W. O. U.       Germany   Sept. 1949  Nov. 1950
Course                Mechanical knowledge
                      with some skill
Activities            Soccer team, member
                      student council


College               Duff's Iron City Pittsburgh  Oct. 1951  Aug. 1952
Course                Clerical-bookkeeping
Activities            Student Council


Technical School      P. T. I.    Pittsburgh    Aug. 1954  July 1955
Course                Industrial and
                      Management Engineering
Activities            Sec. class banquet


Technical Qualifications   tinner, typist
                           bookkeeping


Special Interests     Home mechanics, languages,
                      reading, sports, music,
                      Philatelist


Work Experience Record

Goldman Company       Apprentice tinner    Poland   1939    1940
                      sheet metal

Ghetto-under German   instructor-metal     Poland   1940    1944
Occupation            factory
```

Melvin Goldman's 1955 resume. A comprehensive listing of all education, activities, interests, special qualifications, work experience, and references. (continued next page)

(Early Pittsburgh Years, 1950s, continued)

```
Work Experience (con't)

Concentration Camps          general labor        Germany      1944   1945
UNRRA & American Joint       manager-hospital     Germany      1947   1949
Distribution Committee
Schreiber Trucking Co.       bookkeeping-general  Pittsburgh   1952   1953
                             office work
Rosetti & Rosetti, Inc.      record sheets for                 1953   1953
                             customs duty
Cuneo Press                  bookkeeping machine               1953   1954
                             office work
Home Supply Co.              salesman and collector            1954   1954
YM & WHA                     office work                       1954   1955

References

Dr. T. Rubel         1722 Murray Avenue              6229 Monitor St.    Ja. 1-1132
M. B. Gefsky         Asst. V.P. Washington Bank      5th Avenue          Ex. 1-1700
                                                     257 McKee Place     Mu. 1-7916
A. J. Auerbach       Exec. Director YM & WHA         115 S. Bellefield   Ma. 1-6500
                                                     6570 Forest Glen Rd.
Mrs. H. Fruendt      Teacher, Forbes School          1100 Forbes Street
                                                     1924 Monongahela    Br. 1-3770
J. Roy Jackson       Guidance Director, P.T.I.      355 East End Ave.
                                                     Beaver, Pa.         Spruce 4-1354
```

Paul Cherner - 1955-1957 MG selling soft goods store 715 5th Ave.

Globe Trading apr 15 1957 - 1961 - June 30

In Part 1 of this book, Melvin mentions working at May Stern & Co starting in September 1952. His resume above doesn't list May Stern as an employer, but it does include Schreiber Trucking Company for 1952 to 1953. He appears to have worked in both places before going to Chicago.

(Early Pittsburgh Years, 1950s, continued)

Melvin Goldman becomes an American citizen, March 22, 1956.

Naturalization photo, age thirty-three, March 1956.

(Early Pittsburgh Years, 1950s, continued)

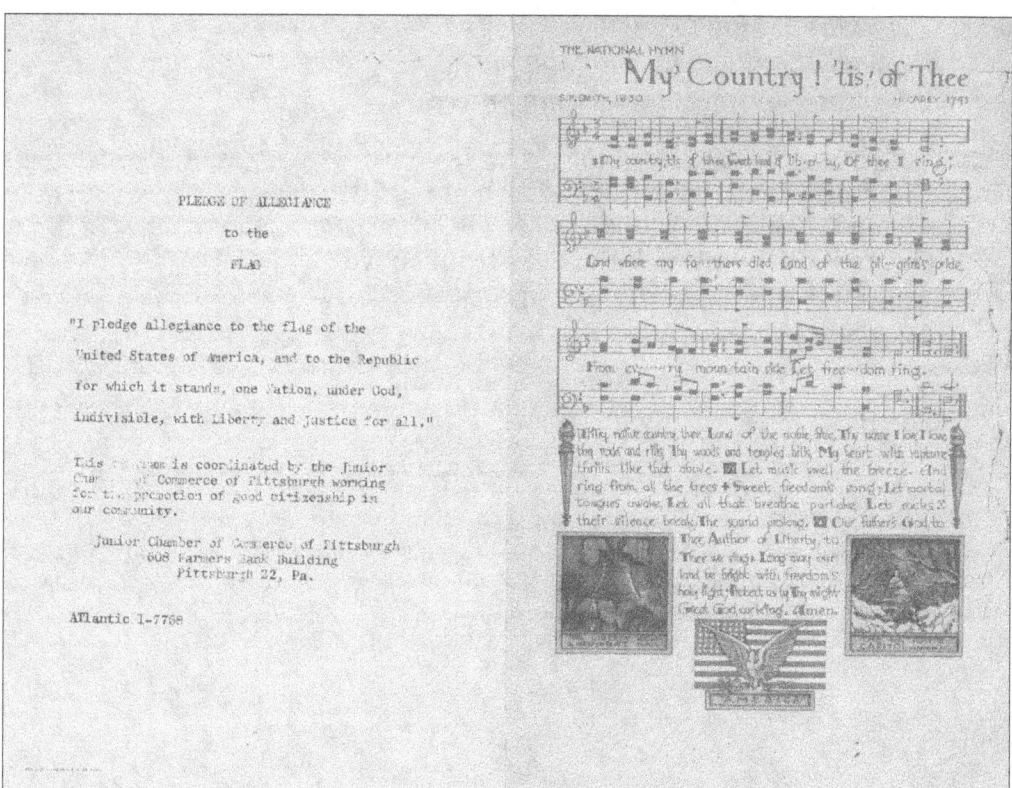

The program for Melvin's special day.

(Early Pittsburgh Years, 1950s, continued)

Like Melvin, Irving Berlin (born Israel Beilin) was a Jewish refugee to the United States. In 1893, when Berlin was five, his family emigrated to New York from the shtetl of Tolochin in Russia, to escape the anti-Jewish pogroms. Berlin wrote literally hundreds of successful songs, including the one Melvin loved to hear. While readers may not be familiar with the first stanza (in italics below), these words were part of the original composition. They were often included in early performances, sometimes sung, and sometimes narrated over background music.

God Bless America

While the storm clouds gather far across the sea,
Let us swear allegiance to a land that's free.
Let us all be grateful for a land so fair,
As we raise our voices in a solemn prayer.

God bless America, land that I love
Stand beside her and guide her
Through the night with the light from above
From the mountains to the prairies
To the oceans white with foam
God bless America, my home sweet home
God bless America, my home sweet home

Relatives Abroad

－ －－－

Melvin's uncle Joel Goldman who had moved to Israel from Poland. The note on the back of the photograph, translated from Polish, reads: "February 18, 1950, Tel Aviv, Israel. For memory from your Uncle and Aunt. Joel."

—

Melvin's first cousin Mario Ekman, son of Chaja Sura Ceder Ekman. The family lived in Argentina. Translation of Yiddish note written (not known by whom) on the back of the photograph: "For my dear son to his dear cousins whom he wishes to meet in person. Mario Ekman."

(Relatives Abroad, continued)

The Ekman family. Translation of Yiddish note writtten on the back of the photograph: "Dear nephew [Melvin], I'm sending a picture of us. And next to my dear son stands my brother-in-law, my dear husband's younger brother. From me, your aunt, who wishes you all the best. Chaja Sura [Ceder] Ekman. September 1, 1950." Chaja and her husband (seated) are in the photo as well as Mario Ekman and his wife, Celia.

Left to right: Chaja Sura (Ceder) Ekman, Mario and Celia Ekman, Chaim Ekman, unknown, 1956.

Restitution and Reparation Efforts

```
           INTERNATIONAL TRACING SERVICE
                   HEADQUARTERS
           APO 171                    U.S.ARMY


Case       :  T- 93936              Date :  25th August 1949

Your ref.  :  Your letter dated 18.7.1949

Subject    :  Certificate of Imprisonment

To         :  Mr. Mietek GOLDMAN
              (13b) Bad Wörishofen
              Hildegardstr. 10
              Germany


        1.  With reference to your request for a certificate
of imprisonment in a concentration camp for :  yourself,


we regret to inform you that for lack of adequate evidence available
in the International Tracing Service no such certificate can be
issued.


                              For the Director of I.T.S.

T-55 (Rev.)
T-55/rev/sch
```

In 1949, the International Tracing Service could find no evidence that Mietek (Mieczyslaw) Goldman had been confined at a concentration camp: "We regret to inform you that for lack of adequate evidence available in the International Tracing Service no such certificate can be issued." Melvin worked hard, and started early on, trying to obtain documents attesting to his war-time experiences.

(Restitution and Reparation Efforts, continued)

> IRO Rehabilitation Center, Bayerisch Gmain
>
> Bayer.Gmain, den 27.4.50
>
> An das
> Amt. f.d. Erfassung
> d.Kriegsopfer
> Berlin – Charlottenburg
> Hardenbergstr.10
>
> Betr.: KZ-Inhaftierungsschein für Mieczyslaw GOLDMAN.
>
> Unser Schüler MIECZYSLAW (Motek) GOLDMAN, geb. am 21.1.23 in Lodz/Polen, erhielt vom INTERNATIONAL TRACING SERVICE, wohin er sich wegen Ausstellung einer Inhaftierungsbescheinigung für die Zeit seiner KZ-Aufenthalte gewandt hatte, den Bescheid, sich in dieser Angelegenheit an Ihr Amt zu wenden, da Sie über die erforderlichen Unterlagen verfügen.
>
> Da der Schüler Mieczyslaw GOLDMAN kurz vor seiner Ausreise steht, vorher aber noch in den Besitz eines KZ-Ausweises gelangen muß, bitten wir Sie, ihm die betreffenden Papiere anhand Ihrer Kartei auszustellen und uns zu übersenden.
>
> Seine KZ-Aufenthalte waren unter anderen :
>
>   Ravensbrück : v.Ende März 45 – 23.4.45
>   Wöbbelin b.Ludwigslust: 23.4.45 – 2. 5.45
>
> Sollten Sie auch für das KZ Wattenstedt Unterlagen besitzen, wo sich Obgenannter v.Jan.45 bis März 45 im Revier befand, so bitten wir auch um diese Bestätigung.
>
> Für die baldige Erledigung im voraus Dank.
>
> Hochachtungsvoll
>
> Oskar Urbach
> Deputy Administrator

In 1950, Melvin received verification of his concentration camp imprisonments in Ravensbrück and Wöbbelin, including dates, as shown by this letter from Germany.

(Restitution and Reparation Efforts, continued)

> Einlaufnummer: .... 15. Jan
>
> **Antrag**
> auf Grund des Gesetzes zur Wiedergutmachung
> nationalsozialistischen Unrechts
> (Entschädigungsgesetz)
>
> 38573
>
> An das
> Bayerische Landesamt für Wiedergutmachung
> Generalanwaltschaft der rassisch, religiös und politisch Verfolgten
> (Anmeldebehörde)
>
> **München**
> Arcisstraße 11
>
> Aktenzeichen: VV 05121
>
> Zur Antragstellung nach dem Entschädigungsgesetz werden folgende Angaben gemacht:
>
> I. Angaben über den Verfolgten:
>
> Familienname: Goldman   Vorname: Mieczyslaw
> Bei Frauen Mädchenname: entfällt   Staatsangehörigkeit: ....
> Geboren am 21.1.1923 in Lodz   Kreis Lodz   Land Polen
> Erlernter Beruf: Schüler   derzeitig ausgeübter Beruf: Schüler
> Jetziger Wohnsitz: Ort, Straße, Kreis, Land Bayerisch Gmain, Rehabilitation Center
>   Kreis Berchtesgaden, Bayern
> Wohnsitz oder gewöhnlicher Aufenthalt am 1. 1. 1947: Bad Wörishofen, Bayern
>
> bei Flüchtlingen: Tag und Ort der Einweisung nach Bayern: ....
> bei Ausgewanderten: vor der Auswanderung polizeilich gemeldet
>   in .... von .... bis ....
> bei zurückgekehrten Emigranten: Wohnsitz vor der Emigration: ....
>   von .... bis ....
>   Rückkehr aus der Emigration: ....
>   wann .... wohin ....
>   in Bayern seit: ....
> bei DP's: Tag und Ort der Ausstellung der Kennkarte:
>   Ind. Card. No. 681580, Augsburg, 28.1.1949
>   Tag und Ort der Meldung beim Arbeitsamt bzw. Anmeldung eines Gewerbebetriebes oder freien Berufes beim Gewerbe- und Finanzamt:
>   (Belege beilegen) Wohnt im Rehab. Center, Bayerisch Gmain
>   bei bereits durchgeführter Auswanderung letzter dauernder Aufenthalt
>   vor der Auswanderung: (nicht Durchgangslager) ....
> bei Verstorbenen: letzter inländischer Wohnsitz: ....
>   von .... bis ....
>   Ort und Datum des Todes: ....

From a five-page document in German, listing Mieczyslaw Goldman's various rehabilitation hospitals, 1945–1950, and imprisonments, from 1940–1945. (continued following two pages)

(Restitution and Reparation Efforts, continued)

Aufenthaltsnachweis (durch die Polizeibehörde bzw. IRO-Dienststellen auszufüllen):

a) Die Ortspolizei in .... bestätigt, daß
   Name: .... geb. .... in ....
   am 1. 1. 1947 seinen rechtmäßigen Wohnsitz oder gewöhnlichen Aufenthalt in .... hatte.

   (Stempel)   Unterschrift

b) Die Ortspolizei in .... bestätigt, daß
   Name: .... geb. .... in ....
   seit .... in .... ansässig ist. (Derz. rechtmäßiger Wohnsitz)
   Zugezogen von .... am ....
   Kennkarten-Nr. .... ausgestellt von ....
   Flüchtlingspaß-Nr. .... ausgestellt von ....

   (Stempel)   Unterschrift

c) Die Lagerleitung des DP-Lagers in .... bestätigt, daß
   Das IRO-Center Nr. 7 in Munich, Ingolstadterstr.19B
   Name: GOLDMAN Mieczyslaw geb. 21.1.1923 in Lodz, Poland
   am 1. 1. 1947 rechtmäßig seinen Aufenthalt im DP-Lager Bad-Wörishofen hatte.

   (Stempel)   NELL CROWN
                                    RECORDS OFFICER
                                    Area No.7 HQs   Unterschrift

d) Die Lagerleitung des DP-Lagers in Bayerisch Gmain, Rehabil.Center bestätigt, daß
   Name: Goldman, Mieczyslaw geb. 21.1.1923 in Lodz, Polen
   seit 12.8.1949 im DP-Lager Bayerisch Gmain, Rehabilitation Center
   ansässig ist und die DP-Karte Nr. 681580 ausgestellt am 25.1.49 von IRO
   besitzt. Er kam vom DP-Lager Bad Wörishofen am 12.8.1949

   (Stempel)   Peter Friedl
                                                          Unterschrift

Inhaber des landeseinheitlichen Ausweises: Ja — nein   Wenn ja: Nr. ....
Anerkannt bei Kz-Betr.-Stelle/BHW-Außenstelle in ....   Nr. ....
Mitglied der NSDAP oder einer ihrer Gliederungen: Ja — nein
Wenn ja, welcher: .... von .... bis ....
Rang: .... Mitgliedsnummer: ....
Spruchkammerbescheid: Jude Kammer: .... Datum: ....
(Begl. Abschrift des Spruchkammerbescheides beilegen)

(Restitution and Reparation Efforts, continued)

An das
Bayerische Landesamt für Wiedergutmachung
Generalanwaltschaft der rassisch, religiös und politisch Verfolgten

38573 * C

Betr.: Anmeldung von Ansprüchen gemäß Gesetz zur Wiedergutmachung nationalsozialistischen Unrechts.

C.
§ 15 und 16, **Schaden an Freiheit.**

I. Angaben über den Verfolgten:
   Familienname: Goldman   Vorname: Mieczyslaw
   Bei Frauen Mädchenname:
   geb. am 21.1.1925 in Lodz   Kreis Lodz
   Gegenwärtige Anschrift: Bayerisch Gmain, Rehabilitation Center

II. Angaben über den Freiheitsentzug:
   Ich war meiner Freiheit beraubt durch:
   Gefängnis ___ von ___ bis ___
   Zuchthaus ___ von ___ bis ___
   Konzentrations-Lager Auschwitz, Braunschweig, Ravensbrück, Lyons von 15.8.1944 bis 2. Mai 1945
   Ghetto Getto Lodz von Mai 1940 bis 15.8.1944
   Zwangsarbeits-Lager ___ von ___ bis ___
   Wehrm./OT.-Strafeinheit ___ von ___ bis ___
   Haftanst. gleichzus. Lager, ähnl. Institutionen und
   Zwangsarbeit ___ von ___ bis ___
   insgesamt 60 Monate.

III. Nachweise:
   1. Ich bin Inhaber des landeseinheitlichen Ausweises für rassisch, religiös und politisch Verfolgte, ausgestellt vom Landesamt für Wiedergutmachung, Generalanwaltschaft (vorm. Staatskommissariat für rassisch, religiös und politisch Verfolgte)
      am ___ mit der Nummer: ___
      Sämtliche Haftbescheinigungen liegen dort auf.
   2. Ich besitze den landeseinheitlichen Ausweis des Landesamtes für Wiedergutmachung, Generalanwaltschaft, nicht und lege folgende Nachweise für die aus politischen, rassischen bzw. religiösen Gründen erlittene Haft vor: Eidesstattl. Erklärung von 2 Zeugen, von IRO Berul Gmunweiler, 7.11.1949

IV. Antrag:
   Ich beantrage für die erlittene Freiheitsberaubung von insgesamt 60 Monate vollen Monaten Haftentschädigung gemäß § 15 des Entschädigungsgesetzes.

   Ich erkläre hiermit an Eidesstatt, daß alle in der vorstehenden Anmeldung enthaltenen Angaben nach meinem besten Wissen und Gewissen genau, vollständig und der Wahrheit entsprechend gemacht worden sind. Die Bestimmungen des § 48, Ziff. 1 u. 2 und § 49, Ziff. 1, 2 u. 3, sind mir bekannt.

   Bayerisch Gmain, 24.10.1949
   Ort und Datum   Unterschrift

(Restitution and Reparation Efforts, continued)

Notarized Copy

U.R> No. 1834.

Declaration of an oath

In front of the notary, Franz Michael Eßlinger, in Bad Reichenhall, the following dates and indicated people appeared in Bad Reichenhall in order to make a claim for the authorities or particular public bodies or, likely, to give a statement.

Notaries are responsible for taking a statutory declaration < 24 R.N.O.> A person who makes a statutory declaration and knowingly makes a false oath or refers to someone who made such a false oath will be punished by jail time between one month and three years. <156, 160 R. St G.B.>

To the best of my knowledge and belief of the undersigned of these documents no passing of rights, requirements, properties of person whose ability through military government is off-limits or a payment through such person and decrease or impact of such power was implicated.

The truth of the foregoing information is the declaration of an oath.

I, a notary, confirm this declaration as correct.

Today, on November 2nd, 1950 it appears that:

1.) Mr. Marjan Cudkiewicz, engineer, in Bad Reichenhall, Rink Street 7, born on 31. October 1907 in Łódź, Poland, identified through his identity card B 08978, issued by City of bad Reichenhall on 18 of September 1946,

2.) Mr. Leon Menson, student, in Bayerisch gmain, Hotle am Forst, born on 27th of April 1927 in Łódź/Poland,

identified through his registration card No. 0549, issued by Imigration department Munich, Maria-Theresia Street 11, on 30th of March 1950 produced his identity card No. 708082.

These person explain herewith about the stay of Mr. Mieczyslaw Goldman, precision mechanic, a resident of Bayerisch Gmain, Hotel am forst, born on 21st of january 1923 in Łódź/ Poland the following pflights as shown:

    I, Marian Cudkiewicz, got to know Mr. Mieczyslaw Goldman in May of 1940 in the Łódź Ghetto. I was with him:

between 5th of May 1940 until 1943 in the Łódź Ghetto,

between August 1944 and November 1944 in the concentration camp Auschwitz,

between November 1944 and January 1945 in the concentration camp Braunschweig,

between January 1945 and the end of March 1945 in the concentration camp Wattenstaedt,

---

Translated testimony of two individuals who were with Mieczyslaw Goldman throughout his atrocious experiences. Mieczyslaw excelled at planning ahead: he obtained the testimony, and had it notarized, before leaving Germany for America. (continued next page)

(Restitution and Reparation Efforts, continued)

between the end March 1945 and the end of April 1945 in the concentration camp Ravensbrück,

between the end of April 1945 until 2nd of May 1945 in the concentration camp Woebbelin,

including the American combat support hospital at Ludwiglust until June 1945.

I, Leon Menson, got to know Mr. Mieczyslaw Goldman in May 1940 in the Łódź Ghetto. I was with him:

between 5th of May 1944 and July 1944 in the Łódź Ghetto,

between August 1944 and November 1944 in the concentration camp Auschwitz,

between January 1945 and the end of March 1945 in the concentration camp Wattenstaedt (Central Neuengamme),

between the end of March 1945 and the end of April 1945 in the concentration camp Ravensbrück,

between the end of April 1945 until 2nd of May 1945 in the concentration camp Weebbelin near Ludwiglust, where we have been liberated by the American Army.

In the Łódź Ghetto, we have worn the yellow Star of David on the left side of chest and on the back. In Auschwitz, we have not worn any badges. In the Braunschweig camp, we had red badge "X" on the back. We had in the lft side of chest a red "V" badge. Directly over the badge "V" was a yellow bar that created roughly a triangle between one arm of "V" with the other arm of "V." Over the yellow arm was the prisoner number. The prisoner number as well as the triangle were stitched on. Moreover, we had to wear a metal necklace with the prisoner number. I – Leon Menson - cannot remember my prisoner number and I don't remember the prisoner number of mr. Goldman. Also, our hair was cropped for the width of the hair clippers, from the forehead to the spine in the back of the neck. We got the same badges in Wattenstaedt, Ravensbrück and Woebbelin. In Wattenstaedt, Mr. Goldman was in the camp district.

We, Marian Cudkiewicz and Keon Menson, confirm the accuracy of our above-mentioned information in the deposition.

Also, we confirm in our deposition that we are not related to Mr. Goldman neither by blood nor marriage.   Leon Menson   Fees: 16.50DM (German Marks)

Marian Cudkiewicz

Notary, Eßlinger

The notarized copy of the aforementioned declaration of an oath was given by Messrs Majan Cudkiewicz, Engineer, Bad Reichenhall, Rinck Street 7 and Lean Menson, student, in Bayerisch Gmain, Hotel am Forst. Bad Reichenhall, 6th of November 1950. Seal: Franz Michael Eßlinger

(Restitution and Reparation Efforts, continued)

The statement, in German, by Leon Menson on May 8, 1950 (translation, previous page), affirming that he was with Mieczyslaw Goldman in the Łódź ghetto and in imprisonments at various concentration camps until their liberation by American troops. Mr. Menson describes the various identification badges prisoners were made to wear at each location.

(Restitution and Reparation Efforts, continued)

Correspondence Concerning Claims.—The Commission will acknowledge receipt of each claim, and notify the claimant or his attorney of the claim number assigned to it, which number should be used on all further correspondence and papers filed concerning the claim.

Payment of Awards.—After a determination is made by the Foreign Claims Settlement Commission that the claimant is entitled to an award, such award is certified to the Secretary of the Treasury for payment. Payments are to be made in full of the principal of each award of $1,000 or less from the Polish Claims Fund. On any award the principal amount of which exceeds $1,000, only $1,000 will be paid initially. After such payments are made, payments will be made on the unpaid principal in ratable proportions. No payment of interest will be made until principal amounts of all awards have been paid in full.

Clerk of the Commission.

10. Has evidence of claimant's United States nationality ever been filed with the Foreign Claims Settlement Commission? **no** (Yes or no). If answer is yes, identify claim in which such evidence was filed

11. Has claimant ever lost his United States nationality? **no** (Yes or no). If yes, attach a statement of the circumstances, reasons, and present status.

12. If claimant is a corporation or other juridical person, attach a statement regarding ownership and qualifications in accordance with the conditions of eligibility set out in the Agreement Annex. Has the corporation or other juridical person been reorganized through judicial proceedings after the property was nationalized or taken by Poland? _____ (Yes or no). **NOT APPLICABLE**

13. Detailed description of the property, rights and interests upon which claim is based. (Nature, location, street, number, city, county, lot number, area, etc., itemize personalty. Show the value of each item at the time of loss.)

    Mothers fur coat (persian lamb), diamond set, pin, bracelet, necklace earrings, mens ruby ring, household goods, appliances and clothing $1,111.00. Household furniture, chairs, living room, suits, dining room suites, bedroom suites, pictures $2,77.00. Machinery and equipment at #33 Wolborska, Lodz, Poland, this is equipent and machinery in in the sheet metal and building construction business under thetrade name of Chaim Goldman $3611.00. Raw materials, merchandise, supplies and inventory at #31 Wolborska, Lodz, Poland, this is merchandise supplies and inventory which my father stored in the warehouse at #31 Wolborska, $3,333.00. Equipment, furniture, office equipment merchandise, supplies, inventory located in #2 Cegelniana, Lodz, Poland. My father in addition to his own business located at Nos.

14. When and how property was acquired:

    (a) If purchased, when **not purchased** consideration paid _____
    (fathers death)
    (b) If inherited, when **Sept. 1944** from whom **Chaim Goldman**

    _____ Value at time inherited (in zlotys) **695,000 zlotys**

    What was nationality of the previous owner? **Polish**

    (c) If acquired by inheritance was claimant's title officially recorded by a court? **no** (Yes or no). If yes, identify court and give date, attaching the decree as an exhibit. If no, on a separate sheet give a family tree or outline showing from whom and when you acquired your interest.

    (d) Cost of improvements (not repairs), if any, made since acquisition **unknown**

On September 12, 1957, Melvin Goldman submitted a claim to the Foreign Claims Settlement Commission of the United States in Washington, DC, in an attempt to be reimbursed for the property stolen from his family during the German occupation. Shown here is a description of the property, including "Mother's fur coat (persian lamb)," jewelry, household goods and furniture, and machinery and raw materials related to his father's metal business. (continued next page)

(Restitution and Reparation Efforts, continued)

#13, (Cont)

31 and 33 Wolborska, Lodz, Poland, was also equal partner with Mr. Mojsze Chaim Senderowitz in a sheet metal business with its office and warehouse located at #2 Cegelniana, Lodz, Poland. My fathers interest in this business was $3,888.00.

Urzad Stanu Miary in Lodz Poland (Bureau of weight measurements) measuring cups called as "Liter" $8333.00.

U.S. called "air purifiers" known as Rozpylacie Powietrza" $11,111.00.

Debt owned to my father from Oscar Cohen Mfg. Co. for air purifiers delivered to Oscar Cohen Mfg. Co. but not paid for $6,944.00.

,r. Goldman was honorary secretary for 15 years of the Sheet Metal Masters of Lodz, Poland. Member of Board of Examiners of the Sheet Metal Trade of Lodz. (Director of Board was Mr. Dobosh). Teacher in the preparation of sheet metal trade at Jarociniski Scool #44 Pomorska, Lodz, Poland.

Family lived in apartment adjoining the business and property at #33 Woborska, Lodz Poland. The family lived at this address until September 1944 at which time the entire family of 9 was sent to Auschwitz Concentration Camp. The brothers Melvin and Aron were then sent to slave labor camps and the remaining 7 members of the family were gassed.

Also in the claim application, Melvin noted that seven members of his family were gassed.

(Restitution and Reparation Efforts, continued)

1410 S. Negley Ave.
Pittsburgh 17, Pa.

May 23, 1960

Dr. S. Gringauz
U.R.O. 1241 Broadway
New York 1, N.Y.   ref: BM SG

Dear Dr. Gringauz:

I am enclosing herewith the forms which I have filled out to the best of my ability. I cannot supply you with affidavits of witnesses about my fathers death because the people who were with my father in Auschwitz were killed with him and the ones who are alive could not possibly have seen what happened to him and anybody who came into a transport into Auschwitz like my father knows that the ones who went to the left went to the gas chambers. As a matter of fact we tried all over Europe to find my father or any of our family from 1944 without results.

On question C, affidavit of witnesses about his economic and social circumstances I do not have that kind of witnesses either because there are very few people alive. I cannot fill out in the forms about this, but the German Government can check up on it. We had a sheet metal shop in Lodz Poland at Wolborska #33 and also a shop at #36 Wolborska and were partners in a sheet metal shop at Ciegielniana #2. We employed at least four people steady and the last building my father finished was Zichtiger at Zavadzka #53 which amounted to 50,000 zlotys.

We also had two patents, one for measurements, the only one in Lodz and the other for Oscar Cohen Co. He made at least 25,000 zloty a year. He was 15 years honorary secretary of the sheet metal masters association. That is all I can tell you about it.

Enclosed find copy of my birth certificate. I hope that you will be able to go ahead with my case.

Very truly yours,

Melvin Goldman

This cover letter for a claim to the United Restitution Organization gives an idea of some of the difficulties in providing the information requested.

(Restitution and Reparation Efforts, continued)

United Restitution Organization (URO)
NEW YORK OFFICE
1241 BROADWAY • NEW YORK 1, N.Y. • Phone MUrray Hill 5-5900 • Cable Address: Amfedera, New York

June 14, 1960

Mr. Melvin Goldman
1410 S. Negley Avenue
Pittsburgh 17, Pa.

Our Ref.: BM SG
To be quoted in your reply.
(Angabe dieses Aktenzeichens dringend erbeten.)

Dear Mr. Goldman:

In your indemnification case we received a ruling of the Entschaedigungsamt in Munich according to which all your claims as an heir and beneficiary of your late father Goldman, Chaim are rejected. Insofar as the "Haftentschaedigung" of your father and the claims for property and profession are concerned, the rejection is correct already from the formal point of view because your father had never had residence in Bavaria. The claim concerning an orphan's pension was rejected with the following explanation:

"The claimant was born on January 21, 1923. In 1944 - the year of his parents' death - he had already completed his 16th year of life. The claimant stated in his application for damage to health that*he was employed by his father as a metal and zinc worker at a weekly salary of 20 - 30 Zlotys, and that, in addition, he received room and board. He also made then statements concerning a completed elementary-school education as well as the attendance of evening school classes in technical instruction during the years 1937 till 1939.   *prior to the persecution

"These statements were also confirmed by the witnesses Arnold Zweig and Sam Silberstein. It may therefore be assumed that the claimant had completed his school and professional education and training prior to the persecution. Moreover, also the claimant's brother declared in connection with the application for indemnification that neither he nor his brother (the claimant) had participated in any school or professional classes since 1939."

As I wrote you several times, I was very doubtful about your claim for an orphan's pension. Now, as I see from the ruling, there are moreover different statements of your brother and of yourself that practically give us no possibility to pursue this claim

Melvin received an explanation for why his claim was rejected. (continued next page)

(Restitution and Reparation Efforts, continued)

Mr. Melvin Goldman   - 2 -   6/14/1960

From this rejecting ruling you are formally entitled to file an appeal to the court. The space of time for filing an appeal expires on November 29, 1960 - that means, that an appeal must be in the court at least before the end of Octobdr 1960. - I beg to advise you that our office in Munich will not file an appeal because they regard an appeal as practically hopeless. If you nevertheless want to file an appeal to the court, you have to do it either through a private lawyer or by yourself. If you do it by yourself, you have to send the brief of appeal to the Landgericht in Muenchen, Entschaedigungskammer, Promenadenplatz 2. You have to mention the registration number (Aktenzeichen) of your case in the court: EK 9941/53.

Enclosed I am sending you, for your information, excerpts from instructions on the procedure in the filing of appeals.

                    Very truly yours

                    Dr. S. Gringauz

li
Encl.

(Restitution and Reparation Efforts, continued)

INSTRUCTIONS TO CLAIMANTS ON
THE FILING OF APPEALS. *

Insofar as the claim was rejected by a ruling of the Entschaedigungsamt, the claimants living in the United States may – within an emergency term of six months, beginning with the receipt of the ruling – file an appeal against the Freistaat of Bayern. The notice of appeal is to be sent to the Landgericht Muenchen, Entschaedigungskammer – Muenchen, Wagmuellerstrasse 12; present address: Muenchen 35, Promenadeplatz 2.

The only way to file an appeal is either by submitting a brief of appeal to the court mentioned above or orally before the clerk of the Munich court. If the appeal is lodged by a brief of appeal, the brief must contain the following data:

(1) The designation of the parties and of the court;

(2) the registration of the case in the Entschaedigungsamt

(3) the exact specification of the claim and its basis, as well as a specified petition.

It serves the acceleration of the court procedure if two copies of the brief of appeal and of the ruling in question are enclosed in the original or as copies.

The space of time for filing an appeal is not considered as having been met if the appeal is lodged with another court or another indemnification agency, or by a complaint or petition addressed to another court.

For the lodging of the appeal and the further pursuance of the court procedure the claimant may, without charge, retain as his representative

        the Offizialanwalt fuer Wiedergutmachung
        Muenchen 2, Perusastrasse 5/III,

provided the claimant gives him a general power of attorney for the entire court procedure.

Instructions for filing an appeal for the claim rejection.

(Restitution and Reparation Efforts, continued)

AFFIDAVIT

This is to certify that I, Arnold Zweig, born November 20, 1921 in Lodz, Poland, now residing at 1167 Wightman Street, Pittsburgh 17, Pa. have known Mieczyslaw (Melvin) Goldman since we were children as we lived only a few blocks away from each other in Lodz, Poland and attended the same schools, Magistracka 6. I have also known his father and his family as I came into their home often.— We were in the Ghetto Lodz together and it is to my knowledge that when I met the family in Auschwitz in the fall of 1944 the father, mother and children were gassed. The only person I have seen since that time is Mieczyslaw (Melvin) Goldman. I certify that Chaim Goldman, father of Mieczyslaw (Melvin) Goldman was gassed in Auschwitz in the fall of 1944.

I swear the above statement is true and correct.

Arnold Zweig

An additional affidavit by Arnold Zweig in support of Melvin's appeal.

(Restitution and Reparation Efforts, continued)

> 1320 S. Negley Ave.
> Pittsburgh 17, Pa.
>
> April 22, 1964
>
> Dr. E. Weil
> U.RO.
> 1241 Broadway
> New York 1, N.Y.
>
> re: A (r) PL-(Dr.W.)hg
>
> Dear Dr. Weil:
>
> In reply to your letter of April 13, 1964, I would like to advise you that in November 1940 the Gestapo came to our house and asked for valuables, especially diamonds, gold, furs, etc.
>
> These are things that were taken from our home. My fathers 1.80 Ct. cents ring valued at 600 Zloty. 1 Gold Tissot 18 gold watch 200 Zloty. 1 fur coat for 150 Zloty. My mothers valuables were a 2.25 Ct. Marquise engagement ring and wedding band to match at 3400 Zloty. 1 14 K gold wedding band plain setting 10 Zloty. 1 diamond watch at 330 Zloty. 1 Persian lamb fur at 450 Zloty and 5 $20.00 gold pieces American and 60 English Pound Sterling. 1 ladies medallion set with rubies and 1/2 Ct. diamond at 120 Zloty.
>
> All of these things were taken by the Gestapo at gunpoint. I understand that I was a minor at that time and would appreciate if you would introduce an inheritance claim as you pointed out in your letter.
>
> My father and mother died in the gas chambers in Auschwitz in 1944. I only have one surviving brother and his name is Aron Goldman born September 27, 1925, residing now in Pittsburgh, Pa. U. S. A.
>
> I hope to hear from you very soon and hope you will be able to proceed with this case. Thanking you in advance I remain
>
> Very truly yours,
>
> Melvin Goldman

This letter provides an example of Melvin's inability to provide proof of the crimes committed against his family. He notes, "All of these things were taken by the Gestapo at gunpoint" and "I cannot supply you with affidavits of witnesses about my father's death because the people who were with my father in Auschwitz were killed with him."

(Restitution and Reparation Efforts, continued)

FOREIGN CLAIMS SETTLEMENT COMMISSION OF THE UNITED STATES
WASHINGTON D.C. 20579

CERTIFIED MAIL

14 SEP 1964

Melvin Goldman
1320 South Negley Ave.
Pittsburgh 17, Penna.

Re: Claim No. PO 5880

Dear Mr. Goldman:

Enclosed is a copy of the Proposed Decision on your claim.

Where the Proposed Decision denies a claim, in whole or in part, or approves a claim for less than the full amount claimed, the claimant may, within twenty days of service of the decision, file objections and in addition may request a hearing before the Commission for the purpose of presenting oral argument, the taking of evidence or both.

Although objections need not be submitted in any particular form, it is essential that the reasons for each objection be clearly stated. Each instance of alleged error in the Proposed Decision, whether of law or fact, should be set forth clearly.

The statement of objections must clearly indicate whether a hearing before the Commission is requested. Such hearings are conducted by one or more Commissioners at the office of the Commission in Washington, D. C. If a hearing is requested, the claimant or his counsel will be notified as to the time when the hearing will be held.

If objections are filed, but no hearing is requested, the objections will nevertheless, be thoroughly considered by the Commission before the issuance of a Final Decision.

If a brief is filed, four copies should be submitted. If a hearing is requested, the brief, if any, must be submitted at least 15 days prior to the date scheduled for the hearing. If no hearing is requested, briefs must be filed within two weeks from the filing of objections.

If no objections are filed, and unless the Commission otherwise orders, the Proposed Decision will be entered as the Final Decision of this claim upon the expiration of 60 days.

Copies of the Polish Claims Agreement of 1960, pertinent portions of the International Claims Settlement Act of 1949, as amended, and of the Commission's regulations are enclosed.

Very truly yours,

Francis T. Masterson
Clerk of the Commission

After years of correspondence between Melvin, his lawyer, and several international agencies, this final 1964 ruling came from the Foreign Claims Settlement Commission.

(Restitution and Reparation Efforts, continued)

FOREIGN CLAIMS SETTLEMENT COMMISSION
OF THE UNITED STATES
WASHINGTON 25, D. C.

IN THE MATTER OF THE CLAIM OF

MELVIN GOLDMAN

Claim No. PO-5880

Decision No. PO-

Under the Polish Claims Agreement of 1960 and the International Claims Settlement Act of 1949, as amended

PROPOSED DECISION

This claim, for $38,610.00, is based upon the asserted ownership and loss of personal property located in Lodz, Poland. Claimant states that he has been a national of the United States since his naturalization on March 22, 1956.

Under Section 4(a) of the International Claims Settlement Act of 1949, as amended, (64 Stat. 13 (1950), 22 U.S.C. § 1623(a) (1958)), the Commission is given jurisdiction over claims of nationals of the United States included within the terms of the Polish Claims Agreement of 1960 (Agreement with the Government of the Polish People's Republic Regarding Claims of Nationals of the United States, July 16, 1960, 11 U.S.T. & O.I.A. 1953, T.I.A.S. No. 4545 (1960)). That Agreement provides as follows:

> Claims to which reference is made in Article I and which are settled and discharged by this Agreement are claims of nationals of the United States for
>
> (a) the nationalization or other taking by Poland of property and of rights and interests in and with respect to property;
>
> (b) the appropriation or the loss of use or enjoyment of property under Polish laws, decrees or other measures limiting or restricting rights and interests in and with respect to property. . .; and
>
> (c) debts owed by enterprises which have been nationalized or taken by Poland and debts which were a charge upon property which has been nationalized, appropriated or otherwise taken by Poland. (Polish Claims Agreement of 1960, supra, Article II)

The claim was denied because Melvin was not able to meet "the burden of proof in that he has failed to establish ownership of rights and interests in property which was nationalized, appropriated or otherwise taken by the government of Poland."
(continued next page)

(Restitution and Reparation Efforts, continued)

- 2 -

The Regulations of the Commission provide:

> The claimant shall be the moving party and shall have the burden of proof on all issues involved in the determination of his claim. (FCSC Reg., 45 C.F.R. 531.6(d)(1961))

Claimant has submitted no documentation in support of his claim, although suggestions were made to him regarding the type of evidence appropriate for submission and the sources from which it might be obtained in letters dated September 6, 1962 and April 24, 1963.

By Commission letter of December 6, 1963, claimant was reminded that no evidence had been submitted in support of the claim, and was informed that if no reply were received within 60 days it might become necessary to proceed to a determination of the claim. There has been no submission of evidence.

The Commission finds that claimant has not met the burden of proof in that he has failed to establish ownership of rights and interests in property which was nationalized, appropriated or otherwise taken by the Government of Poland. Accordingly, this claim is denied.

Dated at Washington, D. C.
and entered as the Proposed
Decision of the Commission

SEP 9 1964

Edward S. Re, Chairman

Theodore Jaffe, Commissioner

LaVern R. Dilweg, Commissioner

NOTICE: Pursuant to the Regulations of the Commission, if no objections to this Proposed Decision are filed within 20 days of service thereof, the decision will upon the expiration of 60 days after such service or receipt of notice, be entered as the Final Decision of the Commission unless the Commission otherwise orders. (FCSC Reg., 45 C.F.R. § 531.5(e) and (g) (1961))

PO 5880

(Restitution and Reparation Efforts, continued)

```
Anfragende Stelle:                                                    F - 30a

                    COMITE INTERNATIONAL DE LA CROIX-ROUGE
              SERVICE INTERNATIONAL DE RECHERCHES · INTERNATIONAL TRACING SERVICE
                              INTERNATIONALER SUCHDIENST
                              Arolsen / Waldeck - Deutschland

        ( ) Inhaftierungsbescheinigung           ( ) Krankenpapiere
        ( ) Aufenthaltsbescheinigung             ( ) Auskunft über Auswanderung
        ( ) Suchantrag                           ( ) Sterbeurkunde


           Fragen:                    Antworten:

        I. Personalangaben:        im Konzentrationslager       in D.P.-Lager
                                        (Tarnnamen)

          1. Namen/Mädchenname         Goldman

          2. Vornamen                  Chaim

          3. bei Namensänderung nach dem Krieg,
             jetziger Name u. Vorname    --

          4. Geburtsdatum (Tag, Monat, Jahr)  March 21, 1898

          5. Geburtsort    Lodz, Polen

          6. Beruf         Werkmeister in Metallfabrik

          7. Religion      Jewish

          8. Staatsangehörigkeit    Polnische

          9. Letzte Anschrift vor der Inhaftierung
             (auch Straße und Hausnummer)  Wolborska 33, Lodz, Polen

         10. Name der Eltern
             (auch Mädchenname der Mutter)  Majloch Goldman and Bajnle Kohen

         11. Familienstand z.Z. der Inhaftierung:  Ehemann

          a) Familienstand heute?       ---

          b) Falls verheiratet, Vor-und Mädchennamen der Ehefrau
             Vornamen des Ehemannes?
             evtl. 1. Ehe - 2. Ehe    Balcia Ceder Goldman

          c) Ort und Datum der Eheschließung?

         12. Unterschriftsprobe    wie im Konzentrationslager    wie im D.P.-Lager


                                                                  bitte wenden!
```

Melvin persisted with his search for documentation of the crimes committed against his family. (continued next page)

(Restitution and Reparation Efforts, continued)

II. Angaben über Inhaftierung:

13. Verhaftet am Mai 1940 in: Lodz, Polen durch: Gestapo
    Eingeliefert in das: Ghetto Lodz   Häftl. Nr. stern   Juden-Block Nr.
    am: May 5, 1940   einweisende Stelle: Jüdisches Kwartal
    Überstellt zum: KZ Auschwitz   am: Nov. 44   Häftl. Nr.   Block Nr.
    Überstellt zum: am: Häftl. Nr.   Block Nr.
    Überstellt zum: am: Häftl. Nr.   Block Nr.
    Befreit, entlassen oder gestorben am: vergast in Auschwitz 1944

III. Angaben über Aufenthalt nach dem Kriege:

14. Sämtliche Aufenthaltsorte und -daten nach dem Kriege:

15. Nummer des CM/1-Bogens und die DP-Reg. Nr.?
16. Auswanderung erfolgte:
    a) wann,
    b) von wo,
    c) wohin,
    d) wie (Schiffsnamen - Flugnummer)
    e) mit welchen Familienangehörigen
    f) unter welchem Namen?
17. Jetzige Anschrift?

IV. Bei Anforderungen von Krankenpapieren:

18. Für die Zeit der Inhaftierung   KL (Krankenbau) Ort:
19. Für die Zeit nach dem Kriege   DP (Hospital)

V. Sonstiges

20. Anschrift und Aktenzeichen der
    zuständigen Wiedergutmachungsbehörde
    (Bei Anforderung von ITS Inhaftierungs-
    und Aufenthaltsbescheinigungen
    unbedingt anzugeben.)

Unterschrift

Information on the arrest and death ("gassed") of Melvin's father, Chaim Goldman.

(Restitution and Reparation Efforts, continued)

INTERNATIONAL RED CROSS

Questions: **Answers:**

I. Personal Data   in the concentration camp (code name)
1. Last Name/Maiden Name **Goldman**
2. First Name **Chaim**
3. 3. If name was changed after the war, present last name and first name   --
4. Date of Birth (day, month, year) **March 16, 1898**
5. Place of Birth **Lodz, Poland**
6. Profession **Foreman at the Metal Plant**
7. Religion **Jewish**
8. Citizenship **Polish**
9. Last address prior to incarceration **Wolborska Street 33, Lodz, Poland**
10. Names of parents (also, mother's maiden name) **Majlech Goldman and Bajzle Kohen**
11. Marital status during incarceration **Husband**
    a. Marital status now ---
    b. If married, first name and maiden name of wife or first name of husband? **Balcia Ceder Goldman**
    c. Place and date of marriage

12. Signature

- PAGE 2 -

II. Information on Incarceration:
12. Arrested in **May 1940** in **Lodz, Poland** by **Gestapo**
    Taken to **Lodz Ghetto** Prisoner No. **Jewish Badge**
    on **May 5th, 1940** to the place: **Jewish Quarter**
    Transferred to **Concentration Camp Auschwitz** on **November 14th**

    Released, dismissed or died on: **gassed to death in Auschwitz in 1944**

Translation of previous two pages.

(Restitution and Reparation Efforts, continued)

```
                                           1320 S. Negley Ave.
                                           Pittsburgh 17, Pa.

                                           September 12, 1965


Dr. S. Gringauz,
U.R.C.
1241 Broadway
New York, N.Y. 10001

Dear Dr. Gringauz:

I have just gone through examinations by Dr. Tauber who is representing the
German Government here for the examination of health pension that I am
receiving. I am now receiving $90.00 per month.

As you know and can see from your files the German Government declared me
85% invalid as of 1958 on my last examination. At that time the following
things were wrong with me: I had TB on the left side with pneumothorax
applied for 2½ years in Gauting and TB on the right side. I have had
constant diarrhea since the liveration, very bad pains in my head near my
eyes, shoulder and bones, neuritis and neuralgia and spine curvature.
This was established by them and not by me.

Since the past two years they also found Teitzel disease of the bone, a
hernia on the chest, hemmorhoids and sugar diabetes. I taled to Dr. Tauber
about how I can take care of hospitalization and doctors visits. He advised
me to contact the U.R.O.

Is there any way possible that I can get hospital pay and doctor pay for
constant medical care? Since I was strong and healthy when I went into the
camp all these diseases I acquired during my internment in Auschwitz and
others. I strongly feel that it is the obligation of the German Government
to at least supply hospital and medical care for me. Is there any way that
you can help me in this matter or advise me what I can do. If there is any
legal action that can be taken and if you are willing to do so I will do
anything and give you all the power to go ahead. On top of everything else
a man that is incapacitated by 42 years cannot live on $90.00 per month.

Beside being treated at the outpatient dept. of the Montefiore Hospital
at no cost, from 1951 Dr. T. Tubel also treated me privataly for approxi-
mately 10 years and never received payment from you. I sent in a small
bill twice for $700.00 fees and I never even received an answer and I
think this is really outrageous.
I would very much appreciate if you would help me on this case. I would
be forever greatful.

                                           Very truly yours,


                                           Melvin Goldman
```

Melvin's many physical problems and diseases were eventually recognized as deserving of compensation. (continued next two pages)

(Restitution and Reparation Efforts, continued)

```
from 1945 on:

left side TB, pneumothorax applied 2 years
right side TB
diarrhea-stomach trouble- head pains-very bad- back of head near eyes
shoulder pains
colitis
spine deformation, neuritis neuralgia
pains in all parts of body.

Dr. Ciesnykowski- Kaplan- Krotowski- Silverman - Filipowicz Herman-Gauting

1964 Rubel constant visits
Dr. Lebovitz lung, chest examinations
1965 Dr. Chamovitz hernia, found ulcer, hemorrhoids, special diets,
1965 Dr. Uram West Penn Hospital- found sugar, Tietsel disease on
bone
Dr. Lowy - treating diabetes.
```

(Restitution and Reparation Efforts, continued)

United Restitution Organization (URO)
NEW YORK OFFICE
1241 BROADWAY · NEW YORK, N.Y. 10001 · Phone MUrray Hill 5-5900 · Cable Address: Amfedera, New York

September 30, 1965

Mr. Melvin Goldman
1320 Negley Avenue
Pittsburgh 17, Pa.

Our Ref.: RM : SG: 11
Please quote in all communications.
(Angabe dieses Aktenzeichens dringend erbeten.)

Dear Mr. Goldman:

I received your letter of September 12th concerning your medical expenses.

Your case was settled on the basis of the following "verfolgungsbedingte Krankheiten":

"Lungen-Tbc, Verkeruemmung der Wirbelsaeule chron. Darmkatarrh und Trigeminusneuralgie".

All your medical expenses in connection with these four recognized diseases can be claimed by you. You have to present the necessary receipts of the hospitals, doctors, drug stores etc. I am attaching hereto a "Merkblatt" with instructions on how to proceed in this matter. All these bills you can present directly to the German Consulate in Philadelphia (12 South 12th Street) or through our "Heilverfahrensabteilung" (Mr. Hirsch); they will receive a copy of this my letter.

Insofar as your case concerning confiscated jewelry, etc. is concerned, I am attaching hereto a note which I have sent to our Restitution Department. You will receive from them the necessary forms.

Very truly yours,

Dr. S. Gringauz

(Restitution and Reparation Efforts, continued)

United Restitution Organization (URO)
NEW YORK OFFICE
1241 BROADWAY · NEW YORK, N.Y. 10001 · Phone MUrray Hill 5-5900 · Cable Address: Amfedera, New York

November 4th 1965

Our Ref.:
A (r) FL-(Dr.W.) hg
Please quote in all communications.
(Angabe dieses Aktenzeichens dringend erbeten.)

Mr. Melvin Goldman
1320 S. Negley Avenue
Pittsburgh, PA.

Dear Mr. Goldman:

In your restitution case after your late parents we hand you enclosed the application which we have prepared for you on basis of your information.

Please sign the application on page 8 at the place marked x before a Notary Public, provided that the contents of the application concur with the facts. Then please return the application here to our office so that we may forward same to the authorities in Berlin for their consideration.

We wish to add that we assume that no jewelry, which belonged to you was confiscated at the time in the apartment of your parents. In case this should not be correct, please advise.

Very truly yours,
URO
secretary

encl.
P.S. We enclose also receipt for your
check of $10.00 for registration fees.

United Restitution Organization (URO)
NEW YORK OFFICE
1241 BROADWAY · NEW YORK, N.Y. 10001 · Phone MUrray Hill 5-5900 · Cable Address: Amfedera, New York

March 31st 1966

Our Ref.:
A (r) FL-(Dr.W.) hg
Please quote in all communications.
(Angabe dieses Aktenzeichens dringend erbeten.)

Mr. Melvin Goldman
1320 S. Negley Avenue
Pittsburgh, PA.

Dear Mr. Goldman:

Your letter addressed to Dr. Gringauz, (dated: no date) was transferred to me since the letter of November 4, 1965 which you mentioned in your letter to Dr. Gringauz was also written to you by this Department.

In regard to your inquiry I wish to advise that the so-called "Haerteantrag" for the jewelry which was confiscated from your late parents at the time in Lodz by the Nazi Regime was registered with the authorities in Berlin under the registration number
V 63/52 21 34

As soon as we will hear from the authorities in Berlin in regard to your claim we will get in touch with you.

Very truly yours,
URO
secretary

Melvin gets closer to receiving some compensation. (continued next two pages)

(Restitution and Reparation Efforts, continued)

```
                                        1320 S. Negley Ave.
                                        Pittsburgh, Pa. 15217

                                        July 24, 1967

Mrs. Ch. Bernhardt,
U.R.O.
1241 Broadway
New York, N.Y. 10001
                                re:   A-r FL(DrW)cb
Dear Mrs. Bernhardt:

    I am writing to you again about my case regarding confiscation
of my parents jewelry etc.  I sent you the requested affidavit which
was notarized.

    If you recall, in my previous letter I have mentioned that I am very
much in need of this settlement since I am an invalid.  Since it is
already over four months since I have written to you and you advised
me that you will try to help me as soon as possible in order that
settlement is made, please advise me if there is any further
developments in my case and when I can expect it to be settled.

                                        Very truly yours,


                                        Melvin Goldman
```

United Restitution Organization (URO)
NEW YORK OFFICE

1241 BROADWAY · NEW YORK, N.Y. 10001 · Phone 685-5900 · Cable Address: Amfedera, New York

Aug. 2, 1967

Mr. Melvin Goldman
1320 S. Negley Avenue
Pittsburgh, Pa. 15217

Our Ref.: A-r FL(DrW) cb
Please quote in all communications.
(Angabe dieses Aktenzeichens dringend erbeten.)

Dear Mr. Goldman:

We received your letter of July 24th, postmarked Aug. 1st, 1967, today and regret to state that we have no news for you yet. Please rest assured that you will be informed as soon as any communication comes from Germany.

We had forwarded your affidavit to Berlin on March 27, 1967 with a letter setting forth the fact that you are an invalid and in need of the settlement, and requesting our office to see to it that such settlement may be hastened. This is an exception from our usual instructions never to send a reminder in these cases which take, in general, between 6 and 12 months. Therefore, we are unable to remind Berlin again.

Sincerely yours,
UNITED RESTITUTION ORGANIZATION
i.A.

Ch. Bernhardt

(Restitution and Reparation Efforts, continued)

United Restitution Organization (URO)
NEW YORK OFFICE

1241 BROADWAY • NEW YORK, N.Y. 10001 • Phone 685-5900 • Cable Address: Amfedera, New York

Oct. 10, 1967

Mr. Melvin Goldman
1320 S. Negley Avenue
Pittsburgh, Pa. 15217

Our Ref.: A-r FL(DrW) cb
Please quote in all communications.
(Angabe dieses Aktenzeichens dringend erbeten.)

Dear Mr. Goldman:

We received your letter of Sept. 30, 1967, postmarked Oct. 9th, and wish to advise you as follows:

As you will notice from the statement sent to you, the amount of DM 1200.- awarded to you and your brother is designated as "Vorschuss", i.e. it is to be considered as an advance payment. It is not known to us, at the present time, whether, when and at what time a second distribution will take place.

Apart from this fact, you are under a misunderstanding if you believe that this is a "settlement" which you may accept or decline. The law on the basis of which these so-called "hardship claims" are being processed provides for a lump sum payment, as a token of restitution for gold and silver confiscated in Poland. The sums to be paid are not based on the actual value of the items claimed (at least not as far as the "advance payment" is concerned; whether the list of items claimed will play a part in the computation of the final payment is not yet known), but on the number of persons who suffered damages; i.e. DM 1000 for your father and 20% more for your mother.

We trust that the above explanation is satisfactory to make you realize that the award is based on the law and no complaint can be lodged against it. Therefore, please proceed as per our letter of Sept. 27th so that you and your brother will get the money deposited for you both in the bank in Berlin.

Sincerely,
UNITED RESTITUTION ORGANIZATION
i.A.

Ch. Bernhardt

(Restitution and Reparation Efforts, continued)

1320 S. Negley Ave.
Pittsburgh 17, Pa.

March 28, 1968

Dr. S. Gringauz,
U.R.O.
1241 Broadway
New York, N.Y. 10001

re: BM: SG: li

Dear Dr. Gringauz:

Received your letter of March 25, 1968. I would like to advise you that I do not understand why I have to submit to the German Government a paper showing my income tax or that of my wife.

I have been married 14 years and have a 10 year old daughter as you can see from my files. Also the German Government forms which I fill out each year shows that I am only living on the subsistance that the German Government gives me every month, with the exception that my wife works and my child is a dependant going to school.

I cannot understand why I have to submit my wife's income tax return as she feels that they have no right to ask this. Aside from that, I cannot see why the German Government would worry about an income tax return when I am an 85% invalid, having gone through their doctors every year and I have not been getting better, but worse, or what this has to do with anything when I got hurt in German KZ and that they should give me what is due me that they themselves arrived at.

I hope that you do not put me through any extra pressure because I have enough problems as it is with my health. I hope that you can straighten this matter out.

Very truly yours,

Melvin Goldman

Even after Melvin began receiving compensation from the German government, he continued to be faced with frustration, yet he pressed on in his pursuit of justice. (continued next page)

(Restitution and Reparation Efforts, continued)

United Restitution Organization (URO)
NEW YORK OFFICE
1241 BROADWAY · NEW YORK, N.Y. 10001 · Phone 685-5900 · Cable Address: Amfedera, New York

April 22, 1968

Mr. Melvin Goldman
1320 S. Negley Avenue
Pittsburgh, Pa. 15217

Our Ref.: BM : SG: 11
Please quote in all communications.
(Angabe dieses Aktenzeichens dringend erbeten.)

Dear Mr. Goldman:

I acknowledge receipt of your letter of March 28, 1968.

According to the law, you have to present evidence of your income, of your wife's income and the number of persons you have to support. The income must include income from work, income from capital, from real estate etc., as well as income from Social Security or from German pensions, if any.

It is certain that nobody can force you to present evidence of your income; but in that case the German authorities are justified in paying you only the minimum pension provided for in the law.

Very truly yours,

Dr. S. Gringauz

(Restitution and Reparation Efforts, continued)

SWORN AFFIDAVIT

I, Melvin (Mieczyslaw) Goldman, born January 21, 1923 in Lodz, Poland do hereby state the following facts concerning my imprisonment from May 1940 until May 1945 from the Nazi Government in power at that time.

This is to certify that on May 5, 1940 I was taken into the Ghetto Lodz, Poland by the German occupation troops where I remained until July 1944. At no time during this period did I leave the Ghetto Lodz.

From the end of July 1944 until November 1944 I was incarcerated in KZ Auschwitz. In November 1944 I was taken to KZ Braunschweig where I remained until January 1945. From January 1945 until March 1945 I was imprisoned in KZ Wattenstaedt (Zentrale Neugamme), Revier. From March 1945 until the end of April 1945 I was in KZ Ravensbrueck. From the end of April 1945 until May 2, 1945 when I was liberated by the American Troops I was at KZ Woebbelin bei Ludwigslust.

I do hereby swear that the above facts are true and correct to the best of my knowledge and conscience.

One of the many statements Melvin had to provide in his ongoing efforts for reparations.

US Holocaust Memorial Museum Testimony, 1994–1995

> My name is Melvin Goldman born in Lodz Poland JAN 21, 1923
> Pre holocaust life
> My Father self employed, mother stayed home with children. He was in partnership with 2 other people in sheet metal factory. Also separate work shop he owned.
> My Father was 15 years honorary secretary of so-called "Cech" for metal workers. He had a secretary Miss Friedman. My mother and father loved to go to the theatre and since I was the oldest grandchild and son I was taken along. And I still remember most of the performances and songs.
> My mother went for the summer to a cottage in the Cherry Mountains I stayed in town with my father. We took Friday at noon we closed the shops, took a horse and buggy, then a train, and another horse and buggy to the place. We stayed till Sunday

Seen here, the first page of Mildred's handwritten transcript of Melvin's dictated testimony for the US Holocaust Memorial Museum. Later, she typed this to prepare it for formal submission. To this day, the museum is actively collecting accounts of experiences during the Holocaust from survivors and families of survivors for their "Behind Every Name a Story" project.

Melvin's wife, Mildred, was of invaluable assistance to Melvin as they navigated their way through the many bureaucratic processes and requirements for submitting Melvin's claims and testimonies. She gladly shared her strong secretarial, bookkeeping, and recordkeeping skills, all of which kept their work on track and well documented.

(US Holocaust Memorial Museum Testimony, 1994–1995, continued)

, 1995

Dear Mr. Rossman

Thank you for your donation of your memoir, which was passed onto us by our Holocaust Jewish Survivors' Registry after you sent your form and memoir back in during a mass mailing in 1994. With your permission we would like to place your donation into our permanent archival holdings in order that researchers can used it in the future.

In order to fulfill our legal requirements, we ask donors to sign agreements with us. I am enclosing two copies of our standard Donor Agreement and/or Deed of Gift forms. One copy of the form is for you to retain for your personal records. Please sign and date the others where indicated (/<u>all</u> pages), then have a witness sign on the cover page, and return one copy of the form <u>to my attention</u> (very important) at the address shown at the bottom of this letter. Please do not have a relative witness the forms. Please include your area code and telephone number, if you have not previously given our staff this information.

Again, we appreciate your generosity in making the donation available to us. Thank you for contributing to our mission of education and remembrance.

Sincerely,

Robert W. Kesting, Ph.D.
Staff Archivist

Donation acknowledgment. Along with the written testimony, Melvin included eight photographs per his attachments list: 1) Melvin, in 6th grade, in Łódź; 2) Melvin with all his siblings, 1938, in the Cherry Mountains; 3) Melvin's mother and her two sisters; 4) Melvin at the Gauting Sanatorium, 1946; 5) Melvin in Pittsburgh in 1952; 6) Melvin becoming a US citizen, 1956; 7) Melvin in 1994; and 8) Melvin with his wife, daughter, son-in-law, and grandson.

286 — Appendix 4

(US Holocaust Memorial Museum Testimony, 1994–1995, continued)

DONOR AGREEMENT (ARCHIVES)

NAME OF DONOR: Melvin Goldman

ADDRESS: 2877 Grandview Dr., Allison Park, PA.

TELEPHONE: 412-443-6635

The undersigned (Donor) does hereby give, donate and convey to the United States Holocaust Memorial Council and its Museum/Archives the material described on Exhibit A of this Donor Agreement. By signing this agreement, Donor does not surrender existing copyright(s) to any of said material or the right to obtain future copyright(s) for any of said material for which copyrights are obtainable.

All material described on Exhibit A of this Donor Agreement will have no restrictions on access and is subject to "fair use" by researchers. "Fair use" allows for publication of relatively short quotes from the material without permission of whomever holds the rights; publication of complete documents requires the permission of the copyright holder or of the author or owner of the uncopyrighted material.

The Donor does hereby represent and warrant that the Donor owns all of said material, has good and complete right, title and interest in said material, and has the unrestricted authority to give, deposit and convey such material to the United States Holocaust Memorial Council and its Museum/Archives.

DONOR'S SIGNATURE _____ DATE 5/3/95
WITNESS'S SIGNATURE _____ DATE 5/3/95

(form revised 3/93)

A Project of the United States Holocaust Memorial Council

Donation agreement.

Acknowledgments

– – – – –

Writing this book has been a long, multifaceted task, and I have been blessed to receive help with so many different phases of the project. The following people went above and beyond in supporting, assisting, and encouraging me, and they have my deepest appreciation.

—

My extraordinary parents, in gratitude for the strong foundation they gave me and the examples they set. They live on in my heart and mind.

My wonderful husband, John, for his never-ending love and encouragement. John believed in me and encouraged me to pursue this project, and later read documentation and my stories, and answered my questions both in Łódź and at home. He gave me new ways to look at things and fresh ideas that I had not thought of. He was a rock for me when sadness crept in.

My outstanding son, Jason, for insisting that I write this book to honor my father's wishes. Jason believed I could accomplish a major goal that was way out of my comfort zone, and he offered support and encouragement, sometimes from long distance. Jason gave me gentle nudges along the way when I felt overwhelmed or stuck. I appreciate his help with research and translations. He listened to my findings on our family with enthusiasm.

Rae Jean Sielen, owner of Populore Publishing Company, for her vision, dedication, and attention to detail as she assisted me in making my father's wishes become a reality. Her expertise helped me throughout all stages of creating this book. I'm grateful to have had her with me every step of the way.

Bonnie Brown, one of the most positive individuals I have ever met, for her energy and optimism, and for leading me to vital resources. A few years ago, Bonnie and I discussed the possibility of this book, which got the ball rolling. I have never looked back.

Several of my father's loyal jewelry customers and personal friends, for reminiscences that help paint a fuller picture of Dad's character and personality: Rose Ann Brown, Robert "Skip" Brown Jr., Falco Muscante, Dorothy Kinner, John Chamberlain, Richard Lasseter, Ken and Pat Aites, June Hayden, and Powel Goldhersz. I wish to especially mention Mr. Goldhersz, a fellow Holocaust survivor Dad first met during his stay at a rehabilitation facility in Germany.

Mark Lystig, for his help, encouragement, genealogical support, and translation assistance. Mark's knowledge of Poland, the Holocaust, and Jewish history were invaluable. He understood what I was trying to capture, and helped guide me.

Ellie Kellman, of Brandeis University, for help including translating all the Yiddish from my father's postcards. *Nirit* and *Yoav Finkelstein,* and *Hal Grinberg,* for additional translation assistance.

Anna Przybyszewska Drozd, of the Emanuel Ringelblum Jewish Historical Institute in Warsaw, for answering many questions about the Goldman and Ceder families, and *Laura Ivanov* of the US Holocaust Memorial Museum, for information on my father's prisoner identification bracelet and for help with the family tree.

Elisabeth Pozzi-Thanner, oral historian in Vienna, for her interest in my project and for sharing her insights—especially related to my father's desire, method, and timing for telling his Holocaust story.

Ada Goldstein, one of our cousins in Israel, for all her information on my grandmother's side of the family. Cousins *Lili Bergstrom, Fanny Kordon,* and *Richard Ceder,* for even more genealogical assistance.

Gil Pietrzak, archivist at the Carnegie Library, for helping me find photographs of Pittsburgh in the early 1950s, and *Anita Napierkowski,* who led me to the archives of the *Pittsburgh Post-Gazette.*

Diane Wagner, for her diligent, patient work transcribing the many hours of my father's tapes.

Laura Kelly, for helping type, research history, and organize content.

Mary Harper, for the detailed, helpful index.

Andrew Rorabaugh, Cathy Samargo, Danny Williams, Joe Ervin, Jenna Britton, and *Jessica Hamon* from Populore Publishing Company, for additional assistance and services, in developing and completing this book.

Megan Kelly, who did a wonderful job designing my website.

Emily the wonder dog, who kept me company while I worked on this project. I call her my cheerleader, and she cheered me up when I needed it.

Sources and Credits

The majority of the material (text) in this book is taken directly from the coauthors' memories and recollections, as well as original documents, including correspondence and official forms. *Wikipedia, The Free Encyclopedia,* was the other main source for information, especially for facts included in Part 1 footnotes and in the appendices. General words and phrases searched include: Allied-Occupied Germany, Auschwitz, Displaced Persons, Holocaust, Łódź ghetto, Nazi Concentration Camps, and World War II, but *Wikipedia* was also used for short descriptions and definitions of proper nouns such as 82nd Airborne Division, Judenrat, and Muselmann. Select other websites accessed include:

> https://www.yadvashem.org (World Holocaust Remembrance Center)
> https://encyclopedia.ushmm.org (US Holocaust Memorial Museum)
> https://kehilalinks.jewishgen.org/lodz (JewishGen KehilaLinks)
> https://www.jhi.pl/en (Jewish Historical Center)
> https://www.jewishvirtuallibrary.org

Unless noted below, all images (photographs, documents, and ephemera) come from coauthor Lee Kikel's personal collection, with copyright held by Goldman–Ceder Forge. To reproduce these, contact Lee Kikel to request permission. Permission is not required to reproduce the maps on pages 209–211 (© Goldman–Ceder Forge). However, reproduction must be accompanied by the following notation: Courtesy of Goldman–Ceder Forge.

Goldman–Ceder Forge can only authorize use of material for which it holds copyright. To reproduce other images, check the credit information below. Inquiries for permission requests or to confirm that an image is in the public domain need to be directed to the source that is cited.

Page 23: US Holocaust Memorial Museum, courtesy of Muzeum Sztuki w Łódźi.[1]

Page 47: US Holocaust Memorial Museum, courtesy of National Archives and Records Administration, College Park.

---

[1] The views or opinions expressed in this book, and the context in which the Museum's images are used, do not necessarily reflect the views or policy of, nor imply approval or endorsement by, the US Holocaust Memorial Museum.

Page 69: US Holocaust Memorial Museum, courtesy of Arnold Bauer Barach.

Page 117 (left): US Holocaust Memorial Museum Collection, Gift of Malwina "Inka" Gerson Allen.

Page 131: Courtesy of Carnegie Library of Pittsburgh.

Page 132: Public domain. From the Pittsburgh City Photographer Collection, 1901–2002, University of Pittsburgh.

Page 142: Courtesy of Carnegie Library of Pittsburgh.

Page 179: Courtesy of Linda Joseph.

Pages 220–225: Wikimedia Commons, public domain. Photographs by Włodzimierz Pfeiffer, from the State Archive in Łódź.

Page 227, top two photos: Wikimedia Commons, public domain.

Index

Note: Photographs and maps are indicated by an italicized page number. Melvin's immediate family members are indicated by a parenthetical gloss. Indeterminate spelling of names from the tape recordings are indicated by a [?].

A

Aites, Ken, 152
Aites, Pat, 152
Allies
  accidental strafing of prisoner transport trains, 62
  German postwar occupation (map), *210*
  liberation (1945), 67, 70, 71n1
  postwar reluctance to accept Jewish immigrants, 98, 118
  trade and health requirements for emigration to countries of, 99–100
Altshtot synagogue, 7, 26, 26n2, 182, 200, *209*, *223*
American Jewish Joint Distribution Committee (JDC), 87, 91–92, 99, 102, 110, *238*
American Red Cross, 72, 82
anti-Semitism
  experiences during childhood, 19–21, 159
  experiences of in postwar Germany, 76–78
  history of, 37
  incidents of retaliation against discrimination, 77
  pogroms, 21, 57
  in postwar Poland, 98, 171
  present-day need for security at synagogues, 191
  Tree of Life synagogue massacre, Squirrel Hill (2018), 189–190
  See also Nazism
Appel, Sarah, 28
apprenticeships, 12–13
Argentina, as possible emigration country, 101
Auerbach, A. J., 94, 113
Auschwitz-Birkenau concentration camp, 47–67, 184
  Block 11 building, *185*
  Block 13 building, *185*
  cramped sleeping conditions, 65–66
  crematoriums, 54–55, 57
  description of, 51–52
  food and meals, 54, 57, 59, 60
  inmate identification, *227*
  Kapos working with SS, 53, 56, 61
  majority of Jews from Łódź sent to, 203
  medical experiments on prisoners, 55, 59
  Melvin as prisoner, 47–67
  morning selection alertness, 55–56
  motto (*Arbeit macht frei*/work makes you free), 52, 185–186
  prisoner beatings/hangings after bombings by Allies, 63–64
  prisoners at gate, *47*
  separation from family, 52–53, 164, 204
  Sonderkommandos, 57, 203
  transfer to Wattenstädt to work in truck factory, 61–62
Auschwitz-Birkenau Memorial and Museum
  cattle car used to transport Jews to camps, *183*

Kikel family visit to, 185–187
memorial stones of fallen victims, *183*
Australia, quota immigration system, 100

B

Bayerisch-Gmain Rehabilitation Center, 93–95
Ben-Gurion, David, *135*
Berger, Rachel, 8, 13
Berkun, Alvin, 189
Berlin, Irving, 250
Berman, Dr., 84, 92
Biebow, Hans, 40, 45, 201–202
Biegelman, Mr., 11, 12
Bonhoeffer, Dietrich, 121
Briggs, L. L., 74
Brown, Audrey, 150
Brown, Bob, 150
Brown, John, 150
Brown, Karen, 150–151
Brown, Robert S., Jr. "Skip," 150
Brown, Rose Ann, 150
brownshirts. *See* SA (Sturmabteilung, Storm Detachment)

C

Canada, emigration requirements, 100
Ceder, Abram, 205
Ceder, Bajla Maria. *See* Goldman, Bajla Maria Ceder "Balcia" (mother)
Ceder, Chaja Sura. *See* Ekman, Chaja Sura Ceder (aunt)
Ceder, Icek (grandfather), 27
Ceder, Ruchla (aunt)
photographs of, *214*
Ceder, Sarah, 205
Ceder, unidentified relatives, *215*
Ceder family tree, 208
Chaimovich (factory director), 39, 40–43, 49–50

Chamberlain, John, 154
Chełmno concentration camp, 24, 39n10, 184, 202–203
Chernew, Paul, 112, 113
cholent recipes, 159, 167
Cieszykowski, Dr., 85, 94
Cohen, Max, 136
"The Commanding Voice of Auschwitz" (Fackenheim), 122–123
Cooky (dog), *141*
Cudkiewicz, Marian
written testimony on Melvin's path of persecution, 258–259
Cuneo Press, 110, 135

D

deaths, due to Nazism, 120, 122
displaced persons (DPs), postwar, xiv, 70, 80, 82, 90, 118
See also United Nations Relief Organization, Relief and Rehabilitation Administration (UNRRA)
Displaced Persons Act (1948), 98
Drachman (factory master), 50
Duchess (dog), 139, *140*

E

editor's note, on book organization, 193–195
Ekman, Celia
photographs of, *252*
Ekman, Chaim, 205
photographs of, *252*
Ekman, Chaja Sura Ceder (aunt), 8, 205, 218
photographs of, *214*–*215*, *252*
Ekman, Mario, 205, 215, 218
photographs of, *251*–*252*
Elling, Ethel, 106, 108
Elling, Mr., 106
Elling, Nancy, 106, 108

emigration to Pittsburgh (late 1949–
late 1970s), 97–115
  arrival in snowstorm (12/31/50), xiv,
   105
  attends Duff's–Iron City College, 110,
   111–112
  attends English and assimilation
   classes, 107–109, 123–124, 135
  citizenship (1956), 112–113, *117*, *248–249*
  continuing treatments at Montefiore
   Hospital, 110
  early months in city, 105–108, 134
  employment history, 108, 110, 113, 135,
   136–137, *246–247*
  establishes Lee Trading Co., 113–115
  as lifelong learner, 109–110, 115, 136,
   137, 142, 145, 155
  lives and works in Chicago, 110, 135
  New York Customs processing, 104
  preparation via trade skill training at
   ORT, 99–100
  receives JDC #93744, 102
  sails on USS *General Harry Taylor*,
   103–104, 103n3
  takes train from New York to Pittsburgh, 105
  travels around Western Europe after
   leaving hospital, 99, 102
  Wildflecken, awaiting transport,
   103
  See also Squirrel Hill family years
Engelman, Dr., 74
Erben, I. A., 94
Eugene (Melvin's friend), 108–109
extermination camps, 48, *210*
  See also specific concentration camps

F

Fackenheim, Emil, 122–123, 123n3
family businesses
  in Pittsburgh, 113–115, 140–153, *142*,
   147, *152*, 158, 172–173
  in Poland, 5, 9–10, 13, 15–17, *209*
family trees, 204–208
  Lee's research process for, 190
  Melvin's immediate family, *206*
  Melvin's maternal ancestors, *208*
  Melvin's paternal ancestors, *207*
Filipowicz, Dr., 85, 94
Fisher Scientific, 101
Folman, Lola, 6
Foreign Claims Settlement Commis-
  sion, 172, *261–262*, *269–271*
Fruendt, Mrs. H., 107–108, 113

G

G&S Jewelry, 142, 151–153, 173
Galen, August von, 121
Gavin, James M., 71–72, 150, *231*
Geesthacht, Poles' joy in seeing survi-
  vor Jews, xiv, 75
Gefsky, M. B., 113
Gemological Institute of America, 142,
  144
German Confessing Church, 121
Germany, postwar
  Allied occupation (map), *210*
  Bayerisch-Gmain train station, *79*
  citizen certification requirement,
   77–78
  continuance of anti-Semitism, 76–78
  lack of resources for population, 95
Gestapo, 30, 30n6, 268
"Give Me Your Children" speech (Rum-
  kowski), 202–203
Glick, Hirsh, 230
Globe Trading, 113
"God Bless America" (song), 250
Goldhersz, Gloria, 161
Goldhersz, Powel (Paul), 160–161
  photographs of, *161*
Goldman, Aron (brother)

as Auschwitz prisoner, 52–55, 164–165
childhood years in Łódź, 33
death of, 163, 169
emigrates to Pittsburgh, 91, 100–101, 131
Lee's memories of, 161–165
marries Evy, 91
Melvin's arrival to Pittsburgh, 106–107, 134
photographs of, *3*, *163*, *219*
postwar reconnection with Melvin, 83–84, 85–86, 90–91
postwar recovery of items from Łódź home, 165, *219*
postwar time in Poland, 83, 85
steals food for family with Melvin, 36, 37
visits US Holocaust Memorial Museum, 156

Goldman, Bajla Maria Ceder "Balcia" (mother)
begs Melvin/Aron to stop stealing food, 37
begs Melvin to stop using underground library, 43–44
cousins of, 205
death of, 186
family trees, *206*, *208*
Lee's genealogical research on, 190
marriage certificate, *216–217*
Melvin's memories of, 5, 7–8, 9, 10–11, 12, 49
during Nazi occupation of Łódź, 33, 35, 37, 49
parents of, 27
photographs of, *214*
as prisoner at Auschwitz, 52

Goldman, Barbara (niece), 163

Goldman, Chaim (father)
birth certificate of, *213*
characteristics of, 7
as district chief of civil defense, 18–19
family trees, *206*, *207*
German incorporation of factory of, 40–41, 45
helps thief, Irvin escape police, 56–57
International Red Cross confirmation of death of, *272–274*
as inventive fabricator of metal fixtures and business owner, xiv, 4, 6, 7–10, 12–13, 16–17
lost property, 171–172
marriage certificate, *216–217*
Melvin's memories of, 5, 6–14, 32–33
during Nazi occupation of Łódź, 32–33, 36–37, 39, 49–52
as owner of patents for devices, xiv, 15–16
religious orientation of, 6–7, 11
sang instructive song to Melvin, 14
tortured at Kripo Red House, 30–33
as veteran of Polish–Soviet War, 4, 6, 218

Goldman, Chaja Sura (sister)
photographs of, *3*, *219*

Goldman, Evy Elling (sister-in-law), 91, 106, 134, 163

Goldman, Howard (nephew), 163

Goldman, Joel (uncle), 28, 51, 101, 204–205
photographs of, *251*

Goldman, Josef (brother), 9, 32, 43
photographs of, *3*, *219*

Goldman, Lajb "Laibusz" (brother), 9, 43
photographs of, *3*, *219*

Goldman, Lee Diane. *See* Kikel, Lee Goldman (daughter)

Goldman, Majlech (grandfather), 13, 27–28

Goldman, Melvin
admonition of perseverance, 136–137, 146, 171

contributions to US Holocaust Memorial Museum, 156, 194, *284–286*
contributions to Yad Vashem, 156–157
correspondence regarding restitution and recovery issues, xv, 168, 170–172
death of, xiii, 176–177
family trees, 204–208
as grandparent, 175–177
handicapped status determination, 94–95, 137–139, *138*
health in later years, 173–174, 176–177
Lee's dedication of book to, ix–xi
Lee's memories of, 154–160, 167, 169
marriage to Mildred, 134–136, *134*
Melvin-isms, 158
photographs of, *3, 79, 97, 134, 139–141, 143, 147, 155–156, 161, 166, 173–176, 219, 232–234, 248*
Polish name/nicknames for, xiv, 218
as proud to be American citizen, 159–160
records his childhood memories and as an Holocaust survivor, ix–xi, xiv–xv, 14n1, 194
religious orientation of, 165–166
retirement years, 172–177
support for Israeli statehood, 159
as 32nd degree Mason, 157
timeline of (1923–1996), *212*
volunteer activities, 178
See also family businesses; historical artifacts, from Melvin's life; historical documents, from Melvin's life; Melvin's account; Squirrel Hill family years
Goldman, Mildred Zerelstein (spouse)
cholent recipe, 167
correspondence regarding restitution and recovery issues, *168, 284*
employment history, 135, 136
family trees, *206*
friends' memories of, 151–154
health in later years, 179–180
Lee's memories of, 157–160, 163, 170
marriage to Melvin, 112, 126, 134–136, *134*, 139–140
motherhood, 148
photographs of, *134, 139, 147, 166, 173–174, 176, 178–179*
religious orientation of, 165–166
volunteer activities, 177–179
See also Squirrel Hill family years
Goldman, Natan (brother)
photographs of, *3, 219*
Goldman, Rojza (sister), 33, 52, 53n1, 204
photographs of, *3, 219*
Goldman, Rosy (cousin), 204–205
Goldman, Sala (aunt), 8–9
Granach, Alexander, 6
Gray, Nellie, 110
Gross-Rosen concentration camp, 184
Gypsies, extermination of, 53

H

Hartstein [?], Sasza, 49–50, 82
Hayden, June, 153
Hebrew Immigrant Aid Society (HIAS), 101–102, 102n2
Heydrich, Reinhard, 201
Himelfarb family, 11, 41
Himmler, Heinrich, 40
historical artifacts, from Melvin's life
currency issued by Nazis, 227
inmate indentification, bracelet, *227*
Miracle brand soap (100 years old), *218*
historical documents, from Melvin's life
Achievement Record, Duff's Pittsburgh Technical Institute, *245*
Appeal to URO rejection, affidavit by Arnold Zweig, *267*

Approval for emigration, American Joint Distribution Committee, *238*
Baggage Declaration form, USS *General Harry Taylor*, *239–240*
birth certificate of, *218*
Certificate of Naturalization, *248–249*
Chaim Goldman's birth certificate, *213*
claim letter to United Restitution Organization, *263*
correspondence with United Restitution Organization regarding disability compensation, *275–282*
documents and photographs, *213–286*
Dr. Rubel's letter of permanent disability status, *138*
Elementary School certificate, 226
Emigration application, International Refugee Organization, *237*
Foreign Claims Settlement Commission denial, *269–271*
Foreign Claims Settlement Commission request for reimbursement for stolen property, *261–262*
German documentation of path of persecution, *228–229, 255–257*
Industrial Management Engineering certificate, Pittsburgh Technical Institute (1955), *137*
Institute for the Diamond Certificate, Gemological Institute of America (1967), *144*
International Red Cross confirmation of father's death, *272–274*
Lee Trading Company ad, *152*
letter from General James Gavin, 150, *231*
letter from International Tracing Service, *253*
letter from IRO Rehabilitation Center, Bayerisch Gmain, *254*
map of Wolborska Street area, *181*
New York City to Pittsburgh train ticket, *243*
notebooks of correspondence regarding reparations and restitution, xv, *168*
parent's marriage certificate, *216–217*
photos and postcards brought to America, *162*
Plumbing Trade Certificates, *235–236*
postcards received over lifetime, 194
Precision Engineering Certificate, World ORT Union, *236*
Resume (1955), *246–247*
sixth grade photo of Melvin, hid in chimney, *219*
Taylor Post Souvenir Edition, *241–242*
Travelers Aid Society memo, *244*
United Restitution Organization, claim rejection letter, *264–266*
US Holocaust Memorial Museum testimony donation, xi, 156, 194, *284–286*
written testimony on path of persecution, *258–259*
See also maps
Hitler, Adolph, 70, 121–122, 199
See also Nazism
Hitler Youth, 31–33, 45
Hoffman, Mr., 56
Holocaust
complicity of Judenrat, 38, 38n9, 40, 201
evil and barbarism of, 119–122
mental anguish of survivors, 86–87, 92, 93–94
transport conditions for camp prisoners, 51, 62, 164
See also Nazism; *specific concentration camps*
Holocaust survivor oral histories
Melvin's process, ix–xi, xiv–xv, 14n1, 194

Melvin's submission of written testimony to US Holocaust Memorial Museum, xi, 156, 194, *284–286*
See also Shoah Foundation; US Holocaust Memorial Museum

I
IG Farben, 62
Imperial Cultured Pearls, 149
International Claims Settlement Act (1949), 172
International Red Cross, 64, 65
Israel
  as possible emigration country, 98, 100–101
  relatives living in, 28, 51, 101, 102, 205
  statehood for, 98, 159

J
Jackson, J. Roy, 113
Jarocinski Engineering School, 12, 13
Jewish Family Service, 110
Jewish Federation, 105
Jewish ghetto. See Łódź, Poland
Jewish Historical Institute, Warsaw, 190
Jewish National Fund, 167
Jewish population, extermination of, 120
Jewish Social Service, 102
Judenrat (Jewish Council), 38, 40, 201–202

K
Kaplan, Dr., 82, 94
Kathy (Mildred's friend), 179
Kikel, Elizabeth "Betty," 157
  photographs of, *174*
Kikel, Jason (grandson), x, 133, 148, 157, 166, 169, 175–177, 178–179, 180–185, 189, 190, 205
  photographs of, *174–176, 179–180*
Kikel, John (son-in-law), 133, 148, 157, 166, 177, 180–185, 189, 190, 205
  photographs of, *173–174, 176*
Kikel, Lee Goldman (daughter)
  birth of, 114–115, 139
  book produced to honor father, ix–xi
  celebration of Jewish traditions, 166–167
  correspondence with relatives, 190, 205
  cultured pearl show-and-tell incident, 149
  donations to Jewish National Fund for tree plantings, 167
  introduction to book, ix–xv
  listens to Melvin's tape recordings, x, xiii, xv, 180
  marriage to John, 173–174
  memories of father, xiv–xv, 154–160, 176–177, 182, 187, 191
  memories of mother, 148
  namesake of, 43
  photographs of, *139–141, 161, 166, 173–176, 178–179*
  religious orientation of, 165–169
  visits Auschwitz, 185–187
  visits Łódź, xiii, 180–185
  visits newfound cousins in Sweden, 190
  visits Yad Vashem, 157
  writing process, x, xiii–xiv, 189–191, 193, 194
  See also Squirrel Hill family years
Kinner, Dorothy, 151–152
Klaussner family, 11
Klay, Mayer, 160–161
  photographs of, *161*
Kneippianum Sanatorium, 84–92, 160, *232–234*
Końskie, Poland, 13, 27

the Kripo (Criminal Police), 30, 30n4, 31, 182, 202, 209
Krotowski, Dr., 85, 94, 161

L

Lasseter, Richard, 153–154
Lee Trading Company, 114–115, 140–151, 142, 147, 152
See also G&S Jewelry
Lewitt, Abe "Baby Abe," 160–161
  photographs of, 161
Łódź, Poland, 5–6
  Altshtot synagogue, 7, 26, 26n2, 182, 200, 209, 223
  archives buildings, 180–181, 182, 184
  Aron's memories of, 163–164
  demographics of, 200, 201, 203
  deportations of elderly and children (Sept. 1942), 39, 39n10
  Freedom Square, Plac Wolności, 209, 221
  Great Synagogue, 221
  Green Market area, 222, 224
  as industrial center, 200, 201
  Jewish ghetto, 24, 29–35, 124, 164, 169, 200–201
  Jewish ghetto (map), 209
  the Kripo (Criminal Police), 30, 30n4, 31, 182, 202, 209
  monuments to Jews deported to death camps, 183, 184
  Nad Łodką Street, 222
  Nazi confiscation of Jewish businesses, 29, 40, 200
  Nazi invasion/occupation of, 22, 23–45, 23, 164, 182, 200
  number of Holocaust survivors from, 203
  number of Jews deported to death camps from, 184, 203
  number of Jews remaining in (2015), 184
  Park Staromiejski, 182, 184
  Piotrkowska Street, 225
  under postwar Soviet rule, 98
  Radegast memorial train station, 183, 184, 185, 209
  ration cards, 33–34, 36, 42
  the Red House, where Melvin's father and other Jews were tortured, 30, 30n5, 182, 184, 209
  starvation in Jewish ghetto, 33–35, 39, 169, 201
  Stary Rynek square, 224–225
  36 Franciszkańska Street underground library, 43–44, 181, 184, 209
  Wolborska Street, 180, 200, 222–224
Ludwigslust, 67, 71n1, 103, 120
Lupka, Rajzla (grandmother) 27–28

M

maps
  German postwar occupation by Allies, 210
  Łódź ghetto, 209
  Melvin's journeys in postwar Germany, 210
  Squirrel Hill, Pittsburgh, 211
Match (dog), 141
medical treatment for camp survivors, and Melvin's TB, 71–76
  American Red Cross role, 72–73
  Edmundsthal Hospital, Geesthacht, 232
  expressions of humanity from caregivers, 72
  gradual return to eating, 72–73, 92
  gradual return to walking ability, 74–75, 82, 92, 93–95
  handicapped status determination, 94–95
  multiple moves to facilities and zones, 73–77

pneumothorax treatments, 74, 82, 84, 85
receives care in private home, 73
UNRRA's role, 70, 74, 84, 87
Melvin-isms, 158
Melvin's account
   concentration camps (1944-1945), 47-67
   early childhood (1923-1939), 3-22
   emigration to Pittsburgh (late 1949-late 1970s), 97-115
   liberation by Allies (1945), 69-78, 71n1
   medical care, rehabilitation, and strength of will (1946-1949), 79-95
   Nazi invasion of Łódź, Poland, 22, 23-45
   reflections on past/future (late-1970s), 117-127
   See also Goldman, Melvin; *specific time periods*
Mengele, Josef, 52-53, 54, 56, 186
Menson, Leon
   written testimony on Melvin's path of persecution, *258-260*
mental anguish challenges, 86-87, 92-94, 110, 169
mitzvot (anonymous good deeds), 169
Morgenstern, Dr., 92
Moshe Schneur Choir, 6
Muscante, Falco, 150-151
Muselmänner (starving prisoners), 56, 56n2, 64, 65

N

Names Recovery Project (Yad Vashem), 156-157
Nazism
   deaths due to, 120, 122
   invasion of Łódź, 21, 23-45, *23*, 164, 182, 200
   invasion of Poland, 199-200, *23*
   planned eradication of Jews, 60
   prewar awareness of, 21
   systemic evil of, 119-122
   See also Hitler, Adolph; Holocaust; *specific concentration camps*
never again, use of phrase, x
"Never Say" ("*Zog Nit Keyn Mol*") (song), 230
Niemöller, Martin, 121

O

Oscar Kon Company, 16

P

Passamaneck [?], Mr., 109
Piller, A., 93
Piłsudski, Józef, 6
Pittsburgh, Pennsylvania
   during 1950s, *131*
   Jewish Community Center, 132
   Phipps Conservatory and Botanical Gardens, 148
   Pittsburgh Zoo, 148, 175
   See also Squirrel Hill family years
Pittsburgh Technical Institute, *137*, 245
Poland
   Bureau of Measurements, xiv
   civil defense training leading to war, 18-19
   fascist party, 21
   history of partition, 199
   military service requirements, 17-18
   Nazi invasion of, 199-200
   Polish Claims Agreement (1960), 172
   postwar confiscation of Jewish property, 171
   postwar control of, 83, 98
   reconstitution of via Treaty of Versailles, 199
   refusal to pay restitution or apologize to Jewish survivors, 172

Star of David badge requirement, 29, 44, 117, 200–201
Warsaw Ghetto Uprising (1943), 50, 230
Warsaw Uprising (1944), 203
during WWI, 31, 199
See also Łódź, Poland
Polish–Soviet War, 6, 37
Politics of Hate (Weiss), 171
Prilutzki, Noah, 7

R

Ravensbrück concentration camp, 65–67, 184, 210
reflections on past/future (late 1970s), 117–127
  on America, 123–127
  "The Commanding Voice of Auschwitz" (Fackenheim), 122–123
  on fighting hatred, 121, 122
  on Germany, 120
  on Jewish ghettos in Poland, 124
  on Jewish heroes, 120–121, 230
  on religion and church responsibility, 121
  on systemic evil of Nazi Holocaust, 119–122
rehabilitation and Melvin's strength of will (1946–1949), 79–95, 210
  as Bayerisch-Gmain Rehabilitation Center patient, 93–95
  as employee helping manage Kneippianum Hospital, 87–92
  Frankfurt Jewish displaced persons camp, 82
  as Gauting Sanatorium patient, 82–84, 85
  journeys in postwar Germany (map), 210
  as Kneippianum Sanatorium patient, 84–92, 160, 232–234
  mental anguish challenges, 86–87, 92, 93–94, 110
  reconnection with Aron, 83–84, 85–86, 90–91
  as Schwabing [?] hospital patient, 84
  travels to American Zone, 81–82
  as Sonnenhof hospital patient, 92
Richter, Hans, 74
Rockman, Lilka, 75, 81–83
Rosetti & Rosetti, 110, 135
Roth, Gladys, 102
Rubel, Theodore, 110, 112, 113, 137–139, *138*
Rumkowski, Mordechai Chaim, 40, 201–203, *227*
Rydz-Smigly, Edward, 18

S

SA (Sturmabteilung, Storm Detachment), 31, 31*n*7
Sachsenhausen concentration camp, 123*n*3, 184
Senderovicz, Moshe Chaim, 11
Shoah Foundation, ix–x
Sielen, Rae Jean, 193–195
Silverberg family, 11
Slawkin, Elizabeth. *See* Zerelstein, Elizabeth Slawkin (mother-in-law)
Soviet Union
  invasion of Poland (1939), 199
  postwar control of Poland, 83, 98
Spielberg, Steven, ix–x
Squirrel Hill family years
  Beacon Street residence, 140
  Buick cars, 152, 153, 154
  current demographics of, 132
  description of neighborhood, 131–134
  family memories, 139–140
  jewelry business, 114–115, 140–153, *142*, *147*, *152*, 158, 172–173
  Jewish identity of neighborhood, 132–133

memories of local businesses, *132*, 133–134, 142
movie theaters, 133, *142*
recreation time, 148, 175
residences (map), *211*
South Negley Avenue residences, 139–149
SS (Schutzstaffel, Protection Squadron), 31, 31n7
stamp collecting, 158
Star of David badge, 29, 44, *117*, 200–201
starvation, in Jewish ghetto, 33–35, 201
"Stuttgart Declaration of Guilt," 122n2
Stutthof concentration camp, 53n1, 184, 204
suicides, 35, 164, 165
Sunnock, Ella "Aunt Ellie," 139–140, *140*
Sweden, reuniting with cousins in, 190–191
Swedish Red Cross, White Buses, 191
synagogues, security of, 191
Szmulik (Melvin's friend), 75, 81–82
szpera (mass confiscations and deportations), 39, 39n10

T

Talmud, 13
Taub, Moniek, 10, 56, 60, 102
timeline of Melvin's life (1923–1996), *212*
Travelers Aid Society, 105, *244*
Tree of Life synagogue, Squirrel Hill
  location of (map), *211*
  massacre (2018), 189–190, 191
tuberculosis diagnosis. *See* medical treatment for camp survivors, and Melvin's TB

U

United Nations Relief Organization, Relief and Rehabilitation Administration (UNRRA), 70, 74, 84, 87, 91–92, 99
United Service for New Americans (USNA), 101–102, 102n2, 104
US Army
  82nd Airborne Division, 71–72, 71n1, 150, *231*
  liberation of concentration camps, 69
US Constitution, 124
US Holocaust Memorial Museum, ix, x, 156, 194, 284–286
USS *General Harry Taylor*, 103–104, 103n3, 239–240

V

Volksdeutsche, 25–26, 25n1, 74
Voss, Mr., 16, 225

W

Wattenstädt subcamp, 62, 120
Weiss, John, 171
Wightman School, 140, 149
Wöbbelin concentration camp, 67, *69*, 71n1, 120, *210*
World ORT (Association for the Promotion of Skilled Trades), 99–100, 99n1
World War I, 31, 199

Y

Yad Vashem, World Holocaust Remembrance Center
  awards titles of "Righteous among the Nations," 27n3
  Victims' Names Recovery Project, 156–157
Yale University, Fortunoff Video Archive for Holocaust Testimonies, ix
Young Men's and Women's Hebrew Association (YMWHA), 106, 106n6, 113

Z

Zerelstein, David (father-in-law), 136, 165–166

Zerelstein, Elizabeth Slawkin (mother-in-law), 135–136, 165–166

Zerelstein, Mildred. *See* Goldman, Mildred Zerelstein (spouse)

Zerelstein, Rose, 136

Zerelstein, Sam (Gershon), 136

Zweig, Arnold
    Appeal to URO rejection, affidavit for Melvin by, *267*

About Lee Goldman Kikel

John, Lee, and Jason.

Lee with Emily.

Lee Goldman Kikel grew up in the Squirrel Hill neighborhood of Pittsburgh, where her early years revolved around school—Wightman School and Taylor Allderdice High School—and the family jewelry business.

Lee recalls her time in the store with great fondness and can measure her life's progress through those happy memories. As a little girl she played jacks on the floor, while her father crafted jewelry and waited on customers, and her mother handled the books as well as sold merchandise and helped with day-to-day business operations. Soon, Lee matured from playing to helping, then to a more regular job, continuing through her college years at the University of Pittsburgh. She remembers earning her father's hard-won approval to wait on customers as an exciting milestone in her life. Even as an adult, she would help out after her day job or on weekends during the busiest times.

Lee earned a BS in psychology and a master's degree in education, then worked in the mental health field as a rehabilitation counselor. Now retired from that career, she is an avid traveler, gardener, and muscle car enthusiast. She lives in suburban Pittsburgh with her husband and son, and their two dogs, Emily and Bryce.

www.ingramcontent.com/pod-product-compliance
Lightning Source LLC
Chambersburg PA
CBHW051147290426
44108CB00019B/2633